JONATHON PORRITT
and
DAVID WINNER

THE COMING
OF THE GREENS

FONTANA/Collins

To all those who have the influence, and who know
how to use it wisely for the future.

First published in 1988 by Fontana Paperbacks
8 Grafton Street, London W1X 3LA

Printed and bound in Great Britain by
William Collins Sons & Co. Ltd, Glasgow

CONTENTS

ACKNOWLEDGEMENTS

We would like to thank all the following for sharing their knowledge and ideas with us when we were researching *The Coming of the Greens*.

Hazel Barbour, Tony Benn, Murray Bookchin, John Boorman, Julie Christie, Linda Churnside, Victoria Cliff Hodges, Sue Clifford, David Cope, Richard Creasey, James Cutler, Paul Ekins, Harold Evans, Nick Gallie, Paul Gerhardt, Hugh Goyder, Carol Haslam, Simon Hughes, George Lewith, Ken Livingstone, Christine McNulty, Troy Kennedy Martin, Hugh Montefiore, Margaret Morgan, G. F. Newman, Mike Newport, David Nicholas, Richard North, Tim O'Riordan, Sara Parkin, Fred Pearce, Patrick Pietroni, Jonathan Powell, David Puttnam, Liz Rigbey, James Robertson, Anita Roddick, Robin Sadler, Victor Schonfeld, Walter Schwarz, Peggy Seeger, Posy Simmonds, Andrew Smith, Heather Swailes, William Waldegrave, Fay Weldon, and Bob Worcester.

Our thanks too to Christopher Maume and Jane Dibblin for their work on Chapters Seven and Two respectively; and to Jane Judd and Caroline Heaton for their encouragement.

FOREWORD

A cautionary word may well be in order. *The Coming of the Greens* has been written as an analysis of the extent to which green ideas have penetrated different sectors of British society. It is *not* an academic treatise, nor does it attempt to make any detailed exposition of what green politics are all about, either in terms of general principles or specific policies. (If your interests lie in either of those directions, then we have made various recommendations in the bibliography.) It is not, therefore, a basic primer in all things green, but a snapshot of what's been going on in the UK and on the international scene over the last five years or so.

Although we have attempted to cover all the major areas of concern, we are very conscious that there are some omissions. For instance, we have not been able to deal either with the built environment or with the whole question of 'greening the cities'. Our problem was simply this: there is really no area of social or political concern in the UK today that hasn't been touched in one way or another by the coming of the Greens, but the limits of this particular study had to be drawn fairly tightly.

The last point we would like to make is that we felt it best to present the state of the Green Movement as it really is, warts and all. We have no illusions about the difficulties that still have to be faced up to, and are convinced that the hopes which we identify in the final chapter will only triumph over the fears if and when that facing-up is properly done.

You will find the list of all those whom we interviewed in the process of writing *The Coming of the Greens*. Some are easily identified as self-confessed, fully paid-up Greens, but most are not particularly well-known for their green sympathies or interests. It is around such people that the Green Movement of the '90s will be built, and we are enormously grateful to them for the inspiration they gave us as we tried to stitch together the astonishingly vibrant patchwork quilt that is the Green Movement today.

The joy of being green lies in shared commitment, in a shared vision of the future, and somewhere in the Earth itself. In that respect, *The Coming of the Greens* has been a wonderful book to write. We hope you enjoy reading it.

Jonathon Porritt and David Winner
June 1988

INTRODUCTION

Not so long ago, 'greens' were the bits of a golf course where the grass was shortest, or the parts of the main course between the roast beef and the baked potatoes. Until the early 1980s, the word rarely passed the lips of British politicians, except among those caring MPs and party leaders who advised their children, 'Go on, eat up your greens.'

These days, however, Greens are a lot less easily digested – but far more politically nourishing. 'Green' refers to a rich and extraordinarily diverse movement with new shoots springing up all over the place. Activities as diverse as becoming a vegetarian, signing a petition to stop a motorway or living under a plastic sheet outside a cruise missile base in Berkshire are all held to be 'green'. Among a plethora of different aims, the most commonplace is simply to improve the quality of life: to be healthier, to save a lovely old building or to protect the countryside. The most radical seeks nothing less than a non-violent revolution to overthrow our whole polluting, plundering and materialistic industrial society and, in its place, to create a new economic and social order which will allow human beings to live in harmony with the planet. In those terms, the Green Movement lays claim to being the most radical and important political and cultural force since the birth of socialism.

Just as definitions of 'freedom', 'democracy', 'peace' and 'justice' vary according to the context in which they are used, so 'green' tends to mean very different things to different people. For the sake of clarity, we would start by identifying two broad categories: environmentalists (or 'light Greens') and radical Greens (or 'dark Greens').

The first and by far the most common perception of 'green' is as a synonym for what is otherwise referred to as 'environmental'. For most people, the Green Movement is exactly the same thing as the Environment Movement. At this level, we find conservationists, preservationists, champions of the countryside, defenders of public parks and stately homes, and all those people who believe that dying forests, polluted lakes, nuclear power stations and the culling of baby seals are 'A Bad Thing' – but who do not necessarily go on to conclude that it is therefore necessary to change the whole basis on which society is organized. This is essentially a reformist movement, based on the premise that industrialism can be perfected, or at least

9

improved, to the point where it no longer endangers the environment. Probably about 95% of the uses of the word 'green' fit into this category, and when newspapers, television and most mainstream politicians talk about 'green ideas', this is generally what they have in mind.

Greens claim, with some authority, to have won the basic argument at this narrowest and most easily assimilated level of interest. The state of the environment has become a legitimate matter for mainstream concern, and few industrialists or politicians now dare to tell us that caring about the environment is a waste of time or resources, or will lead to higher unemployment. Crucially, we also know considerably more about the ecological problems confronting us today than we ever used to. Technical and scientific knowledge of the environmental impact of our industrial society has developed far beyond what was known even in the early 1970s. Scientific understanding of phenomena such as acid rain and the destruction of topsoil has revolutionized our perceptions of the dangers of atmospheric pollution and of inorganic fertilizers in agriculture. We're also more clued-up about the international dimension of environmental problems. The radioactive clouds from Chernobyl and the swathe of chemicals from the Sandoz factory in Switzerland, which severely damaged the Rhine, brought home to many the fact that pollution is no respecter of national and political boundaries. This recognition has underpinned a much greater willingness to act to control such international dangers.

But politicians and civil servants are, of course, past masters at professional lip-servicing. Back in the 1970s, when the caring buzz-word of the day was 'environment', it was duly hijacked as the name for a gigantic new super ministry, the Department of the Environment. The name-change made not a jot of difference to the policies, since the department's established civil servants (by this time housed in their spectacularly ugly concrete carbuncles in Marsham Street) proceeded to pursue exactly the same extremely established and deeply un-green policies. In the same vein, merely dubbing William Waldegrave the Government's 'green minister' did mighty little to improve Britain's record on pollution between 1984 and 1987.

So what's new? At this level, is 'greenness' just the latest in a long line of relatively safe, worthy causes taken up without any real understanding by politicians and trend-setters? It's still too early to judge, but there are enough pointers to indicate that those cynical

10

Greens who dismiss it all in these terms may be their own worst enemy. None the less, the pace of change is still much too slow for all those active in mainstream politics who are pressing for more than a lick of green paint, let alone for members of the UK Green Party. As we shall see in Chapter 3, these dark Greens are now genuinely alarmed that the old guard, with its greater access to the media, will always be able to exploit the narrow environmental interpretation of green to promote its own grey old politics.

Dark green thinking offers a radical, visionary and fundamentalist challenge to the prevailing economic and political world order. At its most ambitious, green politics sees itself as a global life-saver, an urgent response to fast-approaching ecological collapse. It demands a wholly new ethic in which violent, plundering humankind abandons its destructive ways, recognizes its dependence on Planet Earth and starts living on a more equal footing with the rest of nature. It declares the old-style political discourse, based on distinctions and battles between Left and Right, to be diversionary and obsolete. What matters now is for us, as a species, to order our affairs in such a way as to live in harmony with our surroundings – the entire biosphere, that is, not just the local park.

All of which quite obviously means that tackling pollution, acid rain, famine in Africa, the annihilation of the tropical rainforests, nuclear poisoning, the destruction of the ozone layer and all the other environmental crises which face us, is going to require solutions a good deal more radical than a spot of reformist tinkering with the self-same industrial system that got us into this mess in the first place. Reformist environmentalism, as practised by single issue pressure groups and advocated by environmentalists in the main political parties, is nowhere near enough. The danger lies not only in the odd maverick polluting factory, industry or technology, but in the fundamental nature of our economic systems. It is industrialism itself – a 'super-ideology' embraced by socialist countries as well as by the capitalist West – which threatens us.

Even if we could prevent disasters like Bhopal, Seveso and Chernobyl, and end the destruction of all the habitats and life-support systems currently at risk (and there's precious little reason to suppose that industrialism in its present form can do even that), we'll still be stuck with the same basic problem of dwindling resources and the progressive deterioration of the environment. The simple fact is that we cannot expect to continue using up the Earth's non-renewable

11

resources (oil, minerals etc.) and destroying renewable resources (clean water, forests and fertile soil) at the present rate, and expect the system to survive.

For these hardy Greens, stopping pollution or fighting nuclear power are not therefore ends in themselves – only the most urgent of an extremely long list of political and social priorities. Green politics of this kind rejects the visions of Right, Left and even Centre. As a slogan of the West German Greens puts it: 'We are neither Left nor Right. We are in front.'

Beyond both the light green and the dark green is a vaguer, mostly de-politicized spiritual dimension. For some, that arises out of certain strands in the Judaeo-Christian tradition which emphasize human-kind's responsibility to act as stewards of the Earth, rather than our licence to exploit it; for others, it is located in the principles of 'deep ecology'. Ecology, in its narrowest, strictly scientific sense, is the study of the relationships between organisms and their environment. Deep ecology extends this concept into all areas of thought and being, in the belief that all expressions of life on Earth, both human *and* non-human, have value in themselves, and that humans have no right to reduce the richness and diversity of life on Earth except to satisfy vital needs. This spiritual approach has led to an interest in Taoism, Buddhism, pantheism and ancient, pre-patriarchal cultures. Receptiveness to meditation, holistic approaches to health and spiri-tuality, and an explosion of interest in personal growth, all testify to the appeal of these ideas.

Viewed from *any* perspective, the Green Movement has clearly made considerable progress over the last ten years. Yet it is still dismissed, discouraged and ignored in some quarters. From the political Right and Left, and from the heart of the industrial and technological establishment, the more radical green ideas are strongly challenged. The more radical they are, the stronger the challenge. In particular, the fundamental green assumption that the present eco-nomic and industrial world order will drag us into the abyss is by no means shared by everyone. There are powerful academics who argue vociferously that green fears are simply unjustified. 'Crisis? What crisis? Don't worry – we'll pull through.'

This kind of attitude harks back to the Club of Rome's 1972 report, *The Limits to Growth*, which set the tone for the debate about the possibility of eco-catastrophe throughout the 1970s and played a significant part in fuelling the emerging Green Movement. Although its computer-modelling techniques were decidedly primitive, and despite the fact that many of the details of its projections have since been disproved or have failed to materialize, the central thrust of the findings was subsequently confirmed by the *Global 2000* report to the President, originally commissioned by Jimmy Carter in 1977 and then wholly ignored by Ronald Reagan.

While acknowledging that we have not as yet been tipped over the edge into eco-apocalypse, Greens point out that some of their most nightmarish predictions have already been borne out in reality. While academics nit-pick over the theory, the whole continent of Africa is falling into an ecological collapse on a scale more terrible than even the prophets of gloom and doom in the early 1970s had foreseen.

We shall pick up again on some of these hopes and fears in the final chapter. By that time, we shall have encountered many different manifestations of green, discovered many subtle nuances of what it really means to be green, and understood why the central principle underlying the development of green ideas in the UK (namely, *strength through diversity*, or 'let a thousand green poppies bloom') should give rise to much more hope than fear.

CHAPTER ONE

The Green Delta

Greens in each country have enjoyed varying degrees of success. If West Germany has been the green hare of Western Europe, Britain is unquestionably one of the tortoises. Green ideas here have been spreading very slowly by comparison, carried by a jumble of loosely connected organizations and campaigns rather than by a high-profile political movement. Yet the very slowness which radical British Greens often find so painful and frustrating may, in the long run, turn out to have benign consequences. While the success of the West German Greens has been dramatic, the growth of deep hostility among their opponents has been correspondingly high. According to opinion polls, almost a third of the population in Germany feel profoundly threatened by the Greens. Radical green ideas about the nature of work and reordering of the economy represent a betrayal of deeply revered cultural and social values for many conservative West Germans. The seeds of an irreconcilable political conflict have therefore been sown, as so many dragon's teeth, as emotional and intellectual barriers are erected by that 30% to all green ideas. If the objective is not only to arrive at a greener, more sustainable future, but to do so with the enthusiastic participation of an overwhelming majority of people, then the gradualist, less confrontational British model may, in the long run, ensure a smoother and more lasting transition than the West German one.

The way the British Green Movement has been growing is a bit like the slow but steady geological process by which new land takes shape at the mouth of a giant river such as the Mississippi. In the upper reaches of the river, the weight and power of rushing water and pounding rain tears away the river bed and surrounding topsoil, which is carried downstream as sediment. Likewise, in society, ecological anxieties and an increasingly critical view of the quality of modern life are persuading people to question the values and assumptions of industrialism. As the river slows and deposits the sediment when it approaches the sea, so the doubts and fears are leading to new attitudes and ideas. Over time, small islands begin to appear in the delta. From above the water, they appear to be separate, but they are in fact interconnected parts of an emerging land mass. The disparate 'islands' of the Green Movement – environmentalism, holistic health, peace campaigning, green spirituality, organic farming, alternative economics, green consumerism, animal rights activities and all the rest – may not look as if they have much in common, but *potentially* they are all manifestations of fundamental green principles.

Building Bridges

The 'delta hypothesis' provides the most optimistic and dynamic interpretation of the Green Movement in Britain today. Just because we cannot see something distinctly, right now, does not mean to say it is not there. Don your green scuba-gear, and there it all is, if you only know where and how to look for it. As awareness of deeper green issues and ideas continues to grow, so isolated individuals and single issue campaigns will increasingly recognize what they have in common. New coalitions will form and alliances come into being. Cross-fertilization at the level of ideas has been visible in the way different parts of the Green Movement have increasingly reflected some of the wider debates. Throughout the mid-1980s, for example, the Campaign for Nuclear Disarmament's (CND) magazine, *Sanity*, increasingly drew attention to the question of nuclear power, Third World poverty, the arms trade etc. In the same way, Friends of the Earth's publications became more concerned with development and peace issues, and the threats posed by the world economic order.

Greens are often urged to 'get their act together', to come together in larger, fewer, more centralized organizations. The idea gets a pretty cool reception within the movement; with some justification, activists fear that coalitions based on some kind of non-specific green angst would be bland, bureaucratic and less likely to mount effective campaigns on specific problems than the present exotic assortment of mainly single issue pressure groups. At present, each organization has its special area of expertise, and knows the leverage it can exert.

That said, there are scores of organizations whose main aim is precisely to bring together other organizations and individuals. There are several well-known umbrella bodies like the Green Alliance (an all-party pressure group which sets out to use a deliberately exclusive membership to influence MPs and other decision-makers), or Wildlife Link (bringing together all the conservation bodies that have anything to do with Britain's flora and fauna or the countryside in general), or the Campaign Against the Arms Trade, or the International Broad-

16

casting Trust, as well as heaps of less well-known ones, like Common Ground International, which is practically the only forum bringing together representatives of the environment, development *and* population organizations. On top of that, there are also several international bodies such as the European Environmental Bureau or the Pesticides Action Network.

These are just a few of the more or less permanent bridge-builders of the Green Movement. Of equal importance are the ad hoc alliances that come together in startling profusion, some to oppose (or occasionally propose) a specific piece of government legislation or pursue some particular cause, some on a formal but short-term basis (such as the coalition of groups lobbying the Government about the Non-Proliferation Treaty in 1985), and some on an emergency footing, such as the coalition of Friends of the Earth, Survival International and Amnesty International, which came together at the end of 1987 to protest about the Malaysian Government's imprisonment of several environmental activists.

All of these alliances are formally and publicly acknowledged. They represent only a fraction of the co-operative efforts between different organizations that go on behind the scenes, the invisibility of which often leads critics and outsiders to deplore the lack of co-operation between different organizations! In all honesty, however, even the most fervent Green would currently acknowledge that the 'delta hypothesis' demands not only an act of faith but also extraordinarily acute submarine vision. In the first place, the NIMBY (Not In My Back Yard) variety of environmental activism is really a very mixed blessing when it comes to building up the movement as a whole. Time after time, local groups have emerged to fight local campaigns to stop a section of urban motorway, to save a few acres of woodland or to stop an industrial plant threatening their community. Equally often, such groups fade away again, having either succeeded or failed, without ever seeming to make the connections between their cause and what people in other parts of the Green Movement (let alone the rest of the world) are doing and thinking. This impulse to parochialism is a frustrating phenomenon, for it means that British Greens are more likely to get caught in the trap of being permanently on the defensive, of reacting to an endless stream of external environmental threats, instead of developing a critique of the way of life which leads to such threats.

Secondly, it is actually incredibly difficult to bring the disparate strands of the Green Movement together. Richard North, environment correspondent of the *Independent*, gives a specific instance of this:

17

I have hardly ever met any serious informed environmentalists who are members of the Green Party. I don't mean that there are no environmentalists in the Green Party, or that there are no Green Party members who take the environment seriously. But if I go through the list of *professionals* involved with the environment, they are just not members of the Green Party. So, when you have the environmental campaigning movement on the one hand, and you have the Green Party on the other hand, and they simply do not overlap at all – well, you can't really say that it is much of a movement!

Most organizations do indeed feel distinctly insecure if asked to move out beyond their own solid redoubts. Each feels that it has a particular niche in which to operate, and that resources are usually so scarce as to make any diversion from the principal goals of the organization something of a luxury. For instance, while the joining forces of Friends of the Earth and CND on the first anniversary of Chernobyl to organize a very successful joint demonstration in Hyde Park was warmly welcomed, this important act of solidarity was not easy for either organization. Friends of the Earth felt under a lot of pressure since CND had simply decided off its own bat, without consulting either Friends of the Earth or Greenpeace, to hold its annual demonstration on the anniversary of Chernobyl. This opened it up to accusations by some environmentalists of naked opportunism on the grounds that the Chernobyl accident itself had little *direct* connection with the business of ridding the world of nuclear weapons. On the other hand, many CND activists felt equally uneasy about the dilution of their fundamental aims. And Greenpeace (the only organization unequivocally committed to campaigning against both nuclear weapons and nuclear reactors) made it a great deal harder for both CND and Friends of the Earth by refusing to take part – on the tenuous and seemingly narrow-minded ground that 'demonstrations are not our style'. Building the Green Movement is no easy business, and the territoriality that once vitiated so many joint initiatives in the 1970s is still there, ready to reveal its lurking presence if one tries to push too far too fast.

It should, however, be said that these difficulties rarely exist at the local level: co-operation comes far more naturally outside of the pressure groups' London hot-house. The overlap between activists of the different green organizations is much greater locally than nationally, and it is commonplace for the same people to operate on behalf of two or three organizations simply by swapping hats at the appropriate time! In some parts of the country, regional alliances have proved particularly effective, especially in welding together different parts of the anti-nuclear movement. An organization like the Welsh-Anti-Nuclear Alliance, for example, is about as close as we come in the UK to a properly constituted regional organization. With one or two notable exceptions (such as the Wessex Regionalists), broad-brush regional movements in Britain are for the most part pretty puny.

This is a source of considerable consternation to that small minority of 'Fourth Worlders', the anarchically minded green decentralists who believe in autonomous, self-sufficient communities and who are able to compensate for their lack of numerical strength with an unassailable combination of unworldly idealism and indigestible jargon. As it happens, almost *all* Greens are decentralist by inclination; but most support one variation or another of the 'both top-down *and* bottom-up' model of government (with grass-roots initiatives given every opportunity to thrive through appropriate national legislation), and simply endure rather than support the 'manic minusculism' of those who argue that the Green Movement has been diminished, if not entirely done down, by its involvement in national bodies and national politics.

As it happens, the Green Movement in Britain would be absolutely nowhere without its national bodies. It is now estimated that total membership of all environmental and other vaguely green organizations in the UK exceeds 3.5 million, although this figure has to be qualified by the fact that most Greens belong to more than one organization, and some seem to belong to almost all of them! Whatever one may feel about the usefulness of such crude estimates (and the media seem to find them much more useful than the Green Movement itself), there is no doubt that the environmental organizations in Britain today are going through a particularly healthy period. If the delta is indeed forming, then most of the visible islands are predominantly of an environmental nature.

Public Opinion

Tim O'Riordan, Professor of Environmental Sciences at the University of East Anglia, believes that one can identify three quite separate and distinct phases of environmental awareness before this one. The first, he places about 150 years ago at the dawn of the Romantic age, when writers such as Wordsworth, Chekhov, Emerson and Thoreau passionately believed that 'the woods, rivers and mountains had a life of their own, every bit as important as that found in human consciousness'. The first two decades of the twentieth century then ushered in the age of the 'environmental technocrat, who sought to manipulate environmental processes and thereby increase economic wealth. Sustainable yield forestry, soil conservation, irrigation of the great deserts and the emergence of applied ecology are all associated with this period.' The third phase emerged in the mid-1960s, when environmental concerns began to capture the attention of the burgeoning global media. This, according to O'Riordan, was 'the period of institution-building, sweeping environmental regulation and the rise of scientifically respectable, politically articulate and litigious pressure groups'. Certainly there was a hell of a lot going on then; but the achievements of the period look really rather thin in retrospect.

And that brings us to today, to the 'emerging fourth environmental revolution, where the time is ripe for marrying nineteenth-century philosophy together with early twentieth-century pragmatism and the most recent phase of lobbying and institution-building'.[1]

Some historians of the movement argue that interest in the environment in modern times has largely been confined to periods of prosperity. Concern during the late 1960s and early 1970s certainly coincided with a period when the middle classes were enjoying 'the privilege of concern', the leisure and wealth to take a more caring approach to their surroundings. Hence the commonplace assertion that environmentalism is no more than an irregular sequence of spasms of middle-class guilt. Other theorists, however, point out that while this analysis may have held true in the past, we are now in the middle of an entirely new phenomenon, since the present world-wide wave of environmental concern comes at a time of considerable economic uncertainty. The truth is that, underlying the peaks of concern, there has been a quiet but steadily growing awareness of environmental issues.

This is clearly reflected in the way in which public attitudes on important environmental issues have changed over the last few years. A MORI opinion poll, conducted on behalf of Friends of the Earth and the World Wildlife Fund, now the World Wide Fund for

Nature, just before the General Election in May 1987, revealed that 81% of people believed the Government 'should give a much higher priority to protecting the environment'. Even among Conservative supporters, the figure was as high as 77%. The poll also revealed that there are particular areas of concern to the British public: that the Government should set maximum levels of pesticides and residues in food and drinking water; should provide funds to help finance local authority waste-recycling schemes; and should withdraw proposals for the shallow burial of nuclear waste. Each of these statements received over 80% support from the public.

Public concern is further reflected in a number of measures which people are prepared to take: at least a quarter are willing to pay more for petrol to combat acid rain and air pollution, to pay more tax for measures to protect the environment, to pay more in the shops in return for pesticide-free food, and to stop buying wood products unless they can be guaranteed to come from countries that are managing their forests in a responsible and sustainable way.

These findings were borne out by the 1987 *British Social Attitudes Report*, which featured environmental issues far more strongly than in preceding years. And no wonder, if one looks at the following attitudinal shifts:

TABLE I [2]

| | % regarding each of these environmental hazards as 'very' or 'quite' serious | |
	1983 %	1986 %
Industrial waste in rivers or sea	91	94
Waste from nuclear electricity stations	82	90
Industrial fumes in the air	83	89
Lead from petrol	84	85
Noise and dirt from traffic	66	73
Noise from aircraft	30	42
Acid Rain	N/A	86

Detailed questions were asked about people's reactions to changes in the countryside. The degree of concern increased markedly between 1985 and 1986, with as many as 40% of respondents now very concerned about the countryside.

TABLE 2
Concern about countryside by age within sex

	% 'very concerned'		
	1985	1986	% change
Men:			
18–34	29%	38%	+9
35–54	38%	52%	+14
55+	33%	45%	+12
Women:			
18–34	23%	26%	+3
35–54	31%	41%	+10
55+	34%	39%	+5

The respondents were then probed a little more deeply as to how this concern might translate into *action* across a range of different issues, and at this stage the continuing gulf between *passive* concern and *active* commitment becomes very clear. Ken Young, author of the countryside chapter in the report, draws this conclusion:

> As yet, then, the countryside is not seen by the overwhelming majority of the population as a cause for which they would actively crusade. Concern is relatively passive, and seems likely to remain so for all but a minority of people who are already activists, such as members of clubs or organizations connected with the countryside, who are typically highly educated and in non-manual occupations. On the evidence of our survey, the political base of an active 'green' movement – or for the Green Party itself – is still very small.[3]

By contrast, the evidence on public attitudes to nuclear power, post-Chernobyl, would appear to be less equivocal (see Tables 3 and 4).

This was confirmed by another MORI poll, for the *Reader's Digest* early in 1987, on the likelihood of a Chernobyl-type accident happening in Britain. Half the British public thinks it likely that this will occur, and the same poll showed that environmental pressure groups are much more trusted to tell the truth about the impact of nuclear power on the environment than are Government ministers or representatives of the nuclear industry!

TABLE 3

As far as nuclear power stations are concerned, which of these statements comes closest to your own feelings?

	1983 %	1984 %	1985 %	1986 %
They create very serious risks for the future	35	37	30	49
They create quite serious risks for the future	28	30	31	29
They create only slight risks for the future	26	23	26	17
They create hardly any risks for the future	9	8	9	4

TABLE 4

Support for the construction of more nuclear power stations

	1984	1985	1986	% change 1985–6
Total	15%	23%	11%	−12
Identifiers:				
Conservative	24%	39%	18%	−21
Alliance	14%	25%	11%	−14
Labour	8%	10%	4%	−6

Of particular interest are public perceptions about nuclear waste.

TABLE 5

How serious an effect on our environment does waste from nuclear electricity stations have?

	1983 %	1984 %	1985 %	1986 %
'Very' or 'quite' serious	82	87	83	90
'Not very' or 'not at all' serious	15	11	15	8

This must be particularly upsetting to NIREX and the CEGB, who have always believed that people are worried about nuclear waste only because of distortions, half-truths and scaremongering by environmentalists, and that a bit more public education is all that is needed to sort out these gullible fools. Given the figures, this seems highly improbable, and though environmentalists would totally and angrily refute the charges about scaremongering (in the sure knowledge that the scientific and economic arguments against nuclear power are the ones that will eventually win the day), there is no doubt that the imperviousness of people to 'the facts as seen by NIREX' is highly advantageous to the anti-nuclear cause:

> People are not appraising scientific 'facts' about radioactive waste as though they exist in a value-free vacuum. It is evident that beliefs about waste are inseparable from their confidence in management, worries about 'possible' harm in the future, and the relation of technological advance to their already established value system. It is unlikely that the uncertainties surrounding waste management options now or in the future can be countered by scientific argument.[4]

Whatever steps are likely to be taken to establish the 'scientific facts', it appears absolutely obvious that Chernobyl has already made an impression on the people of Britain equivalent to that which the Three Mile Island accident had on Americans. Though this is likely to fade to a certain extent over time, it is unlikely that it will ever dissipate entirely.

Environmental Organizations

Whether it is nuclear power or the countryside, acid rain or recycling, a growth in awareness and concern can clearly be perceived over the last few years. Whether this has come about *because* of the work of environmental organizations, or their increasing influence has come about because of the public's growing awareness, is one of those imponderable questions. All one can say with any certainty is that there is sure to be an environmental organization out there somewhere to suit everyone, whatever his or her own environmental concerns may be. Environmental pressure groups now come in all shapes and sizes, but essentially there are two ways of looking at how they all relate to each other: either in terms of their tactics and campaigning style, or in terms of their underlying beliefs and philosophical orientation.

As regards tactics and style, one can draw a convenient line with the RSPB and the National Trust at one end, and Greenpeace at the other. All the rest fall somewhere in between. The RSPB (with half a million members) remains formidably pukka, with a great reluctance to broaden the frame of reference. It has even refused to get involved in the acid rain debate, deciding not to publish the results of one of its own research projects which quite clearly demonstrated the impact of increased acidification on different bird species.

Despite criticism from David Clark, MP (the erstwhile 'Mr Green' of the Labour Party), the National Trust is actually more concerned about broader environmental issues than most people might assume. The appointment of Dame Jennifer Jenkins as Chair of the National Trust stirred things up quite a bit, and with its membership of 1.5 million (rising from just 600,000 in 1977) the National Trust now has a particularly important role to play in helping to influence some of its dowdier and more tweedily respectable colleagues.

There have also been considerable changes within the World Wide Fund for Nature, the UK division of which (with more than 120,000 members) is far more dynamic and far less panda-obsessed than World Wide Fund for Nature International or other national groups. Its policy of getting things done partly by helping other environmental organizations has been extremely successful, and the gradual shift of emphasis within it, first from species-specific conservation to habitat protection, and then to involvement in broader social and political issues, has provided a useful model for similar organizations to follow.

In much the same way, the Council for the Protection of Rural England (CPRE) so broadened its remit under the firm but gentle hand of Robin Grove-White that it was able to participate as a major objector in the Sizewell Inquiry with the (more or less!) full support of its members. Having centralized its membership in the mid-1980s, it too became far less stuffy and predictable in its campaigning style, and has gained a formidable reputation for effectiveness, particularly within Tory circles.

Friends of the Earth would claim to bridge the divide between the 'respectable' and the 'radical' ends of this spectrum of environmental organizations. With 220 active local groups, it is not always easy to generalize about Friends of the Earth, but since it got off the ground in 1971 it has combined a variety of different tactics on a very wide range of different issues. While successfully pursuing those single issues in the traditional way, Friends of the Earth has always attempted to provide a broader context for deeper green changes in society in recognition of the enormity of the transformation that it believes is necessary.

Despite very rapid growth in both funds and supporters (currently around 60,000), Friends of the Earth always seems to live slightly in the shadow of Greenpeace, which has grown even more rapidly. (After the French sank the *Rainbow Warrior* in 1986, their membership doubled to 100,000 in just eighteen months.) The Greenpeace 'media machine' has made it the best-known environmental organization in the world, and they have alerted millions of people to a whole series of environmental issues through imaginative and courageous direct actions and high-profile campaigning. Equally, Greenpeace comes in for a fair bit of criticism, both from the public and from their predominantly 'light green' colleagues, on the grounds that both their law-breaking and their confrontationalism are counter-productive for the rest of the Green Movement. Even Greenpeace's reliance on the media has been criticized:

> Television is a passivity-reinforcing mechanism which rewards viewers for sitting down and doing nothing other than watching. Greenpeace bears to the right when it just 'bears witness' – the official ideology of change for the group. To base our hopes on television is to leave our movement vulnerable to changing tastes and escalating demands for more entertaining action. Successful environmental organizing lies in uniting communities around commonly felt threats and translating the support into political power. The alternative is to let the folks stay happily planted on the couch, safe in the knowledge that the whales are being taken care of. It's right there on the tube.[5]

Despite such criticism, it must still be said that Greenpeace is uniquely able to instil a particular feeling of inspiration and commitment, particularly in young people. Their policy of not allowing local groups to become involved in any campaigning, but only to raise funds for the national campaigns, may well make Greenpeace one of the most centralist and least democratic organizations in the Green Movement, but given the risks involved in their direct-action style of campaigning, that is perhaps understandable.

The reputation of most green organizations has never been higher with journalists and scientists and there is still a tremendous sense of confidence as regards the future amongst green activists. Moreover, one should also point out that there are many committed environmentalists who choose not to channel their energies through any one organization, and who suddenly find themselves taking up the cudgels in a way they might never have dreamed would be either possible or necessary. Such a person is Margaret Morgan, who ended up on a 33-day hunger strike to protect the wild-flower meadow at the back of her home in the South Wales village of Gowerton.

She began trying to save the meadow in 1983 after hearing that a local caravan company planned to extend its existing site by covering it with concrete. For years she fought single-handedly with the usual protestor's weapons: letters, lobbies, a one-woman demonstration outside the offices of Swansea City Council, appeals to her MP. By February 1987 she appeared to have won. The Council told her they had given the field planning protection. But a week later a mechanical digger moved on to the site to start drainage work. She decided a hunger strike was her only option:

> It was a very personal thing, much more important to me than just being aware of my environment. I've never been one for pleasures which can be purchased by money. I simply like walking my dog in the meadow, just on my little patch which is full of wild orchids and other flowers. But not everyone sees the beauty. I thought the other house-owners who skirt the area would support me in some way. In fact, they have been conspicuous by their silence. Early on, I tried to start up a conservation association, but no one was interested. No one seemed to understand what I was trying to say, as if there were 3,000 people walking around with their eyes closed. They were quite prepared to let this meadow, which was my relationship with nature, be destroyed. I couldn't cope with that. I felt my back was against the wall. That's probably why I did something as extreme as a hunger strike.

During her painful fast, she existed only on water and fruit juice, but continued to cook for the family and do her ordinary round of household chores. Her self-imposed ordeal ended only when she heard that Swansea City Council had asked the caravan company to stop drainage work on the site 'on humanitarian grounds' She has threatened to repeat her fast if necessary, and still isn't 100% certain the meadow is safe:

27

I don't know why I did it. Sometimes I woke up in the middle of the night and felt a trembling around my heart. Then I'd make a prayer. I do know that I wouldn't last that length of time if I went down that road again. I worry about the damage I might have done to my body and don't dare go to the doctor for a check-up in case I find out. It isn't easy being true, not even to myself.

She knows that her extreme protest failed to strike a chord in Gowerton. In addition, her claims that local politics had lost touch with its socialist roots and had become riddled with freemasonry, cosy deals and mutual back-scratching made her few friends:

I imagine my neighbours thought I was mad. My family definitely thought so. I used to be a quiet individual, just doing my own quiet thing and trusting in democracy. But not any more. We had these ideals, but where have they gone? It's not much fun recognizing we don't live in a real democracy. I'm not just fighting for this one little meadow. It's a nice meadow, and it should be left alone. But so should other meadows all over the country. I'm fighting for all ordinary parcels of land which people like me can't protect because the species on them aren't officially rare enough. But they're special enough to me and thousands like me. If this one goes, there'll be another one, then another, until they've all gone.

That kind of personal story, with its poignant postscript, says a lot about the environment movement today. However courageously individuals like Margaret Morgan fight their corner, however confident the leading organizations may be about their prospects over the next few years, the harsh fact remains that it's really very difficult to notch up any substantial progress across a whole range of environmental issues. In certain instances it may even be true that mere activity is being confused with achievement. The monthly edition of ENDS (Environmental Data Services) provides a depressing catalogue of things that are not getting any better (such as hazardous waste disposal or hedgerow destruction), things that are getting worse (such as declining river quality and increased sulphur-dioxide pollution), and things that promise much but achieve little (such as the Government's much-vaunted programme of flue gas desulphurization).

Green Divides

This paradox can only be explained by considering the astonishing diversity of political and philosophical views within the Green Movement. Tim O'Riordan's 1981 classification of modern environmentalism still provides the most useful analytical clues in this respect. (See Fig. 1.)

FIG. 1[6]
The Ideological Structure of Modern Environmentalism

ENVIRONMENTALISM

ECO-CENTRISM		TECHNO-CENTRISM	
gaianism belief in the rights of nature and of the essential co-evolution of humans and natural phenomena	*communalism* belief in the co-operation capabilities of societies to be collectively self-reliant using 'appropriate' science and technology	*accommodation* faith in the adaptability of institutions and mechanisms of assessment and decision-making to accommodate to environmental demands	*optimism* faith in the application of science, market forces and managerial ingenuity
← redistribution of power towards a decentralized, federal political economy based on the interlinkage of environmental and social justice →		← maintenance of the status quo in existing structures of government power →	

By 'techno-centrism', he means a human-centred view of the Earth coupled with a managerial approach to resources and environmental protection. The optimists believe that by a combination of ingenuity and necessity, things can only get better and better; those into 'accommodation' believe it to be possible to reform the existing system to the point where the environmental costs are minimized or even eliminated. 'Eco-centrism' entails a radical transformation of society if we are ever to achieve any kind of sustainable life-style. 'Communalists' put their faith in bottom-up co-operation, while the

29

'gaianists" believe that the Earth is a living, self-regulating organism demands a fundamental shift in our human-centred value systems.

In 1983, O'Riordan was arguing that 'the most significant achievement of the current environmental movement has been to shift policies out of optimism and into accommodation'.[7] Since then, there is little doubt that environmentalists have consolidated their successes in that area, and have succeeded in shifting more of the emphasis on to the *causes* of environmental breakdown, rather than the *symptoms*. Beyond that, we have not really succeeded in moving things further down the line towards the eco-centric alternative. It is here that the underlying tension between light green environmental reformism and dark green holistic radicalism begins to make itself felt. Single issue reformers rightly claim that they are effective only by virtue of their narrow focus, and get very hot under the collar at being accused of what is tantamount to collaboration with the enemy. Dark Greens claim with equal rectitude that it is a question of seeing the wood as well as the trees, and that no amount of single issue 'victories' will actually save the day.

This debate is dealt with in greater detail in Chapter 10. Die Grünen have, after all, managed to split themselves pretty well down the middle on this question of 'realists versus fundamentalists'. It is conceivable that things might go the same way here, but there does seem to be a rather more pragmatic and tolerant approach to differences of attitude within the Green Movement in the UK. Indeed, from a dark green perspective, intolerance of those less green than oneself is really an utterly unjustifiable self-indulgence. Dark Greens often refer to contemporary politics as a three-lane highway, with a right lane and a left lane and a middle-of-the road lane. It really doesn't matter which lane you're in, since this particular highway is heading for the abyss. Everyone in the Green Movement should therefore be actively engaged exhorting people to get off this three-lane motorway, to get out of their car, and to head off instead down a relatively small footpath by the side of the motorway signposted quite simply 'Alternative Route'.

The simple fact is that it is difficult for many people to see where this alternative footpath is actually going, and therefore an act of faith is often required to take those first few faltering steps along it. Indeed, as soon as people start talking to each other some way along the path, it very soon emerges that different people reckon they're headed in very different directions. But people also discover very quickly that they have more than enough in common with others on the path to keep them going on down it, rather than hurrying back to the motorway. As a result, there are people strung out all along that path, and unless the dark Greens are working flat out to help the light Greens advance down it further and further, then one has to question the usefulness of their being green at all.

That does not, of course, resolve the day-to-day dilemmas of how best to pursue specific campaign goals, or how to get the right balance between co-operation and confrontation. Organizations have a natural tendency to be less confrontational as they get more established and as their staff get older. That is by no means a good thing, unless it is done as a carefully thought-out response to changing circumstances. For instance, there is a lively debate within many environmental organizations as to how environmentalists should now be relating to the farming community. Do we simply go on blaming individual farmers, caricaturing them as subsidized whingers, paid to produce food which no one wants to buy, chopping down trees, ripping out hedges and polluting the Earth with agro-chemicals, or do we start shifting the criticism towards the system which has forced farmers into this pattern of destruction, in many cases much to their own distress? Should we be putting the boot in or patting them on the back? The answer to this varies according to any organization's specific campaign goals, but the most canny approach may of course be to do both at the same time, by putting the boot in on the large, over-subsidized grain farmers, and working together with the small, mixed farmers, organic farmers, etc. Not only does this demonstrate a more accurate perception of who's been doing the damage, but it may also serve to produce splits and divisions amongst their own numbers.

The situation gets even more complicated when it comes to dealing with industry, as we shall see in Chapter 6. The length of spoon required to sup with today's industrial devils varies dramatically from organization to organization. At a time when designer environmentalism is all the rage, when closet Greens are coming out like a nettle rash, and when one can actually feel good about being green rather than having to creep around apologetically like a much-reviled Jehovah's Witness, Greens are doubly wise to be cautious. That rock-like question of just who is exploiting or co-opting whom still has to be asked a great deal more often than your average soft-centred Green might like.

But natural caution does *not* mean retreating into some kind of green laager: all campaigning organizations have to recognize that the vast majority of people operate on a pragmatic basis, and view various extremes of greenery as hopelessly unrealistic and thus damagingly self-indulgent. Richard North sums this up from a personal point of view:

> It would be fair to say that I am fairly split as regards this fundamentalist business. I suppose I am a fundamentalist as regards my attitude towards green spirituality, but on the other hand, as I get older, I also want the achievable real accommodation. It may be that I am just at the classic point of my life when one starts becoming an accommodater – for all I know I shall get extremely bored with it, and become a shit-kicking fundamentalist the week after next. But I like to get involved in *winnable* battles; if we have got dirty cars, then it's better to have clean ones, rather than no cars at all. At different times in my life I have been a vegetarian and a vegan, and took it extremely seriously. But increasingly I began to think – 'No, I do want to eat some meat, so let's campaign for better, healthier meat.' I suppose what I really am is a 'betterist'. As my arteries have thickened, I have become more of a reformer than a revolutionary.

In a recent article in *Resurgence*, Richard St George put the same point in a more general, political context:

> In campaigning terms, the bulk of the population operates on a pragmatic basis. Yet the Green Movement has largely resided in an isolated ghetto of no more than 5% of the population, going round and round in small circles, preaching to the already converted and stoking its own belief system. Of course, one can say that the crushing apathy of the mass of the population creates the extremists, but this simply is not tenable. It is precisely because of the activities of the extremists that the general good will of people is never tapped. The British population is *not* apathetic, and the middle ground is actually often very willing to shift. So, let us disown the extremists, and then the Green Movement might actually start to move![8]

There is little doubt that talking to people, gently and persuasively, who are still 'on the other side of the fence' is what much of green politics today is all about: the process of 'building bridges of benevo-

32

lence'. In this context, however, the Achilles Heel of the Green Movement is revealed time after embarrassing time: namely, its inability to position environmental concerns in any kind of viable alternative framework of economic theory and practice. As Tim O'Riordan says:

> When you look at those periods of decline for environmentalists, what seems to be at the heart of them is the fact that the link is missing between the environment and the economy. Unless Greens can deal with different economic policies, with monetarism, with the problems of unemployment or the rehabilitation of inner cities, then they are never likely to be able to talk to people in the kind of language that they can understand.

The attachment of ordinary people to conventional economics is, of course, astonishingly persistent, despite the fact that the world economy is now in a pretty dismal state: wasteful, destructive, racked by debt and unemployment, distorted by the arms race, fruitlessly pursuing infinite growth within the confines of a strictly finite environment. Precisely because conventional economics consistently fails to take account of things that really matter to people, like their health and the quality of their environment, a small but growing number of green economists have begun to develop alternative economic theories designed to meet real human needs better than growth-orientated capitalism or socialism can do. The objective of this work is as revolutionary an objective as one finds anywhere in the whole Green Movement, for it aims to change fundamentally the whole process by which we think about wealth.

By far the best introduction to this fledgling school of 'green economics' is to be found in *The Living Economy*, edited by Paul Ekins. This summarizes much of the work of the *only* green organization taking on the unglamorous business of economics, namely The Other Economic Summit (TOES) and its charitable body, The New Economics Foundation. TOES, set up in 1984 specifically to counter the 'conventional wisdom' emanating from the annual summit of leaders of the Western world, is one of those umbrella groups that really has built some lasting bridges. It has gradually drawn together more and more individuals and organizations, who collectively have tried to impress upon sympathizers just how important it is for the Green Movement to get its economic act together. As with many of the harder aspects of green politics (i.e. those with an uncompromisingly honest message which makes no effort to mollycoddle the kind of people who prefer to keep their heads in the sand), it has proved difficult to gain widespread support for green economics. The truth is often more painful than the lie, even when the lie is known to be a lie.

This is likely to remain a major problem for the whole Green Movement well into the next decade. On balance, however, the prospects for those involved in the specifically environmental organizations within the Green Movement look reasonably good. Tim O'Riordan isolates two important reasons for subscribing to this optimistic view:

> One of the most critical factors in the growth of environmental organizations is the change in technology and science. There has been such a massive improvement in prediction, modelling and general scientific understanding, and this has, of course, rubbed off on both the public and on those environmental organizations who are now able to build up genuine counter-expertise in relation to government departments and industry's scientists.
>
> Add to that the fact that what is going on in Europe will certainly continue to raise the consciousness of people across a whole number of important environmental issues (particularly bio-technology), and I think one can say that environmental organizations are going to be both busy and successful over the next few years.

The importance of the international dimension of the work being done by environmental organizations is picked up again in Chapter 10, but for the time being we need to look beyond what is happening environmentally to see just how far green awareness has reached into other *potentially* green social and political movements. How substantial are those other islands forming in this hypothetical green delta?

CHAPTER TWO

The Common Ground

The Development Movement

Until a few years ago, conventional wisdom held that the best way to improve living standards for people in the world's poorest nations was to help them to live more like us, as industrialized consumer societies. If only enough money could be pumped into these developing economies, wealth would 'trickle down' to the poor, and standards of living would rise. In the decades following the Second World War, 'under-developed' countries enthusiastically embraced the concepts of industrialism and economic growth; throughout the 1970s, Western banks speeded up this process by handing out billions of dollars in loans.

Such development has often proved catastrophic for the people of the Third World, replacing sustainable social and economic patterns with destructive ones which cannot be sustained. Instead of cultivating food for themselves, for instance, more and more farmers began growing cash crops for export to earn foreign exchange. But the world recession, combined with falling commodity prices and the high interest rates of the early 1980s, left debtor nations reeling. Many were obliged by the International Monetary Fund to introduce austerity measures, which invariably hit the poorest people hardest.

As the debt ratio for these countries worsened, commodity prices remained low, so that the per unit value of their export crops has inexorably fallen. Under ever more intense financial pressure, more crops are therefore grown faster and with less regard to environmental circumstances. To increase production, farmers have abandoned centuries-old sustainable agricultural practices. At the same time, minerals are being extracted at an ever faster pace and pollution levels are rising dramatically. We have reached the point where the fundamental logic of conventional economics is to force countries to convert their irreplaceable natural resources into debt interest repayments. In the process of seeing their forests destroyed, their topsoil worn away and their fresh water increasingly polluted, the impoverished Third World has, ludicrously, become a net exporter of capital to the developed world to the tune of billions of dollars every year.

In 1987, *Our Common Future*, the report of the United Nations World Commission on Environment and Development, provided strong evidence for a radical change of approach. It argued that the various environmental, development and energy crises confronting the planet were simply different aspects of the one, interlocking global crisis:

> Environmental degradation, first seen as mainly a problem of the rich nations and a side effect of industrial wealth, has become a survival issue for developing nations. It is part of the downward spiral of linked ecological and economic decline in which many of the poorest nations are trapped.
>
> The environment does not exist as a sphere separate from human actions, ambitions and needs, and attempts to defend it in isolation from human concerns have given the very word 'environment' a connotation of naïvety in some political circles. But the 'environment' is where we all live; and development is what we all do in attempting to improve our lot within that abode. The two are inseparable.[1]

Growing awareness of all these issues has deeply affected British attitudes to foreign aid and the Third World. In the early 1980s, most officials of British development agencies still had implicit faith in 'trickle-down'. They spoke warmly and uncritically about the 'need' to increase the volume of trade and improve access to markets in the developed world for client countries, assuming that such measures would automatically help poor people. Questions about the long-term ecological implications of such trade were simply not on anyone's agenda. Only in the last few years have aid agencies begun to challenge these assumptions. They have restructured their own aid programmes by placing a much greater emphasis on encouraging sustainability, and they have sharpened the criticism of the British Government's aid policies, both for being stingy and for its emphasis on 'bilateral' or 'tied' aid, by which aid is given only in return for agreements to buy British goods or services.

Oxfam, Britain's largest development and relief agency, has for many years concentrated on developing self-sufficient local projects designed to help the poorest of the world's poor. As a result of growing experience in the field and awareness that Western methods and machines were often not appropriate for local conditions, Oxfam's staff were increasingly forced to question their faith in the ability of trickle-down and other Western concepts to provide lasting solutions to poverty, hunger and illness. In recent years, like other organizations in the development movement, Oxfam has been obliged to broaden its horizons even further to take green political perspectives into account. They have adopted a tougher campaigning approach and forged important links with environmental agencies.

Hugh Goyder, former head of Oxfam projects in India and now research and evaluation officer, remembers a moment when the limitations of working on isolated local schemes became painfully apparent:

> In the late 1970s, we were happily funding a small project digging wells in a tribal area of Gujarat. It was a straightforward project with no particular problems which was running nicely and providing good publicity back home. One day, I visited it and the man in charge there told me: 'We're all about to be flooded out by a great dam scheme – what are you going to do about it?' I had that sort of experience more than once. Government decisions, taken outside the area and usually backed by World Bank or British government money, would often threaten our small schemes. Our publicity at that time was all about wonderful achievements: 'Give £10 and provide clean water for ten tribal peoples in India' – that kind of thing. So the dam in Gujarat didn't just flood out our wells; it showed that kind of publicity to be fraudulent.

Goyder believes that both donors and Oxfam workers have become more and more aware of the ecological dimension of poverty. The setting up of its 'Hungry for Change' groups in the mid-1980s was one of the main factors accelerating this awareness. As repression, environmental degradation and poverty have all increased, political activists, environmentalists and aid agencies have increasingly found a common agenda:

> As the pressures have grown, we've all been forced to look for more allies. We've been pushed nearer the Green Movement. We've become better at focussing and articulating and at fitting our experience into a much broader picture. I've been surprised in the last few years how strong our common agenda now is with organizations like the World Wide Fund for Nature and Survival International. In the 1970s, we might have decided it was all a bit beyond us. But now we've expanded our campaigning work.

37

In fact, Oxfam campaigns on three or four issues at any one time, and it's only fair to say that the environment has been no more than one amongst many. Despite quite a fanfare of publicity about their environmental campaign in 1987, it never really amounted to much and recently has been kept ticking over with a very low profile. This is partly explained by budgetary constraints, and partly by the difficulty of establishing appropriate and achievable targets. But the real truth is that Oxfam still approaches 'the environment' in a rather reductionist and reactive way. For instance, it anticipated a much bigger public response to the World Commission's report, *Our Common Future*, and when that didn't materialize, it made very little effort to push the report itself. (This was in marked contrast to the enormous efforts it made at the time of the Brandt Report back in the early 1980s.) Very little of their research has been directed at the environment/development theme, and 'sustainability' remains something of a catch-all, mean-anything abstraction in much of their literature.

Worse still, there remains a lingering suspicion that protecting the environment and promoting the interests of the poor might still be mutually exclusive. Their 1987 brochure on *Oxfam and the Environment* opened with these astonishingly defensive words: 'All over the world Oxfam supports local communities fighting for a better future. No matter how important the threat to plants and animals highlighted by ecologists, Oxfam's prime concern must be to improve the living standards of poor people.' At first glance, one might suppose that whoever wrote that simply hadn't read *Our Common Future*, which time after time hammers home the mutuality of interest between poor people and their environment. To imply that protecting 'plants and animals' might actually constitute a threat to poor people is real Dark Age stuff, and shows exactly how difficult it is, even in an organization as progressive and dynamic as Oxfam, to root out reductionist support for add-on, symptom-curing environmentalism.

That said, Oxfam is still setting the pace in this area, and their own grass roots in the UK as well as their workers in developing countries now lend enormous and highly influential support to the sustainable development movement. By contrast, more conventional organizations like Christian Aid and Save the Children have remained in the familiar philanthropic or charitable mould. Depoliticization is very much the name of the game, and green issues have a disturbing knack of getting very political very quickly. But public perceptions about

38

aid, aroused by the Ethiopian famine and by Bob Geldof's swash-buckling, no-holds-barred crusade, have become increasingly sophis-ticated and increasingly radical. Geldof himself underwent an interesting transformation, shifting the emphasis from short-term emergency relief to long-term grass roots projects giving some real hope for a sustainable future. Such an emphasis was even more clearly reflected in Comic Relief's enormously successful initiative in February 1988. The laudable humanitarian impulse to give money to send food to starving peasants with swollen bodies is being augmented by a much tougher analysis of the politics and causes of poverty in the Third World. The idea that aid means crumbs from the rich man's table is no longer respectable.

Britain's aid record is not exactly one to be proud of. In 1986, the Independent Group on British Aid asserted that while most govern-ments of rich countries acted meanly and with unapologetic self-interest in their dealings with the Third World, 'hardly any has been meaner and more self-interested in its response than the British Government.' Between 1978 and 1986, the value of British aid actually fell by 17% in real terms.[2] In addition, 60% of British aid is 'tied' to contracts with British companies. In other words, it is designed to benefit British exporters at least as much as the countries which receive it. Furthermore, for political reasons, the great majority of British aid projects of all kinds go to comparatively well-off commonwealth and capitalist countries instead of to the poorest countries which need it most.

Yet even here there are signs of improvement. A process of greening has begun to take place even at the heart of Whitehall. Chris Patten, the Minister of Overseas Aid, has become the most notable convert to a more enlightened and greener approach. By March 1987, his department had agreed a series of guidelines to assess environmental considerations in any proposed aid project. Mr Patten declared: 'What is needed is growth that can be sustained. Growth must be pursued within – and not despite – the limits of ecological resilience.'[3] Such sentiments are commonplace in green circles, but it would have been unthinkable even three years earlier to suppose that one might hear them from the mouth of a Tory minister.

In the long term, this conceptual revolution in the development movement is likely to prove of greater significance than almost anything else going on in British society itself. The question it poses is this: if Western-style development in the Third World can wipe out the rainforests, create thousands of square miles of desert, reduce millions of Africans to famine and chronic poverty, and bring much of Latin America to the verge of ecological destitution, then what might it be doing to us closer to home? The answer to that question should reverberate in every corner of our industrial society.

The Peace Movement

Other, equally searching questions about the substainability of our current industrial systems are being asked elsewhere. In April 1987, on the first anniversary of Chernobyl, 50,000 people marched to Hyde Park for a rally organized by CND and Friends of the Earth to protest against both nuclear weapons and nuclear power. As we saw in Chapter 1, the idea that there is a firm link between civil and military nuclear programmes is now so widely accepted that the co-operation between the two organizations was not even questioned by the media. Observers were left in no doubt that this was an unprecedented and genuinely green event.

Yet that degree of co-operation was possible only because of a remarkable transformation inside CND. At its national conference only three years earlier, the mood was so different that members refused even to discuss a proposal to make opposition to nuclear power part of CND's constitution. And just three years before that, when Ecology CND (which later became Green CND) was set up to join Labour, Trade Union, Liberal and Christian CNDs as a special section with its own budget within the organization, the lack of enthusiasm for (and unmistakable hostility to) wider green ideas was palpable. As Linda Churnside, now Chair of Green CND and National Treasurer of CND, remembers: 'CND just wanted to recruit more people from the environment movement, as it saw it. If the term "Green Movement" was used, everyone laughed. Not many people in CND believed such a thing existed.'

From its formation in 1958, CND has been steeped in the politics of the Left. A large proportion of its members and officials came from the Labour Party. It was organized along lines a trade union official would feel comfortable with. When the Labour Party and the trade unions were solidly pro nuclear power, so too, as night follows day, was CND. It is important to recall that CND in the 1950s and 1960s actually campaigned with the slogan 'Atoms for Peace'! Only very slowly did the realization dawn that you can't have 'atoms for peace' without getting 'atoms for war', and even then the issue divided CND along predictable lines. On one side were the trade unionists who feared the loss of members' jobs in the nuclear industry and wanted CND to remain a strictly single-issue campaign. On the other were the Greens and the anti-nuclear socialists who saw nuclear power and nuclear weapons as siamese twins.

By 1986, an anti-nuclear power motion at CND's annual conference was backed by some of the largest affiliated unions and by Trade Union CND itself. The evidence CND presented to the Sizewell Inquiry concerning the military use of plutonium from civil nuclear reactors dispelled any lingering doubts. Since then, Lord Marshall has conceded that plutonium from our nuclear power programme did indeed go into the military stockpile up until 1969, and though Mrs Thatcher persistently claims that no plutonium has been exported or used for military purposes since she took office in 1979, she refuses to comment on what went on in the intervening decade.

A less dramatic but highly significant change has occurred at the organizational level and in the way in which CND reaches decisions. Linda Churnside recalls her extreme anxiety at the first National Council meeting she attended in 1984:

> The whole thing was terribly intimidating. It was held in a long room at County Hall [in London] with all the chairs facing the officers who were sitting at the front. It was a terribly rigid, hierarchical set-up. Everything was done by resolutions and standing orders. That's what was acceptable at the time, the way things had always been done in the Labour Party and in the unions. It wasn't really very democratic, but doing anything differently was considered very strange.
>
> Meetings are different now. We've done away with microphones, we sit in a circle so that everyone has a sense of greater equality. I certainly find it much easier to speak. Others do too. The old attitude was that you hadn't really decided anything unless you'd taken a vote. You either won or lost. But the Women's Movement and the Green Movement have shown that that's not a very good way for a peace movement to make decisions. It's very divisive and undemocratic. Now we try to decide things by consensus, though it's not always possible. CND has come a long way on that. The changes are symptoms of a deeper change on the level of ideas,

41

but it's been very difficult. A lot of people were terribly unhappy about changing, usually men and people on the far left who'd never come across this way of working and who'd not really taken on board what the Women's Movement, or Greenham, or the Green Movement, has had to say.

Easter 1988 marked the thirtieth anniversary of CND (duly celebrated with a nostalgic march to Aldermaston to recall the innocent early days), but the signing of the INF Treaty in 1987 actually represents a more important date for the peace movement and CND in particular. With one or two honourable exceptions, the media simply swallowed the Government's line that the Russians were compelled to an agreement only because of NATO's tough line in introducing cruise and Pershing missiles. CND has yet to fashion a post-INF strategy, and Mrs Thatcher's third election victory has made it harder for CND than almost any other pressure group. It is widely expected that the new 'realpolitik' of Neil Kinnock and Bryan Gould may include some watering down of the Labour Party's unilateralist policy, and the chronic confusion within the Social and Liberal Democrats precisely demonstrates the extent to which the balance of power in the UK has shifted to the right. CND has to cope with the 'Great Fear' of all these politicians: that any party advocating non-nuclear defence strategies and non-alignment will be unelectable.

That makes it very difficult for those in CND who have always thought (as many still do) that CND exists to help elect a Labour Government which will then carry out its aims! As Linda Churnside says, such an approach is now considered somewhat counter-productive:

> CND has become far more diverse over the last few years, Green CND has been very active and a lot more people have come in from different backgrounds: anarchists, Christians, women from Greenham Common. Practically every woman in CND has been to Greenham at some time and they've been a big influence. A lot of people don't trust the Labour Party and are ignoring the political process. They see it as a diversion. And that's why the basic message of the Greens that nuclear weapons are not just the least healthy aspect of an otherwise perfect world but part of a much wider malaise is being taken up by more and more people.

There has, of course, always been a Peace Movement in the UK over and above or beyond CND, and it has almost as many diverse strands as the Environment Movement. Michael Barker's *Directory for the Environment* lists eighty-five different organizations, involving many professional, academic and religious groups, as well as those opposed to the whole arms race and militarism in general. The extent to which green ideas have had any influence here can only be gauged by looking in detail at each organization, but there is a constant creative tension between the need to preserve single-issue campaign goals and the desire to promote broader attitudinal and psychological shifts.

This is more of a problem for national organizations than for local groups. One of the most exciting developments over the last four or five years has been the explosion of local peace or anti-nuclear alliances and umbrella all-purpose green groups. It has proved far easier to establish the links through such grass-roots organizations than through their far more cumbersome and often territorial national counterparts. As regards the next few years, it is likely to be at this level, therefore, that some of the more radical ideas about peace and security will be absorbed. The modern Peace Movement is very much a product of the nuclear age, and has tended to concentrate very largely on nuclear weapons and nuclear disarmament. However, much work is currently under way on extending the notion of 'security' to cover far more than military security. As Paul Ekins, Director of the Right Livelihood Foundation, says:

> There are, in fact, intrinsic problems with military security which guarantee its unattainability on a global scale. It is, at best, zero-sum security. The increase in one country's military security is always a decrease in that of its (perceived) enemies. This leads them to increase their military commitments, so that the security of the first country is correspondingly reduced. A new approach to national security needs to include at least the following four dimensions: military security; civil security; economic security; and ecological security. These securities are obviously interlinked. In particular, ecological security promotes economic security which promotes civil security.

Ecological security is obviously security of a very different kind. Among the basic constituents of ecological security should be counted the quality of any country's soil, water, forests and grass-

43

lands. And because these factors invariably make a nonsense of national borders, the opportunity for nations to discover a new mutuality of interest in the joint care of shared environmental resources is enormous. Paul Ekins:

> If the problem of peace were increasingly to be seen as one of achieving security in the terms described above, rather than of weapons, then there would be a greater chance of convergence between the peace and green movements. For it is only through an integrated approach to security that it is *rational* to disarm, and such an approach has a large economic component which dovetails neatly into the green economic agenda, and into that of no other political movement.

Eco-Feminism

An increasingly important voice in the peace movement over the last few years has been that of the hundreds of thousands of women involved in peace activities of one kind or another. On 12 December 1982, thousands of these women linked hands around Greenham Common Airbase, soon to become home of Britain's cruise missiles. A hand-written call for action, put out from the tents of women camping at the base, asked everyone to bring along symbols of life to decorate the fence which enclosed these weapons of mass destruction. The fence was entwined with photos of children, friends and lovers, nappies, shells, poems, tampons, teddies – treasured things of memory and ritual. The effect was both exciting and scary. Here was an act of creative transformation. And it was dangerous. Women were challenging the death-wish of military institutions with their love of the small, everyday acts of life.

Though the relationship of women with the Peace Movement has been widely debated, there has by comparison been very little discussion about the links between feminism and ecology. There is a basic assumption that the Women's Movement in Britain would be sympathetic to ecological concerns as a matter of course. It would be highly unusual to meet a feminist in favour of nuclear power, dumping toxic waste at sea or allowing industry to pollute the air we breathe. Yet for many, perhaps the majority, these issues have not been seen as a priority for campaigning. There's one simple reason for this: issues such as reproductive rights, freedom from rape, decent

44

pay, housing and childcare, the daily struggle against racism, and so on, are all felt to be more important and more *immediate*.

Some of these issues are of course about the environment, yet remain ignored by most environmental groups, perhaps because they affect the landscape of the inner city rather than the countryside. The cover of *Making Space: Women and the Man-made Environment* shows a woman struggling up a flight of dirty, graffiti-covered concrete steps carrying a baby in a pushchair. The image provokes questions about the availability of transport, design of housing, provision of childcare and safety on the streets; yet the environment with which this woman and others – especially poor and black people – have to struggle is only rarely on the ecological agenda.

Equally, many feminists remain unsure of the basic orientation of green politics. Within Judaeo-Christian societies, a hierarchy has been assumed where white middle- and upper-class men are closer to *culture* (and God), while women, black and poor people are seen as closer to *nature*, and are therefore 'baser'. Thus women are associated with what is messy, chaotic, unpredictable, smelly and dark. Susan Griffin argues that women are not *inherently* more in tune with nature; but the role allocated to women by society means they inevitably spend much time preparing (and in some cases gathering) food, cleaning up the mess of the very young and very old, or attending births and deaths. 'If this association [between women and nature] has been the rationalization of our oppression by a society which fears both women and nature, it has also meant that those of us born female are often less severely alienated from nature than are most men.'[4]

'Nature' is often used as a powerful weapon by the right-wing. Woman's 'nature', it is said, is to bear children and care for them, to be intuitive and closer to her emotions, not to analyse, plan or make important decisions. Worse still, such views are used to control sexuality and to keep women in passive sexual roles. The Parliamentary debates on clause 28 of the Local Government Bill took for granted that heterosexuality is 'natural' and homosexuality therefore a perversion. The peddlers of this particular brand of 'nature' cite the animal kingdom to back them up, ignoring the fact that homosexual affection and sexual activity has often been observed among some other species. Nature, then, is a loaded concept for feminists; wrestling with these myths about the 'nature' of women has been central to the Women's Movement and explains something of the tension in the relationship between feminism and ecology.

There has also been an important difference of emphasis between socialist feminists, who have concentrated broadly on the whole question of gender, stressing the social factors which put pressures on little girls to act one way and on little boys to act another, and radical feminists, who have laid more stress on what it is that makes women so profoundly different from men, rather than emphasizing the extent to which men and women might become more like each other given equal opportunities and equal rights. The fact that intuition, emotional awareness, nurturing and so on are so damagingly under-valued in the male world doesn't mean that women have to take on the attitudes of men in their struggle for justice.

Despite such tensions, the convergence of interests between feminism and ecology has a long history: in the eighteenth century, Mary Wollstonecraft had a terrible and accurate vision of the future destruction of the Earth, when all wilderness would be cultivated, famine would be endemic and the world 'a vast prison'. Many nineteenth-century British feminists were active in the anti-vivisection movement. But such linkages have been made far more compelling by the multiplicity and intensity of threats within our industrialized societies. Ynestra King, one of the most influential of American eco-feminists, gave voice to this new intensity in the early 1980s: 'We're here to say the word ECOLOGY and announce that for us as feminists it's a political word – that stands against the economics of destroyers and the pathology of racist hatred. It's a way of being, which understands that there are connections between all living things and that indeed we women are the fact and the flesh of connectedness.'[5]

One of the main sources of inspiration for eco-feminists has been derived from ancient, indigenous societies – American Indians, Aborigines, Maoris, Pacific Islanders – who traditionally regard themselves as caretakers of the Earth, with which they have lived in harmony and respect. In *Reclaim the Earth*, one of the few collections of eco-feminist writings, Ngahuia Te Awekotuku writes:

> Underlying her relationship with the land was the traditional Maori woman's perception of the environment as a source of emotional, spiritual and physical sustenance, identification and strength. For the Maori, possession of the land was merely custodianship, a caretaking for future generations, and acknowledgement of the temporariness of individual human life ... Nevertheless, Maori society was a warrior society;

46

warfare was glamorous – land and women were its spoils . . . this strong undercurrent of Maori society was a natural avenue for the infiltration of Western attitudes towards land and women; with the descent of the Christian ethos, sophisticated technology and industrial 'civilization', any semblance of pre-contact holistic balance promptly vanished. Female values were entirely eclipsed.[6]

Eco-feminists have also looked to pre-Judaeo-Christian matriarchal, goddess-worshipping cultures to discover other ways of relating to each other and to the Earth, other forms of spirituality not predicated on the subordination of women.

Such insights have rightly encouraged eco-feminists to challenge those male ecologists who talk of 'humans' damaging the Earth, thus conveniently bypassing any examination of who holds power in the world, or the very different situations of the desperately poor African farmers who chop down firewood and the owners of multinationals who devastate rainforests. Nor, they claim, has there been sufficient acknowledgement of the root causes of the ecological crisis, which include men controlling, exploiting and 'raping' the Earth in parallel with and similar to their attempt to dominate women.

Feminists of all types have meanwhile become increasingly alerted to ecological issues which have a very direct impact on women. The dangers of the chemical industry, for example, were brought home particularly strongly by the poisoning of the local population at Seveso in Italy and Bhopal in India. Women have also been particularly active in the campaign against low-level radiation. Many feminists are deeply involved in the work of Friends of the Earth, Greenpeace, the Green Party and the like, but often retain strong reservations about the willingness of these organizations to take on board lessons of the Women's Movement in their ways of working and their approach to campaigning.

For some, this was epitomized in 1985 when first Greenpeace, and then the animal liberationists, Lynx, used an advert showing a woman in high heels and a tight slit skirt, a fur coat flung over her shoulder, standing in a pool of blood. For many feminists, this image resonated with echoes of violence against women in films and hard porn. There was also anger that the advert seemed to be blaming women for the fur trade when, in fact, the people making money out of it were men. The debate raged in ecology magazines and newsletters for a few months. Assurances from Greenpeace and Lynx that the advert had

47

been 'effective' did not stop a large number of feminists from turning away in disgust that ecologists were less concerned about the liberation of women than of animals.

The way in which that debate was fought out caused great anguish to those women who saw themselves as being as committed to the cause of animal rights as to the cause of feminism. Julie Christie epitomizes such a combination, and turned her back on a conventional film career when she found herself completely alienated from the distorted values of that particular world. In her politics she has long been regarded as a feminist and is associated with the Left. But labels make her uneasy:

> Among many left-wingers, there's still a sneery sort of reaction if you say you're green. At the last election I labelled myself as a 'Green for a Labour victory' to show where my major concern lay in a party that's actually not terribly green. I'm also proud of the word 'feminist', but it means so many different things and it's been so badly devalued by the media. I don't go along with the idea of women as earth mothers, goddess types or as nurturers, though we've certainly done a lot of nurturing over the centuries! But a feminist woman is no more necessarily green than a green man is necessarily a feminist!
>
> Ecology and feminism are, in my opinion, essential to all liberation struggles. But a lot of people who are doing fantastic work in unions, in industry or with Third World revolutionary groups are neither feminist nor green. What's important is to add another dimension to what they're doing. Change will come from unimportant little people like us taking responsibility for the way they live their lives. The biggest problem is the way people feel they can't do anything. But we're all capable of taking on the responsibility of living our own lives in a more ecological manner.

She has certainly achieved that in her own life-style, having largely abandoned city living for a small farmhouse on a Welsh hillside which she shares with a family of travelling gypsies from Birmingham and a menagerie of contented-looking sheep, horses, goats, geese, ducks and hens. The animals can look forward to long and happy lives, as she would no more think of eating them than of appearing in an advertisement for British Nuclear Fuels. She also prefers home-grown fruit and vegetables to food flown at great cost and with

48

dubious ecological wisdom from far corners of the globe, and adopts a sceptical approach to the cult of consumer durables:

'We've lost touch with the rhythm of the seasons. For instance, we've lost the great pleasure of eating food in its natural season: first the broccoli, then beans, beetroot, carrots and so on through the year. That's why having fresh strawberries for the first time used to be such an incredible treat. But exactly the same pleasure can be experienced with the first batch of broad beans!

Being green probably started with my mother. She hated wasting anything. She never chucked out food, paper bags, jars or anything else she could find a use for. I think a lot of women used to live that way. My mum brought us up with a knowledge of and sensitivity to the natural world around us. Sometimes I'd be quite frightened by the power and mystery of nature. It was a very real *presence* – far more real than any city I ever visited. It taught me that humans are one tiny interrelated facet of a world in which every human blunder has an extraordinarily distorting effect throughout the world and throughout time. If more people understood that, then a lot of destruction that's going on in the world wouldn't be happening. People seem to think other living things exist purely so that we can exploit them. But I want to live not just in relation to people, but as a part of the *whole* of nature. We have to respect everything in nature, because we are all equally part of this world.

Animal Rights

The British have always prided themselves on their affection for animals. Long before the Greens arrived on the scene, the image of lonely widows leaving their life savings to the Battersea Dogs Home was a cherished symbol of that slightly eccentric concern for animals held to be peculiarly, almost patriotically, British. Foreigners still think we care more about animals than we do about people. After all, we have a *Royal* Society for the Prevention of Cruelty to Animals but only a *National* one for preventing cruelty to children. Which other country's firemen give pets the kiss of life or injure themselves while

49

trying to rescue cats which have climbed up trees? Where else do newspapers lavish such attention on 'human interest' stories about animals?

During the last decade, however, the image of the animal activist has undergone an enormous transformation. Notions of 'animal welfare' dating back to Victorian times have been replaced by much tougher, radical ideas about 'animal rights'. Uses and abuses of animals in farms, zoos, circuses, sports and laboratories, which went largely unquestioned for decades, have become targets for passionate protest by a newly militant breed of campaigner. With some justification, the new activists regarded the traditional welfare societies as rather cosy, private clubs for middle-class hobbyists. Militant new groups, including the shadowy grouping known as the Animal Liberation Front (ALF), began to make their presence felt during the late 1970s. Unlike most of their predecessors, the new activists directed their anger towards the scientists, farmers and industrialists who abused animals for profit or simple expediency. They were outraged by the routine suffering inflicted on millions of laboratory animals for the sake of tests of often dubious scientific value, and disgusted by the philosophy and practice of factory farming. They had little patience for gradual reform and were willing to risk jail to engage in non-violent direct action to get their message across. The Hunt Saboteurs Association and others disrupted fox-hunts; anti-vivisectionists raided laboratories.

The animal organizations have now undergone more than a decade of turmoil. First, the activists clashed with the cautious old guard, succeeding in taking over some of the older organizations like the British Union of Anti-Vivisectionists in 1980 and battling for control of the RSPCA. The period from about 1984 onwards saw the growth of an increasingly bitter and futile series of internal feuds as the radicals fell to squabbling among themselves. In addition, the direct action militants who had gained considerable publicity – and not a little public sympathy – by freeing or photographing suffering animals in raids on laboratories in the early 1980s, began to forfeit general respect and support by turning to quasi-terrorist tactics. The earlier, rigorously observed prohibition against violence against humans went by the board.

The ALF, which has an estimated 1,000 members in 'cells' around the country, deliberately increased the level of violence and now wages a vicious campaign of intimidation against butchers, fur and pet shops and anyone else they accuse of abusing animals. It has

50

planted bombs under the cars of scientists, slashed the wheels of milk floats, damaged cars with paintstripper and windows with etching fluid, and splattered homes with red paint as a symbol of animal blood. In 1987, the ALF's press officer Ronnie Lee and his assistant Vivienne Smith were jailed for ten and four years respectively for their part in a fire-bombing campaign. But there was little sign the violence would end. After the red paint attack on the home of a Labour councillor in Islington, provoked in the ALF's eyes by the council's 'crime' of allowing halal meat to be served to Muslim pensioners in its meals on wheels service, the ALF's new press officer Chris Oakley told the *London Daily News* on 5 May 1987 that anyone who was not a vegetarian was an animal abuser involved in the mass murder of animals. 'In my mind there is no difference between animal abusers and Nazis, and I have studied the Nazis deeply,' he said. (Hitler and other top Nazis were, of course, vegetarians).

Film-maker Victor Schonfeld closely followed the growth of the animal rights movement in Britain and, by making *The Animals Film*, an extraordinarily powerful documentary about animal cruelty and exploitation, contributed significantly to spreading the message to a general public:

> In 1978, people in the movement saw themselves as a vanguard with nothing behind it. They felt they were way ahead of their time and society wasn't ready for what they had to say. The people in the militant groups were mostly working class or lower middle class and young. They could just as easily have got involved in the nuclear issue, but something in the animals issue struck a personal chord with each of them. There was an anarchistic feel to it and a lot of disrespect for scientists. But there were just very small groups of people passionately committed to a cause that was still invisible. Within two years that had changed. All of a sudden, the question of the treatment of animals had become a respectable, mainstream concern.

He cites a raid on an agricultural research institute outside Cambridge in Spring 1980 as a turning point. The activists photographed animal experiments in progress inside and got themselves filmed making the raid. The event made dramatic television and the media devoted considerable attention to what had happened:

51

That event caught the imagination. The choice of target and the tactics broke through some of the barriers which were stopping people from taking the issue seriously. It was clearly an institute for agricultural research, devoted to the business of food production, not to medical research. That broke through the public perception that scientists were only doing experiments on animals to save people's lives. The people who went in didn't destroy the place or steal anything. They just took pictures and gathered information. It made the front page of all the newspapers, even *The Times*. After that, the way the media dealt with the issue of animal exploitation changed.

The broadcast of *The Animals Film* was an important moment in the growth of public awareness of animal exploitation. It was shown for the first and only time in Channel Four's opening week in November 1982. The film's graphic depiction of appalling and unnecessary cruelty – including archive footage of Thomas Edison's public electrocution of an elephant to show off the power of electricity at the turn of the century, and gut-wrenching images of animal experiments and donkeys dying slowly of radiation sickness for the sake of nuclear weapons research – was seen by more than 1,350,000 people and made a colossal impact. Schonfeld remembers:

> There was a tremendous amount of publicity, an extraordinary amount for a documentary, and it was helped by the fact that the IBA decided to censor it by cutting scenes showing a raid on a laboratory before the film was transmitted. Because of the traditional RSPCA-type British sympathy for animals, there was a pool of potential sympathy and receptivity to the issue and the film tapped into it. After the film was shown there was a period of intense activity by the militants. Their numbers swelled tremendously, something which many people attributed to the film.
>
> Then a nasty development emerged: the use of violence against people. Not only had this not been contemplated, it had been actively opposed by all the groups for many, many years. They made a point of being against any kind of violence to living beings, in that it would be inconsistent to be opposed to violence against animals, but allow it against humans. Now that got turned around: anyone involved in animal abuse was 'like a Nazi', and deserved what was coming to them. The first time I heard of an animal rights militia sending a letter

bomb, I didn't believe it. It sounded as if it was a fraud. But it soon became evident that it was really happening. Interviews started to appear where people were saying things like, 'I don't care about people – I care about animals', and all of a sudden the old stereotype of fanatical lunatics had become a reality. The violence halted the growth of the militant wing. It was very counter-productive.

But that wasn't the only problem:

Fighting started inside the organizations. In terms of the focus of energy, that was even worse than the violence. They started expelling each other, calling in the police to evict people from meetings, having membership votes to impeach officers. People who were all working together a few years ago have become bitter adversaries. For example, people disagreed about whether new legislation went far enough to warrant their support, but instead of acknowledging legitimate political differences on the subject, they'd become terrible enemies. The animal rights movement in this country has completely lost direction, but I think there will be a resurgence in a few years because the issue hasn't gone away. What has changed permanently is that the general public, particularly people on the left, environmentally-minded people and people in the anti-nuclear movement, now see animal rights as a legitimate issue. That is a change which can't be erased by the later degeneration among the activists. That change of awareness remains a major achievement.

Education

If there is any one thing that *all* Greens, light or dark, have in common, it is their emphasis on the importance of education. This would seem to be sensible, given that saving the world may take rather more than one generation, and when it comes to the prospects of the next generation making a better job of it than this one, then hope springs reassuringly eternal. As we shall see in the final chapter, such hope is only rarely affected by what little evidence there is on the attitudes and motivations of today's young people, but that is hardly the point.

Despite the fact that many Greens are teachers themselves or involved in education in one way or another, their readiness to convert this expertise into a properly thought-out and practical approach to education has been decidedly limited. One of the classic hallmarks of involuntary alternativism is to seize on ideas that are utterly impossible to implement. With many a bold hurrah, these hunters after the definitive 'green truth' sped off on the scent of Ivan Illich's de-schooled society. This was unfortunate; Illich's book, *De-schooling Society* (which advocates doing away with schools altogether), is essential reading for every would-be teacher, but is hardly the stuff of political maturity. Only in the last two years or so have the less rowdy, more pragmatic practitioners been able to haul green thinking on education back into the real world.

For a start, there's a great deal now going on in terms of the most basic level of environmental education. The curriculum has recently begun to reflect the growing interest in environmental and development issues, and many schools have incorporated new courses or options in this area. What's more (in a way that Keith Joseph can never have originally anticipated), the new GCSE is obliging even mainstream subjects like geography and biology to take up the challenge of environmental problem-solving and awareness. The Council for Environmental Education has developed a prodigious resource-list in this area, providing an invaluable service to both newcomers and old hands. Many new materials were developed under the aegis of the European Year of the Environment, and the separate but closely related fields of development education and peace education have incorporated more and more of the green message in the way that they are now presented.

The synthesizing and deepening of these compartmentalized and often uncoordinated approaches to curriculum reform has been taken on in a delightfully radical fashion by the World Wide Fund for Nature. Their 'Global Impact' programme (based at the Centre for Global Education in York) first carried out a detailed survey of over 800 primary and secondary schools, which produced some fascinating results:

- 46% of teachers indicated that their schools had policies or guidelines which feature environmental education;
- 67% of teachers think that the political aspects of development and environmental education are not too controversial to be dealt with in the classroom;

54

- 78% of teachers think that development and environmental education are central to achieving an understanding of, and active participation in, the world today;

The global impact team (Sue Greig, Graham Pike and David Selby) then went on to produce a superb handbook for teachers, *Earthrights*, which knocks spots off most other teaching aids in this area. Damien Randle (editor of *Green Teacher*, itself an enormously useful and interesting publication) explains why:

> The Centre for Global Education is the country's most exciting and creative source of educational work in the area of interaction between environmental education and development education. For many schools and teachers, environmental education stops with nature studies, and development education stops with a description of Third World problems. The political, economic, cultural, spiritual, and personal issues which must be tackled, with active learning, are often ignored. But not by *Earthrights*.

A rather different approach to getting beyond old-fashioned nature studies is that of an organization called the Institute for Earth Education, which runs impressive workshops and 'earthwalks', 'to encourage understanding and appreciation of the ecological principles which are reflected in life all around us'. Originally developed by a visionary educationist called Steve van Matre in the USA, Earth Education has been successfully transplanted to the UK, and precisely embodies the distinction between light green environmentalism and dark green ecology within the educational field.

Such initiatives can do little about the prevailing ethos of competition and self-interested individualism within so many schools. So great is the despair of some parents that they choose to withdraw their children from school altogether, many turning to an organization called Education Otherwise which was set up in 1976 by a small group of parents and takes its name from the 1944 Education Act, which states that parents are responsible for their children's education, 'either by regular attendance at school or otherwise'. It has now evolved as a self-help organization offering support, advice and information to well over 2,000 families involved in this approach.

Most parents either can't or wouldn't want to withdraw their children, but they know that things could and should be different. Hence the burgeoning interest in Human Scale Education – or 'education as if people matter', following on in the line of Fritz Schumacher's 'economics as if people matter'. The manifesto of this increasingly influential movement includes the following proposals:

- that only in very rare and exceptional cases should village primary schools be closed against local and parental wishes;
- that large schools wishing to subdivide into federations of smaller units on a single site should be supported;
- that existing secondary schools regarded as 'too small' should not normally be closed, and that ways should be explored for them to work co-operatively with other schools and to adopt practices and technologies to compensate for smaller size with supporting advice and services from the local education authority;
- that co-operative efforts by parents and others to restore small infant and primary schools to their villages should be considered sympathetically by local education authorities;
- that small community schools (as in other European countries), anxious to work within the state system, should be viewed sympathetically for funding by local education authorities, and their progress and qualities evaluated as examples of good practice.

It was this sort of approach that inspired Richard North to write his informative and topical book *Schools of Tomorrow*, which highlights some of the best practices already going on in the UK today. Top of his list is the Small School in the tiny village of Hartland in Devon, which has rightly been written up in countless newspapers and magazines as an exciting example of what can be done with minimal financial resources given the right commitment on the part of the community. Colin Hodgetts, the Small School's headmaster, explains something of the magic:

> We have tapped a huge reservoir of talent among parents and villagers, and the school has become the centre of village activity. We discuss everything with the parents. This is how education should be in Britain. It should be small and it should be accessible to all the people. We believe that something exciting is happening here, and we know it could work in every town and city. We could have a nation of Small Schools

where children are no longer lost in the crowd, and education could once again become the joyous thing it should always be.

Richard North also looked in some detail at the example of Denmark, where around 10% of children are educated in independent, state-subsidized schools. These schools do not depend on the affluence of individual parents, since it only costs something like £30 a month to send a child to a Danish independent school. The state funds these schools to the tune of about 85% of their total expenditure. They are set up by parents coming together in a community, some with very liberal ideas, some with very traditional ideas. Each school must appoint an overseer, subject to Ministry of Education approval, so as to ensure that these schools match the performance of state schools.

This is, of course, precisely the kind of initiative which could help to break up the institutional log-jam of Britain's educational system, and there are some who hope that such an approach might soon be with us, thanks to an improbable helping hand from Kenneth Baker and the Conservative Government. Though most Greens would hate to admit it, a monolithic comprehensive system is not necessarily the only way, let alone the best way, to promote the educational interests of children, nor indeed to work towards a more egalitarian, less divisive society. The inflexibility and total lack of imagination on the part of the teaching unions and the defenders of the basic principle of state-funded education have only served to undermine their own cause by making it more vulnerable to intolerant, bigoted attacks from the likes of Roger Scruton.

It is as yet too early to judge what the impact of the 1988 Education Act will be; as Kim Taylor, Director of the Gulbenkian Foundation, rightly asks:

> Will the Conservative Party's election rhetoric about parent power, parent choice and variety in schools, together with their general emphasis on individual initiative, small business and the reduction of public monopolies, now be reflected in the Education Bill? Will a principle which has been argued solely in the context of established schools *opting out* be extended to a more likely source of recruitment, namely newly founded schools *opting in*? That remains to be seen – and vigorously to be campaigned for.[7]

And even if all works out best in this respect, the imposition of a national curriculum by the Conservative Government represents a fearful increase in centralized control, which will certainly make it harder for schools to introduce more radical and progressive curriculum reform.

It is appropriate to conclude this survey of the Green Movement firmly back in Westminster. It has been convincingly argued that much of the most effective opposition to Mrs Thatcher's Government for the last nine years has come from pressure groups in the voluntary sector, rather than from the opposition parties themselves. The Green Movement has been at the forefront of providing that kind of opposition, and whatever one may feel about the strength of it, *as a movement*, or the speed with which the Green Delta referred to at the start of Chapter 1 is now coming together, few would deny success in terms of straightforward damage limitation.

But that, of course, is not enough. One can't go on simply protesting and saying 'no' for ever. It is time, therefore, to see what's going on in the political parties themselves, and to consider the extent to which green ideas have permeated the UK's political system.

CHAPTER THREE

The Greening of British Politics

NF ACCUSED OF JUMPING ON BANDWAGON WITH
'GREEN' POLICIES

The National Front is moving into 'green' politics: organizing vigorously in rural areas, joining the protests against acid rain, seal culls and straw-burning, and claiming figures such as William Morris, the nineteenth-century Utopian socialist, among its philosopher forebears.

The Front's change in focus, described as a 'deliberate policy' of concentrating on the countryside, has been developed over the past year. Its disclosure in party literature elicited dismay from leaders of Britain's more traditional 'Green' Movement.

Mr Jonathon Porritt, Director of Friends of the Earth and former co-chair of the Ecology Party, said he found the news 'appalling'. But Mr Phil Andrews, a member of the Front's national directorate and national organizer of its youth section, denied that the Front was 'jumping on the bandwagon'.

He added: 'We have always been ecologically-minded. We are concerned with the benefit of our people and the health of our nation. The countryside affects both.'

He acknowledged, however, that the environment had been accorded too low a priority by the Front. 'We were too concerned with urban problems. But the cities are dying and the country towns are thriving. Ideologically, we have developed somewhat.' New recruits were also stressing 'green' issues, he said.

Successful new membership drives claimed by the Front include Suffolk, where numbers are said to have quadrupled, the West Country, Wales and the Border country, rural Scotland and Hertfordshire.

The current issue of *Nationalism Today* contains a new section, 'On the Green Front,' which is to become a regular feature. Subjects covered in this and in *NF News* range from acid rain, straw-burning and the Alaskan seal cull to waterways, rural bus services and the village corner shop.

The Front has also espoused industrial co-partnership and aligned itself with 'green' groups against the American nuclear presence in Britain. Its own view, however, is that Britain should have an independent nuclear deterrent.

This article appeared in *The Times* on 20 October 1984, and William Morris wallpapers up and down the land must have been spinning in disbelief. However improbable it may now seem, this initiative on the part of the National Front was the first in a veritable barrage of publications, speeches and headline-grabbing stunts on behalf of various political parties to prove just how 'green' they really were.

This one turned out to be very much a one-off from the National Front, and much good it did them. Perhaps their supporters just died laughing at the notion that the real problem with Dutch Elm disease was less to do with the fact that it had decimated our elms than that it came from a 'foreign source'! Looking back on it now, the fact that such nonsense, even from so abhorrent a source, elicited 'dismay from leaders of Britain's more traditional green movement' is faintly ludricous. But that too became part of the pattern; every time the major parties laid the remotest claim to a few square inches on board the green branwagon, the Green Party would instantly weigh in dismissing such claims as opportunist, dishonest and specious.

The source of such frustration is simple. For members of the Green Party, and many other active Greens outside the party, green means *the lot*: international relations, the economy, health, education – you name it, successive Green Party manifestos have had it. Holistic green politics is nothing if not whole. However, for 95% of people in this country, the word 'green' is used almost exclusively in reference to the environment. A process of totally logical linguistic evolution has transformed the old-fashioned Conservation Movement first into the Environment Movement of the 1970s and then into the Green Movement of the 1980s.

The latest wave of environmental concern started in the early 1980s, and has gradually and impressively grown since then. As it happens, the Green Party itself was actually slower to respond to this trend than the mainstream parties. There are good historical reasons for this. From its birth in 1973, the Ecology Party (as it then was) struggled endlessly to demonstrate that its brand of politics was much, much more than straightforward environmentalism. Nothing annoyed the 1979 spokespersons more than reference to the 'Party of

60

the Environment'. At the time, this was wholly justifiable; fewer people cared about the environment then, environmental concerns were of zero political importance, and the UK Ecology Party had rightly taken on the critical job of establishing what *global* eco-politics was all about.

Ecology Party stalwarts were therefore slow to see what was in the wind. Conference motions in 1983 and 1984 to change the name of the party to the Green Party were defeated. Despite assiduous efforts by some to 'talk a Green Movement into being' (simply by asserting, with absolutely no supporting evidence at that time, that conditions were now right for bringing together the different strands of the environment, peace and development movements in a brand new Green Movement), the Green Party itself did nothing to substantiate its own environmental credentials.

Reality finally dawned in 1985: the Ecology Party eventually became the Green Party at its September AGM, though by the narrowest of majorities, and only after a basinful of constitutional and procedural wrangling. Tony Jones, then the Party's Press Secretary, honestly acknowledged that this was as much a defensive move as the brandishing of a bright new political standard: 'If we do not change our name, "Green" will mean exactly what William Waldegrave or Bill Rodgers [then Environmental Spokesman for the Alliance] want it to mean. We have a classic opportunity here to put all the other major parties on the run.'

As he himself well knew, the opportunity for that had already been lost. The green genie had already been stroked out of the bottle by environmentalists left, right and centre, though not, at that stage, by all. Some continued to see this green business as 'trendy', 'intellectually sloppy', 'politically subversive'. At the Conservation Society's 1985 AGM, John Davoll, who had been one of the most influential environmental figures of the 1970s, defiantly declared that the Conservation Society was '*not* a green organization'. Even Friends of the Earth needed some persuading that it was OK to go green; in February 1985, some of the more reactionary staff members of that time protested vociferously at the relatively innocent wording in a new membership leaflet, that Friends of the Earth was 'a major force behind today's growing Green Movement'. They soon left to find greener pastures in more traditional environmental organizations.

Even after the name-change, most party activists went on regarding the environment as a matter of peripheral interest. Despite policies

61

on literally everything else, the Green Party's environmental policy cupboard was all but bare, with nothing on acid rain, pesticides, water quality, rainforests etc. Only a spate of hurriedly taken motions at its 1986 Annual Conference saved the Green Party from the deep embarrassment of going into the 1987 General Election with less comprehensive environmental policies than either the Alliance or Labour.

In the mean time, all those wicked opportunists in the other parties got on with the job of chasing the green vote. 1985 and 1986 were enormously busy years for those organizations that shared a specific strategy of using public concern about the environment as a useful lever on the political process. The following quote from a *Guardian* editorial in August 1986 is typical of the sort of 'let's-all-egg-'em-on' mentality then in vogue:

> Labour has identified a trend of thought which is fast taking hold throughout Western Europe and North America. To latch on to it is not mere electoral opportunism. It is a response to what voters say they want. In the big league it is now the Conservatives who are lagging in the ecology ratings, with Labour challenging the Liberals for first place.[1]

How successful were we? It can be convincingly argued that before the General Election itself, things looked far better than they had ever done before. The opinion poll carried out by MORI in April 1987 on behalf of Friends of the Earth and the World Wide Fund for Nature came up with a fascinating confirmation of the potential power of the green vote. Not only did 81% of people feel that the Government should be giving a much higher priority to protecting the environment, but when asked how important a political party's environmental policies would be in determining the way they would vote in a forthcoming General Election, three in ten people felt them to be crucial or very important. If one includes those who felt that a party's environmental policies would be *fairly* important, a total of seven out of ten expressed this belief.

As we shall see, things didn't quite pan out in line with these predictions. The 1987 General Election was a distinctly un-green affair, and since then a very uncertain picture confronts any analyst of the green scene. The prospects for further or deeper greening of the major political parties in the future (bearing in mind that critical distinction between vaguely green environmentalism on the one hand, and the far deeper hue of radical green politics on the other) are so vague as to be almost imperceptible. These uncertainties have more to do with the current state of confusion within the opposition parties than with any loss of momentum within the Green Movement, but the upshot of this is the same: a temporary loss of direction and a crying need for new co-ordinated initiatives for the next decade.

The Labour Party

Casting one's mind back for a moment to those halcyon days before the 1987 General Election, who can claim to have carried off the treasured winner's rosette in the Green Stakes? Considering just how far back they started, the Labour Party moved further and faster than any of its rivals. It went into the 1983 election still making only the most tentative noises about the environment. The party still favoured a 'balanced' energy programme (i.e. a programme dependent on nuclear energy), and had nothing of any significance to say about any of the major environmental issues. Even at the most superficial level, green politics was a complete irrelevance to the Labour Party at that time.

Four years on, the Labour Party stance on green issues had changed dramatically. Years of solid, if somewhat unimaginative, beavering away behind the scenes by SERA, Greenpeace and Friends of the Earth had at last borne fruit. A high level joint policy committee, on which representatives from all of these organizations joined sympathetic trades unionists and local party activists, carried out one of the Labour Party's most intensive and constructive policy reviews ever. And at an intellectual level, the example of the new green parties in Europe, particularly Die Grünen in Germany, had stirred up a lot of interest.

Underpinning all of this was the realization that instead of destroying jobs, taking more care of the environment could be one of the best ways of generating new employment. The Labour Party's *Charter for the Environment* in October 1985 called for increased intervention in practically every sector of the economy, with hundreds of thousands of new jobs as the promised bonus at the end of it. This document was justifiably welcomed as something of a breakthrough. The days of knocking environmental issues as the exclusive preserve of the namby-pamby southern middle classes were apparently over; talking green within the Labour Party became almost respectable. But for all that, it was still a flimsy document, ritualistically putting the blame for environmental degradation on capitalism, and primarily designed to allay the fears of the hard Left about Labours's interest in green issues.

The hard Left has always had an almost complete blind spot when it comes to the environment. For instance, many of the GLC's radical and imaginative green policies were greeted with derision by Militant supporters in Liverpool, on the grounds that providing bicycle lanes, investigating alternative energy sources and fostering respect and tolerance for gays, lesbians and ethnic minorities was a diversion from the all-important socialist class struggle. As it happens, the most radical green policies yet seen in British mainstream politics were carried through by the Labour GLC between 1981 and 1986.

The popular perception was that the GLC belonged politically to the hard left. Conservatives and Fleet Street vilified its high-profile leader, Ken Livingstone, as 'Red Ken'. Yet many of the GLC's policies had at least as much to do with green ideas as with any kind of strict, old-style socialism. There is a bright green streak in Livingstone himself which many in the Labour Party still regard with great suspicion, partly because they find it so hard to classify. As a genuine ecologist, he comes at things from a rather different and extremely refreshing perspective:

> One of my main reasons for coming into the Labour Party was the realization that all the work I did on preserving the habitat of the sand lizard or the natterjack toad, my entire life's work, could be swept away at the stroke of some bureaucratic pen. If Mrs Thatcher and Neil Kinnock formed a coalition to ban me from political activity, I think my first choice would be to go off and study an intelligent mammal, perhaps one of the great whales or the great apes. It appalls me that we will most probably spend thousands of years in the future scouring around the universe looking for other signs of intelligent life, having just obliterated all the other intelligent species on *this* planet!

As the leading protagonist of the green cause within the Labour Party today, Livingstone is optimistic about the prospects for change. But sometimes this optimism comes across as the obligatory hopefulness of a man who *needs* to believe that others will eventually see things his way:

64

It is true that Labour Party people often saw environmentalism as a block to job creation. That is largely because all they have ever seen is environmentalist groups fighting to prevent something awful being done to the environment. They have never yet seen a national administration committed to an environmentalist perspective *and* to the jobs that would create.

Equally, fifteen years ago, most people in the Labour Party would have just dismissed the importance of decentralization and democratization. The objective was to get a Labour government elected and change Britain from the top down. My generation just does not believe that any more; they have seen Labour governments fail to do it. But what we have not yet done is to put together a package based on the practical day-to-day business of how this new politics will work. That is really what the radical Left, Greens and some radical Liberals have got to do in terms of putting together the agenda for the future. Labour has been decisively rejected partly because it is so old-fashioned; even though Kinnock was young and used a lot of modern techniques, the message was stunningly 1950s. And there is no 1980s or 1990s message that is not green.

The emphasis on *local* green action is one that has been taken up with considerable enthusiasm by several Labour authorities over the last few years, especially some London boroughs such as Haringey and Lambeth, and this will undoubtedly provide a model of enormous importance for many other local authorities during the course of the next few years.

Beyond that, Livingstone is prepared to take his arguments into the heartland of socialist ideology. He rejects as inadequately narrow the Marxist concept of alienation in the workplace; a much deeper and more serious alienation from his point of view is the emotional alienation which is a direct product of our urbanized industrial existence. Livingstone's emphasis on personal relationships, feminism and the quality of our emotional life represents a dramatic leap beyond the traditional boundaries of Labour Party thinking:

> If it does not offend both groups, I tend to lump feminism and green politics together. I think the two are indissoluble, largely because of women's attitude to what they do in the world, and the much stronger life orientation of women. It inevitably

65

means they will always be at the forefront of green politics until men change. The impact of environmentalism and feminism on my politics and my life-style is overwhelmingly more important than anything that happens in the Labour Party, and has been for the last fifteen, twenty years.

London, until 1986, was therefore in relatively safe green hands. At the national level, it was not until August 1986 that the joint policy committee, ably chaired by Tom Sawyer, published its full proposals for consideration by that year's Party Conference. It was packed with green goodies: powerful new enforcement agencies; a new Ministry of Environmental Protection (but *not* at Cabinet level); a new Wildlife and Countryside Act; an extension of planning controls to cover agriculture and strengthen regulations to deal with air and water pollution. Environmental organizations responded warmly, which is hardly surprising, given that the document brought together many of the policies that they had been advocating for many a long year. They were even more delighted when the draft document was passed by that year's Annual Conference.

The 1986 Conference also marked a decisive change in Labour's nuclear power policies. The decision to phase out nuclear power by closing down the ageing Magnox reactors, by scrapping Sizewell and by building no new nuclear power stations must rank as one of the quickest and most momentous changes of mind by any British party on any subject since the war. In terms of the deeper greening of the Labour Party, the importance of this policy shift cannot be over-stated. The symbolic significance of nuclear power is enormous. Faith in nukes implies faith in a very particular high-tech vision of the future; renouncing them means questioning all the old technological values and assumptions. A non-nuclear policy clears the way for creative new ways of thinking about energy and wealth creation, and makes it possible for new approaches to technology and the structure of the economy to flourish. When the anti-nuclear activists finally achieved their objective at the 1986 Party Conference, the Conservatives accused Labour of naked opportunism, claiming that the party had jumped on to a post-Chernobyl populist bandwagon. The charge was bogus. Anti-nuclear voices in the party had been growing increasingly loud throughout the 1980s, particularly in local government as many Labour-controlled authorities refused to implement the government's civil defence programmes and declared themselves 'Nuclear Free Zones'.

A vote to scrap nuclear power had in fact been passed at the 1985 Conference, but without securing the necessary two-thirds majority. During the following twelve months, environmentalists lobbied hard and at the highest levels both within the Labour Party and within the key unions to increase the vote to the required levels. By the time Chernobyl went up, the Labour Party was already decisively anti-nuclear, though it is true that the popular wave of anti-nuke sentiment which followed the disaster helped to persuade the waverers that an anti-nuclear energy policy was a likely vote-winner, unlike the party's anti-nuclear weapons policy.

Of particular importance at this time was the role of some of the larger unions, such as the TGWU, without whose support the anti-nuclear motion would not have been carried. The clinching argument for these unions was not Chernobyl, but jobs: the alternative strategies put forward within the party's policy statement (based on conservation, energy efficiency, combined heat and power schemes, and the development of renewables) would clearly create more jobs than the continued dependence on nuclear power.

The role of trade unions in helping or hindering the growth of green awareness within socialist circles remains a controversial area. On the one hand, one can hold up the inspiring work of the likes of Tom Sawyer (of NUPE) and the excellent record of a union like the National Union of Seamen (NUS), who were instrumental in thwarting the Government's policy to dump nuclear waste at sea, and have since then taken a strong line on both nuclear and toxic wastes even when jobs are not the central issue. What is more, several unions have become increasingly involved in health and safety issues in the broader environment, as witnessed by their involvement in the coalition of groups campaigning against the use of pesticides and in their support for the environmentalists' opposition to the privatization of water.

But on the other hand, whatever greening is going on is usually at a most superficial level, and most of the bumf coming out of the TUC's policy unit is impregnated with predictably nonsensical notions about the regeneration of Britain's industry. Worse still, the TUC over the years has done nothing to further the case that jobs and environmental responsibility are not mutually exclusive, and invariably goes out of its way to argue its case in utterly unreconstructed growthist terms.

Fortunately, things have moved somewhat faster within the Labour

Party itself. In early 1987, David Clark, newly appointed as Labour's *official* Environment Spokesperson, produced a discussion document (reworking some important OECD research) on the job creation potential of pollution control and environmental protection. Dr Clark's report to the Shadow Cabinet itemized various initiatives, costing £10 billion over ten years, which would create 200,000 jobs.

It was understandable therefore that the widely accepted assumption at that time was that the Labour Party intended to give its new green policies a high profile in the run-up to and during the General Election. Their own opinion polls had indicated a large number of voters ready to be swayed on green issues, and they had no intention of being outflanked by the Alliance in this respect. Hopes ran high that they would help ensure that the environment would be in there battling for electoral attention with the old favourites such as jobs, inflation and the bomb.

It was not to be. The party's election manifesto duly left out most of the commitments made in their environment statement, and though this statement was published separately in the first week of the election, none of Labour's leading spokespersons made the slightest effort to deal with environmental or energy issues. Just one year after Chernobyl, energy policy in the UK was a very dead duck as far as the election was concerned.

With Dr John Cunningham as Labour Shadow Environment Secretary, perhaps that is hardly surprising. The 'Chairman of the Friends of Sellafield' has been one of the most assiduous defenders of the nuclear faith over the last five years, and is even now engaged in a consistent and not unsuccessful campaign to water down the party's anti-nuclear policy. To him alone can be attributed the ludicrous ambivalence of the Labour Party's policy on the THORP reprocessing plant at Sellafield, which is to permit the plant to be completed, but not to be used for reprocessing spent-oxide fuel!

Neil Kinnock's own position remains deeply ambivalent. Though a dab-hand at eco-rhetoric ('It's a question of treating natural resources with more respect. Every tree, every bird, every animal should be treated as precious' . . . 'I go down to the river at the bottom of my garden on a nice winter's day and it is like listening to your favourite piece of music. It's bloody beautiful')[2], he did not hesitate before squashing any ideas that a Minister for Environmental Protection should have Cabinet rank, apparently out of concern that environmental groups might reduce his freedom of action as Prime Minister!

He has doggedly stuck by Jack Cunningham, despite the unnecessary embarrassments this has caused, and since the election has replaced David Clark (who did sterling work in rather difficult circumstances) as Environment Spokesperson with the rather less enthusiastic Allan Roberts.

Time after time one comes across Labour activists who suggest that all will be well once certain internal matters are properly sorted out. This is nonsense; it is precisely the inability of the Labour Party to dig itelf out of its own fossilized form of in-fighting which understandably makes Greens doubt that they are likely to embrace green politics at anything more than the most superficial level.

So dramatic a failure of political imagination never ceases to boggle the average green mind. As Tony Benn has often pointed out, 'that thin green line within the socialist tradition' – running through from John Ball and the Peasants' Revolt, the Diggers and Levellers, Thomas More, Robert Owen, William Blake and William Morris – has made an enormously fertile and inspiring contribution to socialism. Add to that the equally rich tradition of municipal socialism, the practice of the co-operative movement and the early history of the trade unions, and the essential ingredients for a red/green alternative are clear to see.

But despite the powerful advocacy of Benn ('One of the great failures of the Labour Movement has been its failure to find proper space in its philosophy for the very long tradition of green politics'), Livingstone, David Blunkett, Robin Cook, Jeremy Seabrook and a few others, the green line of socialism is as thin today as it has ever been. Benn is unapologetic about trying to build a new constituency for his brand of socialism through the 'rainbow coalition' approach. But he is quick to point out that simply lumping together greens, women, blacks and sundry disenfranchized minorities can be a meaningless and opportunistic process:

> You have to take on board the basic tenet of Marx: that you cannot understand the world you live in unless you understand the conflict between those who create the wealth and those who own the wealth. Until the basic principles of socialism are re-established (equality, democracy, accountability, internationalism and morality), one cannot build non-opportunistic, genuine realistic relationships with movements which are themselves divided over the primacy of these principles.

69

Most Greens would agree wholeheartedly with that, but would not hesitate to fling that challenge straight back at socialists today: for is it not the case that conventional, GNP-determined, male-dominated, growth-fixated, consumerist industrialism *necessarily* promotes inequitable, undemocratic, unaccountable and immoral little-Englandism? And if *that* is accepted, then why do so many mainstream socialists witter on so aggravatingly about regenerating precisely that kind of industrialism?

Ater attending the Socialist Conference held in Chesterfield in October 1987 (organized by Benn as the start of a process of broadening and redefining socialism), that is exactly the sort of question that was put by the forty or so members of the Green Party who attended the conference. One of those was Jon Carpenter, the editor of *Green Line*, who raised some critical questions about any possible realignment of the Reds and the Greens in a devastating critique of the Chesterfield Conference:

> The overwhelming message of the Conference was that Labour needs more of the same old politics. Statist, centralist, authoritarian, confrontational, and centred on traditional relations of male power, these socialists are nothing if not establishment.
>
> They ignored the fact that the working class is a diminishing phenomenon; that people increasingly refuse to identify as working class; that working-class men are increasingly inclined to vote Tory, or that women are increasingly voting Labour; that in our patriarchal society and economy, men as individuals as well as a class are the net beneficiaries of women's disadvantage and oppression in work and in the home, in this country and abroad; and that many workers believe themselves to be the beneficiaries of the capitalist system. I found myself in an environment where women's rights were on everybody's lips, but the reality of feminism was just a mirage on a receding horizon.
>
> Any Green who went along to find just how much of the alternative economics these socialists have taken on board would have had no difficulty in reaching an answer: none. It was not apparent that any thought had been given to economic questions for some decades.
>
> Perhaps the Green Movement will provide a home for increasing numbers of socialist discontents, a place where socialism can be reinterpreted as a concern for all people, not

just one group composed largely of men, and as a power base for a community as a whole, not just a tiny competing male élite struggling for leadership roles for themselves and a perpetuation of the patriarchal base for society at large.[3]

The message for Greens intent on taking their politics into the heartland of socialism is surely clear: there is a long, long way to go.

Liberals and Social Democrats

Whether the new Social and Liberal Democrats will provide a more promising environment for green politics remains, as of now, a matter of pure conjecture. If they have looked anywhere, non-socialist Greens have traditionally looked to the Liberal Party for evidence that mainstream parties are sufficiently flexible to take on board at least some radical green principles. But it is a brave person today who would claim to know where contemporary liberalism finds itself, let alone where it might be in five years' time. Members of both the Liberal Party and the SDP, including hardened seen-it-all-before activists, were quite literally traumatized by the events of 1987 and early 1988, and although ostensibly engaged in fashioning a *new* party, they are about as interested in anything genuinely new as a laboratory rat that has been taught only one way through the maze to get its evening meal.

The record of their involvement in environmental issues over the past few years can be briefly recorded; it is far more predictable and far less dramatic than the Labour Party's. To its short-lived credit, the SDP was first off the starting block in the green stakes with the publication of *Conservation and Change* in August 1985. It was, in retrospect, an insubstantial document which took the SDP's predilection for fence-sitting on any remotely controversial issue to a new height, though many of its proposals were indeed sound and certainly set the pace on institutional reform by promising a new Department of Environment Protection, headed by a minister with *full* Cabinet status. It also gave birth to that appealingly alliterative slogan, 'green growth', which has since been made so much of by the more conservative elements of the Environment Movement. For any party still committed to unchecked economic expansion, industrial growth, increased competitiveness and consumerism, all such a slogan really

71

amounts to is a promise to carry on raping the Earth in as environmentally sensitive a manner as possible.

No sooner was the document on the streets than the Green Party comprehensively flagellated the SDP for this 'cynical exercise in vote-catching'. Surprise, surprise. Various wets within the Tory Party used it as a lever to launch a mini-campaign along the lines that the SDP's environmental fervour threatened to undo them in vulnerable marginal seats in the South-East. The most interesting, but least publicized, reaction was that the Liberals were decidedly miffed to see their would-be partners overtake them in the green stakes.

They promptly set about dealing with this by convening an Environmental Co-ordination Group under the chairmanship of Simon Hughes, their Environment Spokesperson, to review all policy in this area. Environmental organizations were invited to comment on the first draft (published in April 1986) of the resulting statement on a 'select committee basis'. Comments were mostly favourable: the Liberals quite justifiably claim the best track record as regards environmental policy. But there was deep concern about 'an unmistakable element of complacency', as Friends of the Earth put it in their response:

> We are particularly concerned that in many crucial areas this document favours somewhat pious generalization rather than specific policy proposals. Moreover, the implications in some of these generalizations are rarely followed up. 'In no real sense can GNP be considered a measure of the quality of life' – this is, of course, a reasonable assertion, but what alternative indicators does the Liberal Party intend to put in its place? How do you plan to account for the depletion of non-renewable resources? If it is indeed true that 'high oil consumption resulting from low prices is environmentally harmful in both the short and the long term', what are the Liberals going to do about it? Does this comment constitute a commitment to set oil prices at a level above market values, or is it just another blip of non-specific eco-angst?[4]

Such questions highlight the divide between vaguely green environmentalism and radical green politics. There are only so many patch-up, symptom-solving environmental reforms one can legislate into being before having to look at *inherent* causes in the industrial system. Of all the major parties, the Liberals are the only ones ever to have acknowledged such an uncomfortable truth; their 1979 Assembly resolution to that effect (which stressed unambiguously that 'economic growth as conventionally measured is neither desired nor achievable') has long been the totem pole around which Liberal Greens ritualistically dance. Unfortunately, in the intervening years, that particular resolution has never been referred to by any of the Liberal leadership, and little work has been done on the alternative economic strategies that it would seem to call for.

Despite this, their final environment statement was a good strong document; it *should* have provided the basis for the Alliance's environmental policy in the General Election, but even at this level of light green environmentalism, the bland hand of the SDP caused many of the more radical statements from the Liberals to be toned down or dropped altogether. This was particularly true on the question of nuclear power, with the SDP still favouring an old-style 'balanced' energy policy pending 'several years' worth of further deliberation in the light of the Chernobyl disaster. Green Liberals were hopping mad, but that, as ever, cut little ice with the Alliance apparatchiks.

At that time, 'don't rock the boat' was the order of the day. As a consequence, the Alliance had nothing much to say about the environment, or indeed about energy policy. Simon Hughes was shuffled off into some other job, and literally not a word was heard from Baroness Stedman, the all-but-unknown SDP representative who took on the job as Alliance Spokesperson. Far from it being a big election issue for both the SDP and the Liberals, it therefore became a total non-issue.

Compounded by Labour's simultaneous failure to get anything moving in this area, this ensured – yet again – that the environment simply disappeared off the election agenda. Environmental organizations looked on aghast as the much vaunted Green Stakes failed to get under way *at all*. Despite all that pre-election posturing and prancing in the paddock, they never even made it out on to the course. Friends of the Earth's Green Agenda for the General Election, which encouraged people to write in for details about their candidates' opinions about a whole range of environmental issues, together with a detailed analysis of all the party manifestos, had a good response from the punters. But in most constituencies, there just weren't any runners to follow.

After the 1987 Election débâcle, Alliance activists were the walking wounded of the British political scene. They were then promptly knee-capped by their own leaders during the merger fiasco in January and February 1988. The history of this astonishing episode (with David Steel and Robert Maclennan attempting to foist on their respective parties a policy document that was almost totally alien to Liberals and Social Democrats alike, only to have to withdraw it amidst tears and deep recriminations) has rather obscured the real significance of the eventual decision by the Liberals to merge with the Social Democrats.

Such a merger may have become 'inevitable' by January 1988, but that merely served to demonstrate the extent to which it confirmed the triumph of Liberal pragmatism, of that special brand of middle of the road, steady as she goes, tough and tender, all things to all people oppositional politics. This is epitomized by the statement on nuclear power in the final policy document which was accepted by both parties:

> Our 1987 judgement that 'we see no case for proceeding with a PWR at Sizewell or other nuclear power stations at the present time' looks increasingly sound. We recognize that the government will set the pace and direction for the nuclear industry into the 1990s, including research and development on the fast breeder reactor, and nuclear fusion. We will monitor closely the government's decisions in this area for, as we made clear in the 1987 manifesto, we accept that the economic prospects and environmental implications of the civil nuclear power programme must be thoroughly and independently reviewed in order to assess the potential for safe nuclear energy.[5]

It's astonishing to think that this was really the best the Liberals could put their name to after more than a decade of committed opposition to the nuclear power programme in this country, but such skilful equivocation must have been music to the ears of David Steel, whose attitude to matters green is just about as ambivalent as that of Neil Kinnock. His close advisers kept telling everyone that he was 'genuinely sympathetic', but since the traumatic debate on defence at the 1986 Liberal Assembly, he hemmed himself in more and more narrowly on what he saw as the 'safe' middle ground of British politics.

Green activists within the Liberal Party are themselves not blameless for the current green go-slow. Groups like the Liberal Ecology Group, the Young Liberals and the SDP Greens have never really made the most of the openings and opportunities that were undoubt-edly there in their respective parties. Their collective contribution to the merger debate was so sotto voce as to be all but inaudible. Only Simon Hughes made any real effort to remind Liberals that there was a tradition of liberalism rather different from that on offer by way of merger with the Social Democrats. He remains by far the greenest of the Liberal MPs, with a quite distinct and deep green philosophy. His contribution to the pre-merger debate was highly significant:

> My politics is therefore about working with all creation, holistically, respectfully, to do all that I can to ensure that every living creature has the best possible quality of life. My daily concern must be to lead people away from the distraction of believing that, apart from the basics of food, shelter, housing, clothing and health, other materialistic possessions are fundamentally important, or necessary to true happiness, self-discovery, or self-fulfilment.
>
> For me, pacifists and unilateralists, those who believe in a sustainable economy and no growth, those who believe in the abolition of national boundaries and national armies, those who believe in the fundamentally shared possession that is land and the wrongness of private land ownership, those who are opposed to inherited wealth and to consumer-dominated, demand-led economics, all must be embraced and welcomed.[6]

Given such strong beliefs, it was perhaps rather surprising that Simon Hughes eventually went along with almost all the rest of them in voting for the merger. He did so, however, with a courageous and very public acknowledgement of his real sympathies and a warning about his future in the new merged party:

> At some moments, when the outcome of merger has looked unacceptable, I have wondered about offering myself as the first Liberal and Green joint party candidate. After all, there are Labour and Co-operative Members of Parliament, so joint sponsorship by two political movements is not without recent British precedent. If the party I love with the ideals that I share was not to be arguing fundamentally the same political philosophy in 1988, or 1989, or 1990, as it is now, then clearly conscience would prevent me from putting on the new colours at the next elections.[7]

Some disillusioned Liberals may eventually decide to join the Green Party, but the majority will prefer to wait and see, for it is simply too early to judge the extent to which green ideas will feature in the new Alliance. Optimists such as Des Wilson see tremendous scope for infiltrating all sorts of green input during the course of the inevitably lengthy policy deliberations. This, he hopes, will encourage more Greens to join up. Pessimists believe that the amalgamation of the SDP with the Liberals must necessarily produce a political force more cautious and reactionary than were the Liberals themselves back in the early 1980s.

This has a particular bearing on any efforts that will be made between now and the next election to bring Liberals and Greens more closely together, at both a national and a local level. There is a natural assumption among many members of the Green Party that further disarray within the Social and Liberal Democrats will offer a unique opportunity for a realignment of the Greens and radical Liberals, leading to *practical* co-operation in both campaigning and electioneering. For reasons outlined above, such co-operation was never exactly top of the agenda even for the Liberals, and certainly won't be for the new and still deeply confused SDLP. And should it be for the Green Party?

The Green Party

The 1987 General Election was also something of a watershed for the Green Party. At one level, the results looked quite encouraging: 133 candidates polled 89,354 votes (65% higher than the 1983 total of 54,077). With an average of 670 votes per constituency, it indicates that around 500,000 people *would* have voted Green if there had been candidates in every seat. Half a million voters, not one of whom would be under any illusion that their vote would help get a Green Party candidate elected, constitutes a fairly reasonable electoral base under our ludicrous first-past-the-post voting system, especially given the tremendous pressure in June 1987 for people to vote tactically.

Looked at from this perspective, it was enough to get various Green Party spokespersons talking of an 'imminent electoral breakthrough', with hordes of disillusioned Liberals and Labour Party members signing on. But at another level, especially when compared with the 1979 General Election results, things do not look quite so good. The 670 average voters per constituency was in fact 10% down on the

1979 average of 755. The proportion of candidates obtaining over 2.5% of the vote fell from 5 out of 53 in 1979 to 3 out of 133 in 1987. What is more, current party membership of around 7,000 is not much higher than it was in 1979. And there is absolutely no prospect of a move towards a system of proportional representation for a very long time to come.

Little wonder, therefore, that the Green Party is temporarily a little down, though by no means out. Comparisons are regularly made with the Green Party's 'more successful' sister parties in Europe (though Chapter 10 may give some people reason to reflect on such comparisons), but given the unremittingly harsh nature of the electoral set-up in Britain, it is hardly surprising if its role remains a little unclear. A pressure group? Conscience-prickers and consciousness-raisers? A conventional political party? An extra-parliamentary catalyst? All of these at the same time?

Unfortunately, there is a serious lack of genuine political debate on these questions. An interesting poll of Green Party members in 1984 revealed that 80% of them had never belonged to a political party before joining the Green Party. To be so generously endowed with political virgins may initially be a great advantage, but to go on denying them the prospect of fruitful political intercourse leads inevitably to frustration. For instance, a determination to avoid the sterile inanities of class politics is fine, but *only* if one can establish how green politics might come up with answers to the predictable but still legitimate demands of today's weary old class warriors. By virtue of being so far removed from power, there has always been an irrepressible streak of utopianism within the Green Party. A good thing too, some would say, in a visionless age. But this utopianism has a tendency to degenerate into 'impossibilism', manifested in a series of green-prints for the future which seem to be entirely oblivious of where we are starting from in the present.

Confronted with such problematic issues, Green Party activists would do well not to panic. The party simply *has* to continue with its electoral activities (otherwise why bother to set oneself up as a separate party?), and there are good grounds for arguing that it is at the local level that it is most likely to be successful. What is more, the Green Party in the UK has no need to compromise with other political parties; it should hang in there as fundamentalist as the day it was born. It is still the only organization taking the *full* green message to ordinary people, however unwelcome that may sometimes be, and whether one sees the gradual greening of the other parties as cynical opportunism or the first, very welcome, steps in a much longer evolutionary process, it is crucial that an appropriate yardstick is there against which one can assess rival green claims.

The Green Party's time scale is necessarily different, measured more in generations than in monthly fluctuations of the opinion polls. Either the basic green analysis is *right* (in which case the progressive deterioration of our life-support systems and people's real quality of life will in turn progressively deepen people's responsiveness to the green alternative), or it is *wrong* (in which case, sit back and enjoy the health food and organic wine with the best of them!). Those seeking instant success are better off elsewhere, for their equally instant alienation is rarely productive.

Right or wrong, like it or not, the Green Party's unique role is as 'defenders of the faith'. That does not mean it should just relax, pompously defending the faith until overtaken either by apocalypse or apotheosis. Though any projected realignment of British politics, bringing together Greens, radical Liberals and green socialists, may at the moment be no more than a great green pie-in-the-sky, one thing is still certain: it is a pie that will not get baked on Earth unless sufficient momentum is built up to start bringing the different ingredients together. The best the Green Party can do for this process is to carry on doing better what it already does.

It will not, of course, have escaped the alert reader's attention, whether in the baking of pies or the weaving of rainbow coalitions, that several important political components are still missing. Most important of these, in the long run, may be the SNP and Plaid Cymru, among whom there are many green sympathizers. Though the environmental policies of their 1987 manifestos were no better or worse than those of the other mainstream parties, their commitment to devolution and comprehensive decentralization gives them a critical deeper green advantage. It is unlikely, however, that they will be in the vanguard of any major realignment.

The Conservatives

That still leaves the Tories. Why no blue in this gleaming new rainbow? Is the Conservative Party totally immune to the sort of internal pressures within the other parties which allow one, however tenuously, to see the green tendencies emerging? As of 1988, one can

78

only say that Mrs Thatcher's hegemony is so powerful as to provide her with all but total immunity. Concerns about the National Health Service; rebellions over the poll tax; coded declarations of allegiance to 'One Nation Toryism' – these are the predictable and wholly manageable manifestations of discontent within a party that sees no reason why it should not still be in power at the turn of the century. There is no more chance of a deep green tendency developing within the modern Conservative Party than there is within the Socialist Workers Party.

The implications of this are surely clear: if the Tories *are* to be with us until the year 2000, Greens should not automatically expect the 1990s to be any better than the 1980s. This is not the place for a detailed critique of the Thatcher Government's environmental record; Friends of the Earth produced just such a document in June 1988, and it makes extremely grim reading. Despite some important achievements (such as the implementation of Part 2 of the Control of Pollution Act, the establishment of Her Majesty's Inspectorate of Pollution, the introduction of Environmentally Sensitive Areas, the Food and Environment Protection Act, increased funding for the Nature Conservancy Council (NCC) and the UK 2000 initiative), the other side of the balance sheet is too long and too painful even to begin to enumerate.

It is only fair to say, of course, that it is a damn sight harder to be green in government than it is in opposition. No one seriously supposes that a Labour government would implement all that wonderful greenery which was carried with such acclaim at their 1986 Conference; we would be lucky if we saw 25% of it put into practice, and that would be a 25% improvement on what they did when they were last in power. But this Government has consistently gone out of its way to show its contempt for the cause of the environment and for environmentalists themselves. Back in 1985, the Prime Minister spoke with her usual passion of the dangers posed by 'the enemy within', among whom she specifically included environmentalists. (Shortly after that, she invited six leading 'enemies' from the Environment Movement to lunch, but made up for this inconsistency by giving them all a drubbing for being so negative and devoid of any practical ideas! It was, apparently, a traumatic and chastening experience.) In September 1986, Douglas Hurd, the Home Secretary, warned of the growth of all pressure groups: 'They are like serpents emerging from the sea to strangle Laocoön and his sons in their coils.' He was particularly worried that any freedom of information legislation would merely allow pressure groups to exert further pressure, 'pressures which do not necessarily add up to the general good'. And in December 1987, Nicholas Ridley, Secretary of State for the Environment, who tends to see all Greens as 'pseudo-Marxists', launched a ferocious attack on the 'extremists' within the environment lobby who had the temerity to criticize the Government's record on the North Sea and other pollution issues.

It is cause for considerable concern to many, both within the Department of the Environment and the Conservative Party itself, that the Government seems to revel in such a brutal image. Back in 1984, as part of a confidential but comprehensively leaked review of policy options for the Government, Dr Martin Holdgate, Chief Scientist and Deputy Secretary within the DoE at that time, bewailed the fact that:

> Ministers do not yet understand what has been happening to the environmental concept. We have had a DoE for ten years: it has not gained general acceptance as an environmental department in the context of the political movement. The Government (by which I mean the past four administrations) has not convinced the public that it is succeeding in caring for the countryside or in curbing pollution. We are now being pressed to adopt policies (e.g. on acid rain, marine pollution, water quality, ozone depletion) which are costly and challenged economically – yet appear to have a consensus of support in other developed and European Community countries. It is difficult to contend that we can be so consistently out of step and yet right.[8]

As an historical footnote, it was interesting to see how the DoE agonized about its own internal 'greening', not knowing what to call this policy review: 'The title "Green Issues" seems on reflection to take us too far into the camp of the environmental lobby. Whilst we shall be tapping their ideas, it might be wiser to adopt our own terminology. We propose "Safeguarding the Environment" as an alternative that strikes the right note.' It simply will not do for some people to be seen to be too green in public!

From within the Conservative Party itself, the number of voices raised exhorting the blues to go green have been few but persistent. The Bow Group published an excellent document (*Conservation and the Conservatives*) just before the 1984 Party Conference, combining acute criticism with the warning that the SDP would sweep the green vote in rural and suburban seats if the Government did not get its act together. Its author pinned much of the blame for the bad image of the party on 'Cabinet intransigence'. But the privilege of being in government is being in a better position to call the shots, and they did just that. Through a sequence of new initiatives and decisions, they did just enough to placate their own critics and to limit the campaigning opportunities for both Labour and the Alliance. They announced an investment programme of £600 million to fit anti-pollution equipment to Britain's three largest coal-fired power stations; they set in train the establishment of Her Majesty's Inspectorate of Pollution (HMIP); they withdrew proposals for the dumping of low-level nuclear waste at Elstow, Bradwell, Fulbeck and South Killingholme; they started to make more positive noises about additional funding for conservation-oriented farming; and in the election manifesto itself, they declared their intention of setting up a new National Rivers Authority (NRA) to oversee the privatized Water Authorities. It did not look too much like a co-ordinated campaign, but when the election duly came, it did exactly the defensive job they must have intended it to, completely taking the sting out of what was already a virtually stingless opposition line-up.

What is more, their manifesto took the opportunity to go on to the offensive: 'Conservatives are by instinct conservationists, committed to preserve all that is best of our country's past. We are determined to maintain our national heritage of countryside and architecture.'9 The key words here are 'instinct', 'preserve' and 'heritage'. Though most Greens would consider it difficult, it not impossible, to reconcile the Government's actual record with this brand of 'instinctive conservation', they would do well to stop the knee-jerking just for a moment and consider the seductive strength of this sort of approach.

It has best been articulated in a pamphlet by Andrew Sullivan published by the Centre for Policy Studies in September 1985, entitled *Greening the Tories*. Mr Sullivan is an erstwhile leader writer for the *Telegraph*, and in July 1985 it was his unmistakable style which produced this rich offering:

> For many Conservatives, the word 'green' conjures up the most disagreeable images. Legions of eccentric, muesli-crunching peace fanatics in open-toed sandals are hardly the stuff of which Conservative Party majorities are made. Nor still are the Germanic intellectuals of the far Left, the animal rights campaigners or, even worse, the benign socialist

environmental planners with little respect for private property.

But the real 'green' tradition in this country is a completely different matter. To be British and to be green is far more accurately reflected in our national passions for fishing, gardening and country walking, than in any radical, ecological fervour. We are indeed a green nation, but not in the way the Left would like. We care about the details of our immediate surroundings, street corners and hedgerows, our parks and fens, our rivers and hillsides – small pockets of quiet sustenance – which protect our sense of community, of history, and of beauty. We care too most of all for our own property – and widespread property ownership is the natural friend of environmental responsibility. Above all this, there is a deep patriotic pride in the natural beauty of these islands which, as George Orwell observed, the intellectual left could never understand.[10]

It is one of the most galling things for dark Greens to have to acknowledge that, in a country as conservative as this, he has probably got it about right. Of the 3 to 4 million people who are said to belong to environmental organizations in Britain, by far the largest number would be environmentalists of precisely this kind rather than of the Friends of the Earth/Greenpeace variety.

It is this understanding which made William Waldegrave such a formidable operator when he was Minister for Environment, Countryside and (briefly) Planning. He fully understands the importance of what he calls 'landmarks' in people's everyday lives, but is realistic enough to accept that such an approach can often result in unfortunate outbreaks of the NIMBY (Not In My Back Yard) syndrome. Though thousands of people are involved in many different kinds of struggle for their own particular patch of England's green and pleasant land, their readiness to extend this commitment to the next door village, let alone to somewhere at the other end of the planet, is often extremely limited. (An ironic but pleasing exception to this developed in the communities threatened by the Government's proposals for the disposal of low-level nuclear waste, in that they very quickly transformed the defence of their own back yard into a much broader appreciation of the dangers posed to the *whole* of the UK by the nuclear industry.)

Waldegrave is one of those who seems to have prospered as much

82

under Mrs Thatcher as under Ted Heath. He remains an 'old-fashioned High Tory', but has managed to find so metaphysical (and sometimes abstruse) a way of rendering this as to ensure not only survival but continuing success.

> Those aspects of the Tory tradition that are most sympathetic to the environment are the genuinely Tory bits of it! Most environmental disasters are the result of grand plans that somebody has imposed on others, often against the rather inarticulate conservatism of people who say to themselves, 'I am not quite sure what is wrong with this, but I know something is.' Just consider today the pain and grief of traditional country people about modern farming.
>
> At its worst, this can be a terrible sort of know-nothing attitude that prevents *any* change. But at its best, it ensures we move ahead carefully, respecting the past, tradition and memory.

Such an approach (which Waldegrave refers to as the 'Burkean' side of the Tory politics) may explain why the Government has been able to hold the line on the defence of the Green Belt. Not only has the amount of officially protected Green Belt land been doubled since 1979, but since August 1983, when Patrick Jenkin issued a couple of circulars which seemed to hint that it would be all right for local authorities to turn a blind eye to Green Belt incursions, and instantly found himself on the receiving end of at least eighty Conservative MPs signing an Early Day Motion to warn him off, the Green Belt has remained sacrosanct. Given other changes to the planning system, this is not particularly logical, and it is universally acknowledged (though never admitted by most environmentalists!) that some areas of Green Belt are really not worth protecting at all. But pragmatism has triumphed over consistency here, and the environment is almost certainly the better for it:

> You would need a brave and confident minister to try to change the policy now, to point out that there is actually quite a lot of derelict land in the Green Belts, so why do we not try and create something attractive instead of, for instance, these terrible old gravel pits. The trouble is, everybody believes that this would be seized upon as a wonderfully convenient opening by the developers. It's like the First World War: any

movement might produce a huge collapse. So it has become almost impossible to change it.

With the exception of the Green Belts, an apparent dislike of directives and definitive planning axioms, combined with the often asserted desire to limit central government intervention in local planning decisions, is the hallmark of this Government's approach:

> You can make out a very strong argument that most unsatisfactory environmental outcomes are usually the result not of the market working, but of interference in the market, most often by the state in one way or another or by some monopoly interest. If people want to understand *genuine* market economics, they should read Adam Smith and see what he says happens when two or three businesses get together – that it always turns out to be a conspiracy against the public good!

That said, this non-interventionist claim is a particularly difficult one for this Government to maintain. Over the last few years the Government has quite ruthlessly used its powers on an unprecedented scale to overrule the decisions and green policies of local planning committees. The number of planning refusals subsequently reversed on appeal to the Department of the Environment shot up dramatically during 1984 and 1986, simply as a result of the Government transforming the appeal system into a direct instrument of policy in order to get more houses built.

As he was moved from Environment to Housing after the 1987 General Election, this is something Waldegrave himself will now have to take responsibility for. As one might expect, he has already started to make some interesting noises in this respect:

> I have tried to say, as Housing Minister, that I am very much averse to the numbers game. I would rather that there were fewer houses built during my period in housing, even if it meant political aggro, and that those houses were still occupied by people who wanted to live in them a hundred years hence, rather than that we have got to pull them down again simply because they have been badly built, or built in the wrong places. And the key to resolving some of the conflicts between conservation and new development, particularly in rural areas, is to ensure intelligent, high quality design.

The means by which such quality criteria will be encouraged, let alone enforced, have not yet been revealed. Speculation and flagrantly foolish agricultural policies have pushed up the price of land well beyond the point at which most developers feel they are in any position to spend more than the bare minimum on design features, let alone set aside any of the available land to create a more attractive environment.

Waldegrave will be much missed as Minister for the Environment, particularly by those organizations who enjoyed the access they had to him and were only too happy to play along with the game which he invited them to join, enlisting them as supporters of the department in the battles which they had to fight against other Government departments, particularly the Ministry of Agriculture. (The appointment of Lord Belstead as his successor, straight from the Ministry of Agriculture, was seen to be adding insult to the green lobby to injury). What is more, he knew his stuff (which is a rare thing), and felt quite genuinely, if not passionately, about some issues (which is rarer still). But just as one swallow does not make a summer, so one Waldegrave does not make a green government. It is all the others we have still got to worry about.

Lest that be too gloomy a note to end on, it should be repeated that the 1980s have witnessed a spectacular greening of mainstream British politics, at least in the narrow environmental sense of the word. Until the beginning of this decade, few major politicians were prepared to speak up on green issues. From the 1983 General Election onwards, national politicians have been catching up with the popular perception that the environment is an increasingly important issue. Now, according to their manifestos at least, Conservative, Labour and Alliance parties all care deeply about the environment.

There is therefore compelling evidence that we may be witnessing the first stages of real change. One must emphasize 'first stages': with the exception of the Green Party and of as yet small sections of the Labour and erstwhile Liberal parties, the overwhelming majority of British politicians have barely begun to address the more radical challenges of green thinking. They still see economic growth as the only way to solve the problems of unemployment, quality of life, North/South inequality, and even of environmental degradation itself! But one does not get to the end of the road without taking the first step, and that has at least now been taken.

CHAPTER FOUR
Media Matters

If a nation's ecological wisdom were measured by the number of television programmes it makes about the environment, Britain would have little to worry about. We currently produce more environmental films each year than any other country in Europe. Filmmakers have been churning out programmes on every conceivable environmental subject with steadily increasing enthusiasm since the early 1980s, and their collective output now accounts for a significant slice of television time.

The *Financial Times* TV critic Christopher Dunkley sees an historic significance to all this activity: 'If our children do wage the green revolution successfully, and if Spaceship Earth does come through the ecological crisis which is increasingly apparent, television will have played a central role as publicist and preacher.' Dunkley argues that although television is ill-equipped to explain abstract subjects like philosophy or politics, 'it could well have been expressly designed to deal with natural history and man's effect upon his environment.[1]

The 1987 TV schedules were bursting with major documentaries about the environment. These included the BBC's eleven-part *Only One Earth*, a no-holds-barred, self-consciously heavyweight three-parter from Paul and Anne Ehrlich on Thames, entitled simply *Earth*, and David Bellamy's passionate series *Turning the Tide*, the final film of which, a relatively innocuous analysis of green politics, caused some real controversy amongst the upper echelons of Tyne Tees, who were never quite sure what 'politics' was doing there in an environmental series!

Channel Four's main contribution came in the form of André Singer's *Battle for the Planet*, a series of seven films and studio discussions produced by the International Broadcasting Trust (IBT). Conscious of the 'seen-one-environmental-documentary-seen-'em-all' syndrome, IBT and Channel Four were keen to encourage maximum viewer participation, with each programme focussing on a simple yes/no proposition about the issues raised. More than 50,000 people responded by phone or letter.

In addition, regular nature and wildlife programmes have quietly undergone a shift away from the traditional and apolitical 'furry animals' approach. It is worth remembering that the BBC's classic natural history series of the late 1970s, David Attenborough's multi-award-winning *Life on Earth*, devoted only a couple of minutes to the fact that humans were busily wiping out much of the astonishing natural beauty and diversity the programmes celebrated. But as conservation issues have become more urgent in the 1980s, so producers have increasingly tried to inject green ideas into their programmes. In 1983, the BBC's Natural History Unit launched *Nature*, a magazine programme with an explicit brief to tackle environmental issues, subsequently relaunched in February 1988 as a green combination of *Crimewatch UK* and *That's Life*, and presented by TV reporter and newsreader Michael Buerk.

There has been a long-running debate among natural history film-makers about just how far they can go in altering the still highly successful (but, from a green point of view, very old-fashioned) style of nature film-making without alienating their largely conservative and traditionalist audiences. John Sparks, Head of the BBC's Natural History Unit, takes green programme-makers to task for failing to reach a potential audience of 30 million viewers, whilst pointing out the problems for broadcasters:

> There is comparatively little 'good news' around – certainly most of the major problems of the planet appear insuperable. Such a scenario makes for earnest, and relentlessly gloomy, television, which is enough to make any scheduler nervous. At a local level, the majority of conservation schemes make for worthy, dull watching and are not the stuff for *broad*cast-ing. Television thrives on emotional impact, on the sensational and unusual, and that which generates powerful and intriguing pictures. The sad fact is that the producers of the vast majority of green programmes, although imbued with deep concern for the environment, have not yet devised formats and ways of dealing with these weighty issues which will attract and hold large audiences. But green issues *can* be turned into enjoyable television.

However, in launching his new-look *Nature* series, Sparks went to great lengths to preserve the impression of BBC 'balance' by stressing that 'such programmes would not necessarily promote Greenpeace or Friends of the Earth arguments'. To prove the point, he went on to indulge in a spot of eco-thuggery which would embarrass even Nicholas Ridley: 'Nuclear power might be good for us all; rainforests are beastly places, and that's why most of humanity wants to see them felled; and greenshanks might best be nudged out of the Flow Country by quick-growing pine trees!'[2]

Such sentiments, especially when coming from a man whose whole career has been to promote the appreciation of wildlife and natural history, are so obviously tendentious that it would be easy to miss the more serious point.

The objective, value-free approach, in which BBC journalists act as arbitrators in the 'debate' between environmentalists on the one hand and industry and government on the other, is illusory. There is no cosy, consensual middle ground between supporters and opponents of nuclear power, only a deep clash of values. As Harold Evans observes:

> It isn't necessarily to a journalist's credit to deal even-handedly with every subject. To say: 'On the one hand, Strontium 90 is not a good thing, but on the other hand it's not a bad thing either' is not the highest form of journalism, though it is the safest. The object of journalism is to find where the truth lies. Sometimes, that may mean making an extreme statement such as: 'Strontium 90 is very bad indeed for you at all times and in all circumstances, and damn those who say otherwise!' *Fairness* is what you want, not just even-handedness.

Yorkshire TV's James Cutler, producer of a series of important films on the nuclear industry including *Windscale: the Nuclear Laundry* (1983) and *Inside Britain's Bomb* (1985), regards the failure of any journalist to make up his or her mind on the nuclear issue as a 'sign of lack of intellectual activity'. He expands on this provocative statement.

> When I started out, I thought of Windscale as just another social issue problem, like old people's homes or asbestos. But now I am absolutely opposed to nuclear power. Especially after Chernobyl, it would be dishonest for me to claim objectivity. I've researched the subject enough for my own mind to be made up and I make no bones about it.

In addition to the 'flagship' series, green concerns have also been reflected in short series and single programmes about specific environmental issues, and in one-off programmes on wider cultural and life-style issues, such as medicine and food. Important institutional factors lie behind this green documentary surge. Since the early 1980s, for example, the IBA has identified the environment as one of its priority subjects for adult education programmes. Green pressure groups operating within television have also made quite an impact, including the IBT, the Television Trust for the Environment and the Council for Environmental Education. But perhaps the single most important reason why more programmes about green issues are appearing on our screens is that a growing band of passionately committed producers and a smaller number of like-minded commissioning editors and controllers have simply wanted to make these programmes. In the mid-1980s, two key figures stand out in this process: Richard Creasey, controller of features at Central Television, the ITV company which did most to pioneer campaign-oriented programme-making about Third World, aid and ecology issues, and Carol Haslam, former head of documentaries at Channel Four.

Since 1980, Creasey has commissioned some of the finest and most innovative of all ecologically-oriented documentaries. These have included Adrian Cowell's *Decade of Destruction*, a ten-year project on the destruction of the Amazonian rainforests, Charles Stewart's *Seeds of Despair*, which alerted the world (including the BBC and Michael Buerk) to the 1984 Ethiopian famine, and *The Acid Test*, a co-production with Swedish and Dutch TV companies about acid rain, which was shown to delegates at the European '30% Club' emission control forum. He is also responsible for Britain's first and, so far, only grass-roots ecological magazine programme, *Eco*, which has been going since 1983, and founded the Television Trust for the Environment (TVE), which encourages and helps to find finance for the making of environmental and ecological films in Britain and around the world.

In television terms, ratings are usually quite small for these programmes; but the audience is growing slowly, and even a film that is seen by only a million viewers (like *Seeds of Despair*) can make an enormous impact.

For Creasey, projects like *Decade of Destruction* represented a conscious progression from earlier films like *The Tribe That Hides From Man*, an award-winning anthropological documentary made by Adrian Cowell in 1975:

> Before going ahead with *Decade*, Adrian and I discussed what we were doing wrong. Frankly, it was part of the whole way

Westerners make TV programmes about the Third World. We'd go off to somewhere like Brazil and be *colonialists*. We'd take our film out, bring it back to the West, show it and say: 'Isn't it great?' Then we'd win lots of awards and the situation would carry on as before – so we could make more programmes about it. TVE was conceived out of that discussion. We wanted to find a way to get those programmes *back* to the countries where they were made and send them to other Third World countries where they would be relevant. We also needed to find ways of telling more and more people what was going on.

TVE was founded with co-sponsorship from Central and the United Nations Environment Programme (UNEP), and with the involvement of such respected international figures as the Commonwealth Secretary, Sonny Ramphal, and Norwegian explorer and marine biologist Thor Heyerdahl, on its advisory council. The aim was to encourage all kinds of film-makers to initiate programmes designed to make a worldwide impact about specific ecological and development issues, and to find ways of extending the life of a film by providing re-edited and different language versions for education and by giving films and series free to Third World TV stations.

Creasey is convinced that his and others' efforts are beginning to stimulate other TV companies to follow suit.

We're not on the crest of a wave: there's an expansion going on. If you develop an audience, that audience wants better and better programmes. People have begun to realize we've rather cornered a market. But I don't think we'll hold pole position for much longer. I get the very strong impression that others will soon follow in our slipstream. The BBC will be coming up with a whole series of programmes concerned with the environment which will compete with *Eco*, and I couldn't be more pleased about it.

Channel Four's commitment to green programming was not actually planned from the start. In 1982, months before the new network was on the air, chief executive Jeremy Isaacs told Carol Haslam: 'We'll have no furry friends on Channel Four. They're very nice, but other people do them very well and we can do without.' Haslam had no special interest in nature films, and was more experienced and interested in health broadcasting and Third World issues. Soon afterwards, however, Isaacs had himself been so enthralled by two natural history programmes, including the prize-winning *The Fragile Earth*, that he contradicted his own instructions and bought them for the channel. Haslam responded by writing a discussion paper (*Four's Furry Friends Philosophy*) in which she argued that if Channel Four was going into the nature business, it should do so with a new kind of policy. Its wildlife films should be more analytical and political than the films traditionally made by the BBC's Natural History Unit in Bristol or by Survival at Anglia.

Haslam's ideas were accepted. As far as the 'furry friends' were concerned, old-fashioned, descriptive natural history films were out. Work reflecting the environmental, political and developmental issues which threatened the animals' likely future were in. Haslam's high point was *Worldwise*, an extended TV festival linking more than seventy environmental documentaries and current affairs programmes, and culminating on Whit Sunday 1985 with a five-hour live event, *The Longest Running Show on Earth*, introduced by David Bellamy, which encouraged viewers to go out and get involved in local conservation and environment projects.

Television documentary producers have also proved themselves more willing to devote money and staff to the kind of painstaking and sustained research required for investigative journalism on environmental issues than newspapers have done. The result has been that television journalists have also taken a lead in exposing ecological problems. Probably the most influential film yet made on the nuclear industry was Yorkshire's *Windscale: the Nuclear Laundry*, broadcast in November 1983. The film, exposing clusters of child leukaemia victims near the reprocessing plant, required a year of painstaking research and had a rolling budget. Producer James Cutler recalls: 'The bulk of the work was done by myself and a researcher. I honestly don't know what it cost, but it was a lot. You'd never get that kind of commitment of resources in newspapers.'

Extensive television attention to environmental issues has been extremely welcome. It has contributed much to educating the public, raised awareness of environmental and ecological issues, and played a significant part in accelerating the emergence of green awareness elsewhere. But there are some difficult questions for the future. Green programmes are still mainly confined to 'ghetto slot' minority sched-ules. With the exception of issues which are seen as major hard-news topics like disasters (Bhopal or Chernobyl), or matters of consistent

91

public concern such as nuclear energy, green programme-making has largely failed to break into the prime current affairs slots, or indeed be shown on the more popular BBC1 and ITV than on BBC2 or Channel Four.

Another question is whether the money to go on making such a large number of ecological programmes will dry up. Paul Gerhardt, former deputy director of the IBT, which made *Battle for the Planet*, and now network education officer for Thames Television, the largest of all the ITV companies, puts it this way: 'I see no evidence that it has penetrated so deep that it will remain a permanent part of the output. Television works in terms of 'sexy' subjects which change every year. At the moment, it's the environment. But the sheer scale of the output in 1987 could be counter-productive in the long term.' Robert Lamb, director of TVE, disagrees: 'The ITV companies and the BBC aren't going to drop this subject. I'm normally a pessimist, but I can't see it disappearing. I find programme commissioners very receptive to making films about the environment. They recognize the environment is terribly important, though everybody's stretched for money.'

David Puttnam, who in addition to his feature film-making and his role as CPRE President is also a director of Anglia Television, thinks the future of green programming is extremely precarious. He observes:

> British television is going through an extraordinary metamorphosis. It's likely to become a very cynical business. The public service ethic was very real until about fifteen years ago, but in another fifteen years it will be extremely rare. We're on the cusp of that change, seeing the passing of people like Jeremy Isaacs, Brian Wenham and, in his own way, Alasdair Milne. With hindsight, we'll see those people to have been extremely noble and special. Without people like that, TV is going to become an increasingly expedient medium.

He argues that in such a harsh TV environment, green programmes rest on a very fragile base. They will continue to be made only if they succeed in attracting audiences and overseas sales:

> Remember that everything in television is economy-driven. At Anglia, the Survival unit exists because of one man, Aubrey Buxton. The Natural History Unit at Bristol exists as an act of faith by the BBC. But both those units could be axed *overnight*. A lot of it is just fashion, and it rests on an economic tightrope.

If the greening process comes to a halt, if audiences start dropping off, then funding could disappear overnight. Someone like Michael Checkland could say, 'The Natural History Unit is too expensive' – and that would be the end of it.

These fears are shared by Carol Haslam, who left Channel Four for an ill-fated spell at Superchannel, the European satellite channel:

Having seen at close quarters the effects of market forces, I think the future is pretty bleak. Once you get into a totally free market, all that matters is the size of the audience. Among ITV advertising people, the word 'documentary' is like a death knell. They just don't want to know. As long as programmes on environmental issues are audience pullers there will be no problem. But there will be no protection for them without large audiences. In a regulated framework where you get Brownie points from the IBA, prestige projects like the Adrian Cowell films carry weight. But good reputations don't necessarily earn money.

Mainstream television news, the most influential of all the news media, has tended to be less enthusiastic about green issues than has been the case with documentaries. As David Nicholas, editor of ITN, puts it:

I suppose we are a bit more conscious of environment stories than we were. But the main reason for that is that there have been so many hellishly good environmental stories like Chernobyl and Sellafield over the last few years. We've done some pretty dramatic stuff on the desertification of central Africa. And we were able to look at green politics during the German elections because there were vivid personalities involved. Whether that represents a 'greening process' or us simply reacting to major events, I don't know. But I've certainly not been aware of any dramatic renaissance or awakening. A lot of this stuff has been around for years. I would count the Aldermaston marches and the Aberfan disaster as environmental stories, and I reckon the best environmental journalist we ever had in this country was Wordsworth. Mind you, we could never have used him because he wouldn't have been able to get it all into a minute and a half!

Nick Gallie, publicity director of Greenpeace, is under no illusions that TV news has gone green. Over the years, Greenpeace has succeeded in drawing attention to environmental issues more dramatically than any other pressure group through spectacular designed-for-TV stunts. The main objective of most Greenpeace actions has simply been to get on to the TV news and campaigners have regularly risked their lives for the cameras:

> Greenpeace has always been inherently fascinating and newsworthy as far as the media are concerned. It presented them with totally pre-packaged, simplistic but very powerful images of confrontation that were very new and exciting. TV news journalists saw it as fascinating and bizarre that people were willing to stand in front of whaling harpoons or under a barrel of nuclear waste being dumped at sea. These activities were seen as heroic and they were an absolute gift for the media. They were packaged in such a way that the media – newspapers as well as TV – could swallow them without having to chew. We still use those same techniques now, but the novelty has worn off. There's in increasing awareness inside Greenpeace that just because you do something spectacular and clever doesn't mean the media are going to pick it up any more. Basically, they don't give a toss about the *issue*. They just want the 'sexiness' of the issue and the picture. The individuals who do genuinely care about what we're saying are few and far between.

Newspapers and Magazines

Some green activists believe this can be accounted for by the generally low level of political debate elsewhere in Britain, particularly in the newspapers. Though this may be true at the 'dark green' level, it certainly isn't the case as far as the environment itself is concerned. It is now considered an important area of concern by print journalists; all the main national newspapers (even the *Sun*) now have environment specialists on their staff. And an increasing number of magazines are reflecting green issues in their pages.

One of the most intriguing shifts towards a greener perspective has come about at the *Daily Telegraph*. In the early 1980s, the paper woke up to the fact that its readers were extremely interested in the specifically rural aspects of green affairs. The arrival of Max Hastings as editor in 1986 triggered a more pronounced change. After investigating the balance between conservation and farming in rural areas, Hastings came to the conclusion that the countryside faced appalling dangers. As a result, the paper has mounted some extremely trenchant criticism of the Government's agricultural and forestry policies. Even Mr Ridley is known to be influenced by the occasional editorial broadside from the *Telegraph*, whereas he would sneer at others saying the same thing. *Telegraph* leaders can still take a pretty acerbic line on radical green politics, but the paper's reporting (particularly that of environment correspondent Charles Clover) has always been commendably straight and accurate – in marked contrast to some papers which might claim to be more sympathetic to the green cause.

Elsewhere in the 'quality' press, the *Guardian* and the *Observer* have led the field in covering green issues ever since the early 1970s. Their dominance of environmental news coverage was so complete for so long that a spot of complacency may well have crept in. The *Guardian* in particular remains something of an enigma to green activists and sympathizers, who continue to read it in their droves. The paper has often managed to be both oddly dismissive and acutely in touch with green issues at the same time. On 22 June 1987, for example, in the run-up to the 1987 General Election, there was a Hayman cartoon on the back page showing an Ecology Party (sic) candidate addressing a pot plant: 'Good evening, I wonder if you would spare me a few precious moments of your time?' while just a few pages inside was an excellent and perceptive article about the greening of Overseas Aid Minister Chris Patten. That said, the *Guardian* has a larger than average number of reporters sensitive to and knowledgeable about green issues, including its religious affairs correspondent, Walter Schwarz, environment correspondent John Ardill, nuclear specialist Paul Brown and James Erlichman. More than most national papers, the *Guardian* accords a remarkable degree of freedom to its writers.

The paper's many separate feature pages also reflect the diversity of views and priorities of the people editing them. The 'Society Tomorrow' page, for instance, is probably a deeper shade of green than anything else in the mainstream British press. In the early 1980s it was full of political policy documents and surveys of the way changes in the law would affect social workers. With a change of editor, and its rise to full- rather than half-page status in 1983, the emphasis changed to a much greener, more intimate, personal and occasionally spiritual approach, with regular columns such as 'Ecologue' devoted to specifically green matters. Chris Dodd, joint editor of the page, explains that this change was not the result of any specific policy decision: 'There has certainly been a shift, but not because anyone was agitating for it. Ideas sort of develop because people sit around and talk about them every now and then.' Similarly, green themes have been making themselves felt with increasing resonance on the Third World and science-based 'Futures' pages. On the other hand, apart from the occasional piece by Jeremy Seabrook, few green voices have made it on to the paper's 'Agenda' page, which is designed to bring in non-journalistic voices from outside the paper.

Melanie Phillips, former news editor, now the paper's policy editor, says:

> On the whole, we are a deep green paper and have been over the whole range of pages over a long period of time. We've led the field for years. There's no laid-down policy, but we've taken a great interest in things like nuclear waste dumping and local pollution. We go on and on and on about it. We do sometimes puncture people's pomposities, but we do that right across the board on every subject.

The *Observer* has maintained its position as one of the papers most devoted to environmental stories, particularly through its green specialist Geoffrey Lean, for many years the doyen of environmental correspondents. Lean himself still produces a stream of important green exclusives. If environmental organizations want an exclusive, they will invariably still try to get their story into the *Observer* first, because they know they are assured of excellent coverage. But, like the *Guardian*, the *Observer* has an irritatingly well-developed knack for reinforcing tired 'lentils 'n' sandals' clichés from an earlier age. Consider this sneering news report of the 1987 Green Party conference in Birmingham by Paul Routledge:

> The argument never gets out of hand, though many of the 300 delegates bring their pints into the conference hall: keg beer in plastic glasses unfortunately. Others prefer to knit ... A stroll among the fringe stalls restores one's faith in traditional Greenery. The anti-vivisectionists claim that Aids was caused by laboratory experiments on monkeys. Social Credit, a long-forgotten political panacea, is peddled by an intense Yorkshire-

man, who won't take no for an answer ... there is a poster offering 'meditation and quiet cogitation in the wimminz [sic] room'. Here, presumably, the ladies can ponder a pamphlet from the British Organization of Non-Parents arguing the case for not having children. Conference organizers must hope that it will catch on. Sometimes the debating hall sounds like a crèche.[3]

Richard North of the *Independent*, a long-time green activist and former editor of the pioneering environmental paper *Vole*, defends such coverage:

> English journalists do, thank God, have a predilection for jokes. Actually, I think I've got a bit better about the Green Party. In 1987, I did three decent pieces about their policies and the joke quotient was pretty low. I held myself back. I told the news editor: 'Got to avoid the jokes here.'
>
> The Green Party *does* command a lot of attention inside newspapers. They all feel that it's worth more space, for instance, than the Royal Society for the Protection of Birds – which has half a million members in comparison to their five or six thousand. If the RSBP had a conference about what it was going to do next year, nobody would take a blind bit of notice; if the Greens do it, they do take notice. The point is that it commands attention *as though it were* a serious political force, which sounds pejorative, but the fact is that at this moment it is *not*.

Since it was launched in 1986, the *Independent* has provided a refreshing and authoritative voice on green matters, due in large part to the impact of the much-respected North as its environment correspondent:

> My line on the *Independent* is that this is now mainstream stuff, this is the way the world wags now. Everybody is taking it very seriously as a matter of day-to-day life. It has grown up to such an extent that there are great chunks of legislation constantly chundering their way through Parliament and it preoccupies Europe to an extraordinary degree. Therefore, you simply cannot afford to have the environment anywhere other than at the heart of your paper. There's a sub-text to that which goes against traditional environmentalism: 'This isn't fur, feather and fairies any more. It isn't brown bread and

sandals. It's *not* alternativism. It's at the heart of ordinary people's lives.'

Greens are continually frustrated that newspapers still treat 'green stories' at the superficially environmental level rather than exploring the deeper clash of values that goes on beneath. North offers this explanation:

It's a primordial truth that we live in a rather too materialistic society. That's not news. It's not even a feature; it's lecturing, it's moralizing at people. Newspapers have a very strong feeling they shouldn't moralize. Even a leader column only opinionates. The 'oughts' of this world have very little place in a newspaper – and a lot of environmentalism is about those 'oughts'. In that respect, environmentalism is very close to religion, but religion has had a few thousand years to earn itself a moralizing ghetto. So if any newspaper's going to moralize, it'll have a God-slot. It will take a while before newspapers develop the modern equivalent, which would be an Environment-slot.

At the other end of what used to be called Fleet Street, the tabloids have generally been a disaster area for environmental stories and are still happy to portray environmentalists as whingeing flat-earthers. In 1985, the *Mirror* had an interesting stab at redressing the balance. As the result of a meeting with Des Wilson and Clive Jenkins (both members of the Friends of the Earth Trust), Robert Maxwell wanted to know why his staff weren't doing anything on the environment. The result was the *Mirror*'s 'Living Britain Campaign', which got off to a lively start on 18 April with an emotive seven-page 'Shock Issue' about dying trees, rivers, forests and wildlife heralded by a skull and crossbones on the front page and the headline 'POISON IN THE HEART OF BRITAIN – OUR KILLING FIELDS'. Inside were plenty of splash headlines and heart-rending photographs.

In best tabloid tradition, the emphasis was on human interest – like a baby born with pesticides in his blood – and animal stories. Unfortunately, although the three-month series was called a 'campaign', the paper had assumed that a couple of old ladies living in Bournemouth would probably be the only people interested, and no one had bothered to put any campaign material together. In the event, the paper was deluged with readers' letters (the response was second only to the Ethiopian Famine Appeal), but could reply only by sending out a list of environmental organizations. Apart from other occasional forays, the paper has, like its rivals, signally failed to pay sustained attention to environmental issues since then. But Richard North has some sympathy for the tabloids' difficulties in dealing with the environment:

> The great problem is that most of the stuff you're dealing with is just not sensational enough. Most of the stuff I deal with is deeply tedious. If I'm successful, it's in pointing out that it is also elegant and important and we should please pay a bit of attention to it. Take the quality of our drinking water: despite the occasional nonsense and deceitfulness on the part of Government, which Friends of the Earth has accurately pointed out, the fact is that you can't prove that anybody's dead. You can't even show they're wounded. You can't even show they've had a day off work. You can't *even* show they've felt ten per cent off-colour any one day! It would be nice if our water was cleaner, but there's a very long way to go before proving that anybody's in serious trouble over tapwater.

As regards magazines, they divide fairly clearly into those aiming at an 'inside market', and those which feature green issues as just one part of a broader appeal. The insiders' magazines have a small but devoted readership, each one catering for a distinct taste. *Resurgence*, for example, primarily addresses the aesthetic and spiritual side of the movement with philosophical, theoretical articles or specific stories about craft industries, decentralism and community living. Under the gentle guidance of its resilient editor, Satish Kumar, the magazine continues to make an influential and inspirational contribution to the Green Movement.

Jon Carpenter's newsier *Green Line*, founded in 1982, is very much *the* insiders' magazine, mostly read by Green Party members and green socialists. Editorially, it remains a bit hit-and-miss with some extremely intelligent and perceptive articles mixed up with a fair smattering of absolute drivel. But it too has made a big impact on the Green Movement, particularly through its attention to and emphasis on the red/green debate, international politics and feminism. Carpenter (a former member of the Green Party) is not averse to stirring things up a bit and positively revels in his political detachment, rightly insisting that the Green Movement will never get anywhere unless it debates its differences openly and constructively.

At the other end of the spectrum, the magazines of the peace and development organizations have, like the organizations themselves, increasingly reflected green concerns. Since about 1985, CND's paper *Sanity* has regularly covered certain environmental issues and has become a reliable and prolific source of information on the 'civil' nuclear industry and the political battles over the nuclearization of the Pacific. In the Third World-oriented development movement, the broadly leftist perspective of the *New Internationalist* has taken on a distinctly green hue, and it has done more than any magazine to bring together environmentalists and development activists.

On the academic side, the *Ecologist*, a child of the early 1970s, is still the Green Movement's nearest equivalent to the *Lancet*, and is approaching the end of the 1980s in particularly strong form, with authoritative scientific papers on every ecological issue from climatic conditions to chemicals and cancer. Not so long ago, a rather stodgy diet of long, turgid and highly technical articles threatened the *Ecologist* with an untimely demise. It turned a corner in the mid-1980s with a series of superb and influential articles about the World Bank and deforestation. Its campaigning editor, Teddy Goldsmith, remains one of the most formidable intellectual heavyweights in the Green Movement.

The definitive popular green publication of the 1970s was *Vole*, an exuberant, inconoclastic mixture of sparky ideas and investigative pieces. The paper featured everything from cartoons, ads for hand-carved clogs and 'pollution-free sailing holidays' to detailed analysis of the philosophy of Ivan Illich and angry, open letters to Prince Charles about the future of Dartmoor. To its readers' lasting disappointment, a mixture of financial problems and mismanagement forced it to close in 1981. The great mystery is why nothing has emerged since then to take its place. Richard North, who took over from Richard Boston as editor in *Vole*'s final year, offers this explanation: 'The need for it disappeared. Any story you'd have wanted for *Vole* could go into any of the national papers now. It's become the mainstream. The intellectual stuff, that vague English anarchism has gone, it's true. But it's gone from the culture as well. It bubbles along underground.'

One reflection of this is to be seen at the *New Scientist*, considered by many one of the greenest magazines in Britain, drawing considerable attention to the scientific side of green issues with balanced, authoritative, clearly written articles which avoid the usual technical jargon. It takes a passionate interest in all environmental issues, with strong features on both specific ecological subjects – ozone, nuclear power, global warming – and broader green issues such as the role of technology in society. Its news coverage is also first rate.

Another measure of the new, quite un-*Vole*-like *respectability* of environmental concern in the late 1980s has been the emergence of the glossy *Environment Now*, launched in October 1987 and published under the auspices of the Conservation Foundation. At the time of writing, it is too early to give more than a first impression of *Environment Now*, but it is well written and clearly intends to eschew the image of partisan alternativism. The first issue included a message to readers from the Minister for the Environment at that time, Lord Belstead ('More and more people believe that the environment should be at the top of our list of current concerns . . .') and advertisements for exclusive Austrian leisurewear from Harrods and several large companies assiduously greening their image. It will be interesting to see how its political line evolves, but it has already provided an intriguing example of the way green ideas are moving into new areas.

A range of glossy but not explicitly green magazines have begun to reflect a growing engagement with environmentalism. One is *Country Living*, which has featured profiles of green activists, excellent articles on such subjects as the future of Britain's rivers, all written in a light, brisk, coffee-table tone. Women's and fashion magazines like *Vogue* and *Harpers and Queen* increasingly touch on green subjects. Whether it's about nouvelle green cuisine or light-touch pieces about alternative medicine, very few life-style magazines like *Company* or *Cosmopolitan* now fail to allude to greenery. In addition, literally dozens of food and health magazines have sprung up, many of them taking a more than pastel-green interest in issues like alternative health, natural food and vegetarian eating.

Many of these magazines take an environmental message into areas it simply hasn't reached before. One example of this process was the launch by Marcus Binney, former editor of *Country Life* and a passionate defender of our architectural heritage, of a new magazine called *Landscape* at the end of 1987. The magazine is stuffed to the gills with expensive advertising aimed at thriving executives, but combines this with some genuinely hard-hitting environmental stories.

Advertising

Over the years, there has been a lively debate in green circles about the ethics and effects of advertising in society. The case against is that advertising is a fundamentally ungreen activity because it fuels materialist fantasies and consumerist desires, persuading people to buy more than they really want and certainly more than they need, and that ways should be found to restrain the power of manufacturers to make people yearn for their products. The anti-advertisers have never quite won the day, but the Green Party did go into the 1987 election with a policy of banning all cigarette and alcohol advertising on health grounds.

The opposite view sees advertising simply as another tool for communication, and one which greens will do well to use. As photographer David Bailey, who was involved in the famous Greenpeace anti-fur advertising campaign, puts it: 'It's ridiculous to be against advertising because you're a Green. It's conforming to all the stupid stereotypes, like always wearing sandals and only driving a 2CV. Advertising is just a form of communicating, like any other way of getting your message across. The Labour Party went on for years about how unethical advertising was. Now they get Hugh Hudson to make their films.'

Political advertising came of age in the 1980s. First, Saatchi and Saatchi's famous efforts on behalf of the Conservative Party alerted everybody to the potential of the medium. Later, Boase Massimi Pollitt's award-winning 1985 campaign for the GLC during its fight against abolition showed how effective political advertising could be for the Left. Pressure groups such as Greenpeace, Christian Aid, Oxfam, the anti-fur campaign Lynx, Friends of the Earth and CND have all tried to make their voices heard through advertising. This has usually been in newspapers and magazines, posters and cinema commercials. Television and radio advertising is more of a problem since the IBA forbids 'political' advertising. The IBA's definition is highly controversial, since it rules out anti-nuclear ads but permits British Nuclear Fuels to promote itself on the same issue.

The green organization which has used advertising with greatest conviction has unquestionably been Greenpeace – and its groundbreaking 1984 anti-fur campaign was undoubtedly the most controversial. Through its advertising agency, Yellowhammer, Greenpeace recruited David Bailey, a production company and a film crew to give their services free. The result was a highly professional and extremely hard-hitting poster and an equally tough cinema commercial at the extraordinarily cheap rate of about £20,000 – a tenth of the cost of going to an ordinary agency. In the cinema commercial, a fur-wearing model paraded on a catwalk, splattering her audience with blood. It was the first commercial ever to carry an X-certificate. As we've already seen in Chapter 2, the campaign created a furore, with feminists attacking Greenpeace and the campaign as being deeply, insensitively sexist, a charge which is still levelled four years on. But the advertising industry was thoroughly impressed, and showered the campaign with attention and awards.

Nick Gallie worked in the mainstream advertising business before joining Greenpeace in 1983, and played a crucial part in the decision to use advertising. He remains proud of the campaign's impact and unapologetic towards its critics:

> It was a deliberately disturbing, hard-hitting image targeted at a particular audience. We picked the image to really stir things up and it did. We were trying to degrade the type of women who wear fur coats, and make them ashamed to wear them. The sado-sexual connotations of the image were a deliberate way of making a point about the mentality of wearing a dead animal for fashion. At the time, it didn't occur to anyone that the image connected in some way to menstrual connotations and the myth of 'unclean women', but that's a product of the creative unconscious.

There is considerable debate as to how effective advertising campaigns can be in raising the profile of a campaigning organization or in changing public opinion. Greenpeace's membership has certainly increased massively since 1983, but whether this was a result of advertising or simply of the organization's high media profile is a moot point. Other large green organizations have found advertising less useful. In 1986, Friends of the Earth's GLC-funded 'Cities for People' campaign, directed against new road-building and the power of the road lobby, had little lasting impact. And a survey for *Marketing Week* in October 1987 found that many campaigning groups 'which have tried to present themselves more coherently to the public by using traditional advertising and marketing techniques still have an unpopular image or only command a low awareness of their activities'. One can only conclude that the contribution of advertising to raising green awareness in the population as a whole has been pretty minimal.

From the other side of the fence, green imagery has increasingly entered the ad-person's repertoire. Advertising copy-writers have long appealed to Romantic notions of Arcadian idylls and natural beauty, but in the last few years, the visual language and rhetoric of mainstream advertising has changed quite substantially to take account of consumers' growing environmental concern. Consider these examples, culled more or less at random from magazines at the end of 1987 and the beginning of 1988:

- half-page SAAB car advertisement in the *Guardian* promoting their lead-free petrol engines. 'In the not too distant future, lead-free petrol will be law for all cars in the UK ... if you drive a SAAB, you're already prepared ... If all cars were this mindful of the laws of nature, perhaps new laws would be unnecessary'.

- General Motors proclaiming their catalytic converters with a picture of a car speeding through a forest glade: 'Nobody is more advanced in cleaning up the air pollution from cars than us ... as well as maintaining our lead in automotive technology, we're giving yet another boost to British Exports. And doing our bit to help protect the environment we live in.' (*Environment Now*)

- Baxter's 'No meat and three veg', promoting tinned vegetarian soup: 'There's something rather special about our new range of soups. It's not what's in them, but what isn't ... enough to satisfy any healthy appetite, made without a trace of meat.' (*Cosmopolitan*)

- One of many green-oriented images from the CEGB's clever 'Electricity – Energy for Life' campaign shows the exterior of a beautiful North Wales mountain which houses the Dinorwig power station. 'As you can see, the principle behind preserving the beauty of the environment needs no explanation at all.'

- In a similar vein, British Gas has a picture of a beautiful bird perched on a wooden post with the headline 'Industrial Landscape' and the copy: '... fortunately for our countryside and wildlife, British Gas has shown consistent concern for the environment during nearly two decades of unparalleled growth.'

- A playfully anti-green Volkswagen ad shows a Polo parked outside the greener-than-thou Neal's Yard Wholefood Warehouse in London's Covent Garden. The cheeky caption, about the car's paint, bodywork and safety features, reads: 'More preservatives. More colouring. More additives . . . Our body is all the healthier for being literally crammed full with preservatives.'

And finally, perhaps the hardest of the lot to swallow without spluttering over the muesli:

- Smiling Labour MP Dr David Clark, clutching a copy of the Wildlife and Countryside Act (which, to the great benefit of Britain's badger population, he helped to amend), is pictured in front of the Houses of Parliament. The product? Barbour jackets – he's wearing one. 'Real country people unquestioningly rely on their Barbours to allow them to function under all conditions . . .'

Some of today's mainstream green advertising is by companies claiming legitimate green credit for their policies or products. Much of it, though, is undoubtedly defensive. It is placed by companies trying to defuse criticisms from environmentalists by presenting themselves as being ecologically sensitive. It can be cheaper to advertise one's green virtue than to earn it. In August 1987, for example, the CEGB, under assault from environmentalists over its appalling record on sulphur dioxide and other emissions from its power stations, increased its annual rate of spending on newspaper advertising from £574,000 to £3,243,600, with a similar amount going on TV.

Shell is an intriguing case. For more than fifty years the company has promoted itself as being interested in the countryside. In the 1930s, Shell produced country guides and nature wall-charts and attracted artists of the stature of Paul Nash and John Piper and poets like John Betjeman to produce work for it. Whilst BP emphasizes its technical expertise, Shell emphasizes its environmental concern. But is this just another cynical route to the same hard sell?

Some of Shell's eco-conscious advertising has been quite preposterous. One particularly distasteful poster appeared in early 1987 advertising the attractions of new Formula Shell on the grounds that it pumped out fewer emissions than other petrols. The poster showed a smiling cyclist drawing in a car's fragrant exhaust fumes like some latter-day Bisto kid; not terribly advisable in real life, unless you also want a lungful of carcinogenic hydrocarbons. On another occasion, 'proof' of clever landscaping at Shell's newly opened Mossmoran oil-cracking refinery in Scotland involved advertisements which showed pictures taken from behind a hill . . . From that angle, the plant, one of the biggest of its kind in Europe, was indeed invisible.

It's only fair to point out that some of Shell's environmental efforts on projects such as restoring the countryside after putting in pipelines has been very impressive. Hazel Barbour, director of the Shell UK's 'Better Britain' campaign, also believes the company's green concerns are reflected as much in its 'community' programmes as in its advertising strategies. (Shell puts about £3 million a year into green community programmes, including recycling schemes and the Groundwork Foundation, which helps small companies improve their local environment. It also works closely with bodies like the British Trust for Conservation Volunteers.) She argues that such environmental concerns have become a *genuine* part of her company's corporate social responsibility philosophy.

Green cynics remain unimpressed; whilst admiring Shell's astuteness in picking 'environmental concern' as the hallmark of their corporate identity, and in being ahead of the field in realizing that being seen to be 'for the environment' would be good news for the company, they can't actually see the practice of Shell being radically transformed as a consequence. Having that particular corporate identity may have some influence on boardroom decisions, in that they're obliged not to be too obviously or overtly insensitive to the environment. But, fundamentally, they're no more concerned about the environment than anyone else in that business. Whatever they do is bound to be marginal because their whole purpose is still to drill for oil and to make money.

British Nuclear Fuels' defensive advertising, urging the public to visit Sellafield to see the plant for themselves, is quite different. According to Nick Gallie:

> That's a straight case of BNFL being under tremendous public attack from Greenpeace, Friends of the Earth and the public, and having scored a spectacular number of own goals. They have a filthy image, and they were under great pressure from the government to clean up their act. Their first response was totally cynical: they showed healthy children running about under clear blue skies, through green fields with blossoms all

106

over the place. That didn't work. They found they had a problem with what advertising people call 'cognitive dissonance': no one believed them. So they had to come up with a 'communication strategy' to bridge the gap between how they are seen and how they want to be seen. In advertising terms, their campaign after that was extremely good. Their problem was that they were seen as unsavoury and secretive. So their advertising campaign had a nice, trustworthy-looking, down-to-earth northern lass saying: 'Why don't you come up and visit Sellafield?'

And what of the advertising agencies themselves? To what extent are they now on the side of the angels? In the wake of the success of the Greenpeace and GLC anti-abolition campaigns, a number of the big advertising agencies have been eager to work for peace, development and green organizations. *Campaign* magazine referred to this as 'avant-garde London agencies looking for a few awards and a little conscience-salving'.[4] But Robin Sadler, a long-time environmental activist who is also a senior account executive in the London office of the world's biggest ad agency, McCann Erickson, argues that some of the cynicism directed at the world of advertising is misplaced: 'The general public sees us as devils associated with the large manufacturing companies. Most ad agencies have never been like that. There has always been a fairly healthy amount of scepticism about clients and their products. There have always been people inside the agencies who take a greener and broader ethical view than clients have.'

Sadler says he 'came out' as a Green in the late 1970s. Rather to his surprise, he found he was able to use his environmental sensibilities to professional advantage:

I've never tried to campaign openly or tell clients, 'You can't do it that way: it has to be green.' I've tried to make people aware of the environmental implications of almost any product, which might become more important to consumers as general environmental concern developed. That perspective has been useful in enabling me to predict some consumer developments. Being reasonably informed, I was able to pick up concern about additives and interest in vegetarianism and 'naturalness', particularly among the young, and to present ideas for the development of new products and food items to companies like Unilever. That was in about 1979 or 1980, long before such suggestions would have seemed sensible to our normal clients. It was a useful if slightly eccentric attribute to be known as the green person in the office.

Nick Gallie remains sceptical:

The industry *is* getting more sensitive to the environment. But it's very much to its own advantage to be so. The whole population is becoming more concerned about green things, so there's no reason why advertising people should be immune from that, particularly as their job requires them to be aware of emerging social trends. The point of advertising is to cast their clients – corporations or particular products – in a favourable light. If society sees green issues as being important, the advertising will reflect it. But remember, the essence of advertising is that it doesn't tell the *whole* truth: it just extracts part of the truth.

CHAPTER FIVE

Towards a Green Aesthetic

If green ideas really are penetrating to the heart of our culture, we would expect to see this reflected in the work of artists and entertainers. Green themes ought to be popping up in films and television soap operas, in art galleries and salerooms, on the stage and in record shops. We would expect a growing army of painters, writers, musicians, sculptors, actors and performers to bring their experience of and questions about nature, technology and the environment to the centre of their work.

Clearly, the notion of 'green art' raises important aesthetic and cultural issues. The concept itself is probably a symptom of the truly desperate degree to which most of us have lost touch with nature. For tribal peoples such as the few surviving Ache Indians of Paraguay or the Penan of Sarawak, all art, their stories and music, their rituals and spirituality, are so intimately connected to the environment they live in that the very idea of 'art', let alone 'green art', as something outside the rest of their lives would be simply incomprehensible.

Nevertheless, there has clearly been some kind of burgeoning green interest in the arts of late. One indication of this is that many of our most creative talents have been increasingly willing to identify themselves with environmental causes. This growing reservoir of green good will among artists has been reflected by the success of organizations which have been providing opportunities for them to become more actively involved.

One such group is The Arts for The Earth (TATE), launched by Friends of the Earth in February 1986 to raise money, publicize environmental causes and extend the green message through the arts. Dozens of artists and performers have now donated their services and talents free to help out on different occasions. Their first event was a cartoon auction involving the work of more than eighty top cartoonists including Gerald Scarfe, Ralph Steadman, Posy Simmonds, Giles, Barry Fantoni and Charles Schultz. A fine art auction a year later featuring only environmental works elicited equally prestigious support. Lenny Henry did a benefit for them at the Albert Hall; Ben Elton compèred a review in the unlikely setting of St James's Church in

Piccadilly. Julian Bream dedicated his 1988 Wigmore Hall recital to TATE. Actors including Diana Quick, Jeremy Irons, Andrew Sachs, Susannah York, Helen Lederer, Bill Oddie, Hayley Mills and Nicholas Woodeson performed in *The Earth Awakes*, an ecological reinterpretation of *Sleeping Beauty* which followed in the fund-raising footsteps of Amnesty International's *Secret Policeman's Ball*. Poets like Andrew Motion, Gavin Ewart, Adrian Henri and Roger Woddis turned out to read green extracts from their work.

By any standards, this represents an impressive line-up of supporters, and with patrons like Placido Domingo, Peggy Ashcroft, Douglas Adams, Tom Stoppard, Yehudi Menuhin and Kenneth Branagh, it is clear that the 'artistic establishment' in Britain has become a powerful force for the good in promoting the cause of the environment. The personal testimony of many of these artists bears witness to a terrible anguish at what is being done to the Earth, and a clear understanding that cultural impoverishment and environmental degradation are but two reflections of today's ruthless materialism. Encouraging people to 'sing again the song of the Earth' is no less of a challenge for artists than it is for environmentalists.

A quick scamper through some of the better-known names and institutions of the art world reveals the degree to which overtly green interests (and even specific campaigning projects) have begun to emerge. In late 1988, for example, the English National Opera is due to stage an opera for children with music by Ilona Sekacz and a libretto by Fay Weldon about the true story of a sixteen-year-old schoolboy who led a campaign to save a patch of wild land in London's Wormwood Scrubs. Plans are well advanced for an exhibition in 1990 which will turn the Hayward Gallery on the South Bank into a multi-media version of the tropical rainforest, with recordings, film and sound effects. That exhibition will recall the now-defunct Earthlife's extraordinary show *Dead Wood*, staged in Kew Gardens in 1986 by the theatre group Lumière and Son, who re-created the atmosphere of the Brazilian jungle to draw attention to its accelerating destruction with brilliant lighting effects and a cast of dozens. The event was followed each night by a special mass in the Palm House.

In literature, recognizably green or greenish concerns are reflected in the work of writers as varied as Paul Theroux, Russell Hoban, Maggie Gee, Melvyn Bragg, Ursula LeGuin, Iain Banks and John Fowles. Doris Lessing, arguably the greatest visionary novelist writing in English today, rejects the green label, but much of her work, particularly *Shikasta*, engages with spiritual and ecological emotions with a force and clarity that most Greens are only beginning to grope towards.

In the pop world, Band Aid and Live Aid reflected genuine and passionate concern for victims of the famine in Africa. They, and all subsequent showbiz spectaculars on the subject, have focussed attention on wider development and aid issues in a way that would have been unimaginable before 1984. Green threads run through the work of performers as diverse as Sting and Talking Heads. Boy George even voted for the Green Party in 1983! In folk music, Peggy Seeger observes: 'People who used to sing about boss-worker relations are turning their attention to the environment'.

Many visual artists have also reflected a passionate engagement with environmental and ecological issues. The late West German artist Joseph Beuys was an inspiration to and founding father of Die Grünen. In Britain, Frank Auerbach, best known for his portraits, is now devoted to painting trees and landscapes of Primrose Hill. Adrian Berg has developed an equally intimate relationship with Regent's Park. Sculptor Andy Goldsworthy reflects his relationship with nature in gentle, transient works made of twigs, logs, fallen leaves and ice. CPRE had no trouble persuading some of the country's top photographers, including Lord Snowdon, Fay Godwin, David Bailey and Patrick Lichfield, to take pictures for a book to draw attention to the plight of threatened beauty spots – *England's Glory: a Journey Through England's Threatened Landscapes.* Greenpeace did a similar job on Britain's coastlines.

Does all this and a plethora of similar activity add up to a greening of the arts? Arts for the Earth director Victoria Cliff Hodges believes 'the bandwagon is just beginning to roll . . . The good will is there; the problem is finding suitable forms in which to express it. Doing that requires courage and hard work, but, as one environmental issue after another strikes home with people, the reaction to what we're doing is becoming increasingly positive.'

Sue Clifford, one of the co-directors of Common Ground, a slightly older and very different green organization involved in the arts, sees it less as a bandwagon than as a process of making explicit what has always been present:

> I see a lot happening now, but an awful lot of people have been doing things for years and no one noticed. Now they are being noticed. I loathe the idea of a 'green art' with a 'message' as

111

part of 'the environmental cause'. That would be so imperialistic! I prefer the idea of holding hands with artists as equal partners. There is so much that poets, artists and writers have always known, have not forgotten. *They* can now teach *us*. That is an incredibly important part of ecology. We are trying to reclaim the central importance of arguments of the heart, our emotions and the subjectivity of well-being.

Common Ground, set up in 1983 and based at the London Ecology Centre in Covent Garden, aims to stimulate people to explore the deeper aspects of their connections with nature. Their New Milestone Project, for instance, encouraged communities throughout Britain to commission local sculptors to create new landmarks for villages and the countryside. Another venture was the Parish Maps Project which asked for unconventional, personalized maps of the places where people lived. The idea was to make people more aware of the textures, sights and experience of their local environments. 'We are trying to focus on the commonplace, everyday experience rather than the special and rare, so as to give people the confidence to fight for things that are special to them,' says Clifford:

> The exciting thing is that in Britain we have enormously rich traditions of a very close cultural relationship with nature and the land. Composers like Elgar, Delius and Holst were all relating to the experience they got from trees and landscapes. We have an incredibly strong tradition of landscape painting with people like Turner and Constable. But in the last 150 years that relationship has been largely broken. Science and technology fragmented everything. One of the things the Green Movement is trying to do is to put things back together again, acknowledging that some artists have kept the relationship going all through that time.

This is not the place to try to define a 'green aesthetic', or the role of art in our society. Nor is it possible in the limited space of this volume to reflect the enormous diversity of green work in all the arts. We hope others will explore these areas. Instead, in the following pages, we will look in more detail at what has been happening in film and television (mass audience, mainstream, populist forms which exist at the point where art and entertainment meet high finance) and the theatre.

Film

In a sense, film-makers have taken an interest in green issues ever since the birth of the medium: if we adopted a very broad definition of the term 'green film', we would be able to claim that each one of the countless works which have explored the problematic side of human attempts to dominate nature or misuse technology and science was part of a green-tinged discourse. That would include everything from Charlie Chaplin in *Modern Times*, or Jacques Tati, or Dr Frankenstein, or Marilyn Monroe in *The Misfits*, to Powell and Pressburger and comedies like *Mr Deeds Goes To Town* and *Crocodile Dundee*. The majority of these films, particularly those made before the 1970s, were clearly not consciously green. Nor were they perceived as being green by the audiences who watched them. But whatever their creators' motivations or the public's reaction to them, many films which are not self-consciously ecological or environmental should, at the very least, be considered as significant symptoms of the cultural landscape from which the Green Movement has emerged and which made it possible.

This is undoubtedly true of anti-nuclear movies, of which there are enough to constitute a genre all by themselves. These range from early 'warning' films about the dangers of atomic technology (like *The Day the Earth Caught Fire* or *Seven Days to Noon*) through to the horror and science fiction films of the 1950s depicting bizarre atomic mutations (gigantic ants in *Them!*, microscopic or gargantuan humans in *The Incredible Shrinking Man* or *The Attack of the 50-Foot Woman*). Many films have attempted to depict the mentality, dynamics and terminal consequences of planned or accidental nuclear war (*Dr Strangelove, Fail Safe, On the Beach, Panic in Year Zero, The Forbin Project, The War Game* (1965), *War Games* (1982) or *When The Wind Blows*). And there have been numerous thrillers about the dangers and secretive nature of the nuclear industry and the nuclear state (*The China Syndrome, Silkwood* or even a crime film like *Kiss Me Deadly*). Such films bear witness to the widely held fear (and, for some, conviction) that we are living at the end of an historical epoch, and quite possibly at the final moments of human civilization on the planet.

Since the 1950s, film-makers have also reflected other apocalyptic anxieties, such as the fear of an accidental release of chemical weapons which is manifest in *The Satan Bug*, *No Blade of Grass* or *The Crazies*. Fears about science and technology took on a particular form in the mid- and late 1970s with the cycle of hugely popular disaster movies like *The Towering Inferno* and *The Poseidon Adventure*.

The era of *Limits to Growth* and prophetic eco-doom generated a group of explicitly environmental movies such as *Soylent Green* and *Silent Running*.

The notion that nature itself might produce monsters to take revenge on polluting mankind became a favourite theme in eco-horror movies of the 1970s, with unscrupulous chemical companies usually depicted as the villains. In *Frogs*, for instance, an environmentally insensitive industrialist played by Ray Milland gets his come-uppance when a plague of killer frogs fight back on behalf of the earth. Revenge-seeking monsters like the bear in *Prophecy* (a film based on the Minamata mercury poisoning tragedy in Japan), or the smog monster in the Japanese children's film *Godzilla vs The Smog Monster* (theme song: 'There's One Solution – Stop Pollution') were used as vehicles for sometimes embarrassingly crude ecological messages and the vogue for eco-horror largely died out by the end of the decade.

It would certainly be a mistake to see such films as evidence of a fundamental greening of the mainstream commercial film industry. There has been none. Indeed, if there is an overall trend in the industry at all, it is probably anti-green. Hollywood, still overwhelmingly the dominant cinema in the world and the source of most films seen in British cinemas, remains rigidly hierarchical and hopelessly addicted to technology, money and raw power. As the former head of Columbia Pictures, David Puttnam, puts it:

> The film industry is probably the least green business in the whole world: wasteful beyond the dreams of avarice – and arrogant with it. Today's Hollywood is a complete mess. It tends toward a corrupt, self-serving oligarchy and, in terms of the quality of its product, it doesn't work. There are noble exceptions, but much of the power in Hollywood resides with people whose idea of an adequate salary is, in human terms, ludicrous and who have no concept of service beyond the desire to serve each other and themselves. That kind of power-obsessed figure exists in Europe, but he's rare. In Hollywood, it could well become the norm.

114

Puttnam also sees little evidence that creative film people are significantly engaging with green issues:

> I've been disappointed in the way my generation of film-makers and people in the arts generally have responded to the environmental movement. At Columbia, I was looking at literally hundreds of projects. I would love to be able to say that there's an emerging environmental trend, but in truth there isn't. Film-makers tend not to be deep thinkers. They're not Utopians and very few have any considered vision of the future. There are no George Bernard Shaws making movies today, though people like John Boorman, Bill Forsyth and Roland Joffe may well prove able to carry that torch. Perhaps it's because of the nature of the industry. The best directors tend to be highly intuitive and to have a good 'media nose'. But their working environment seems to fragment them. They seldom seem left with any world view.

Julie Christie agrees that Hollywood's values are fundamentally anti-green, and that the occasional green-tinged, mainstream commercial film should not be seen as evidence of a deeper greening:

> I don't see many films from Western countries these days, but I do get the impression that green films are very few and far between. There are a few anti-nuclear thrillers like *China Syndrome* and *Silkwood*. The nuclear theme is so mind-blowing that it's possible to make films about it. But it seems to be terribly difficult to make a decent film about ecology without getting didactic. I've seen several scripts about animal liberation, for example. But they haven't been successful. Dramatically speaking, it's hard to make a good film about a subject which boils down to showing how everything we use comes out of ghastly animal torture chambers. I'd love someone to make a really good and moving film about Britain's terrible agricultural policy, but I don't expect that to happen for a few years yet.
>
> By far the best ecological films I've seen are from the Third World, particularly from Latin America and Africa. Because what's happening to their countries is so serious, some of the films are very radical: stories about little farmers fighting big corporations who spray hideous chemicals all over their fields, the farmers falling ill, and so on. But people in Britain aren't

terribly interested in people from Third World countries, so we don't get to see many of those films.

And yet, Christie and Puttnam are prominent members of a small but highly significant group of important individuals in the film industry who are clearly identified as Greens and who strive to reflect their beliefs and concerns in their work. In the United States, major Hollywood stars like Robert Redford, Jane Fonda, Paul Newman and Martin Sheen are publicly associated with environmental issues. The work of the Australian director Peter Weir, who is now based in Hollywood, reflects a deep and green-edged concern about the cultural, spiritual and ecological problems confronting the consumer society. His films (*Last Wave, Witness, The Mosquito Coast*) probe alternative values and beliefs through the eyes of characters vaguely dissatisfied with their own societies who are confronted by other cultures.

Environmental themes have also found their way into the most populist science fiction format. Unlike its predecessors, *Star Trek IV* was an overt piece of eco-consciousness-raising, with Captain Kirk and the crew of the *Enterprise* zipping back in time to present-day California to save the whales from extinction. The boundless technological optimism of *Star Trek* makes it a curious vehicle for such a message, but Leonard Nimoy, the star of both the long-running TV series and the *Star Trek* films, explained: 'There are scientists who are deeply concerned because of a prevalent attitude that, whatever problems we create, science will "fix it". They are afraid that something will go terribly wrong and someone will turn around and say, "Fix it" and they will have to say, "We can't. It's gone too far and it's something we can't control." '[1]

There are few explicit statements of green ideology in film, and even fewer successful ones. One of the best of these is Godfrey Reggio's *Koyaanisqatsi*, a painstakingly crafted independent American project, seven years in the making, which stands as an impressive cry of green angst about the state of modern civilization. The film tells no story in the conventional sense, presenting instead a procession of exquisitely photographed images of natural beauty (clouds, mountains, deserts, flowers) which are contrasted with equally extraordinary images of the ugliness of the man-made environment (electricity pylons, open-cast mines, junk food, factories, nuclear explosions, Manhattan subway stations). The title is a Hopi Indian word meaning 'life out of balance', or 'way of life that calls for another way of living'. Hardly any of the film is shot at conventional speed. Images are either speeded-up or slowed right down and the whole is edited to synchronize with an hallucinatory score by the American composer Philip Glass. In terms of sheer filmic technique, it is unique and undoubtedly moving, but most green movies don't wear their hearts on their sleeve the way *Koyaanisqatsi* does.

Green themes pervade the work of the important British director, John Boorman. Ideas about human relationships with nature lie at the heart of his *Deliverance*; vital and healing nature forms an important background to both the science fiction film *Zardoz* and his Arthurian epic *Excalibur*, which reworks the King Arthur story – 'Britain's most important myth' – from a deep green, Jungian perspective, largely stripped of its Christian overtones.

But Boorman's personal turning point came with the three-year process of making *The Emerald Forest* between 1982 and 1984. The film, a campaigning eco-drama shot in the heart of the Amazon jungle, is the most passionate plea against destruction of the tropical rainforests that has yet been made for the commercial cinema. But it goes deeper than simply putting the environmental case, and tries to portray something of the spiritual richness and perfect harmony with nature of the Indian tribes who live in the forest. The film was inspired by a newspaper cutting from the *Los Angeles Times* about an engineer who spent ten years searching for his son who had been kidnapped by an Amazon tribe. Initially, Boorman was excited by the story alone. But both he and the project changed through the experience of living in the jungle. The experience altered the way he thought about both film and the world:

> I had the sense of suddenly coming into the engine room of the planet. I felt I was witnessing almost continuous Creation, that things were being evolved as I watched. It was like a furnace. You could practically feel the whole thing thrusting and humming and see the multiplicity and interconnectedness of everything. I became completely entranced and obsessed by the forest. Every time I walked into it, I had a tremendous compulsion just to go on walking for ever and I had to force myself to turn back. I also felt that I was walking into the past of the human race and I could see the last vestiges of that past and of the forest being destroyed together. I've always had the feeling that nature has the ability to heal and that harmonious contact with nature is necessary for your mental health. I saw

117

how perfectly the life of the Indians was connected to the life of the forest, and that both the Indians and the forest were being destroyed. The experience of the Amazon brought all my previous feelings, intuitions and psychological tendencies about nature into focus. I came to realize that the planet itself was in grave danger.

The Emerald Forest is a compelling adventure story about the relationship between the father and his son, whom he finds living happily as a respected member of a fictitious tribe. But it is also an investigation of the unequal clash between the forces of corrupt Western 'civilization' (including grinding poverty or death for the indigenous peoples, forced prostitution and annihilation of the jungle to build hydro-electric dams) and the wisdom, magic and spiritual vitality of the people who live in harmony with the jungle. There is no doubt where Boorman's sympathies lie. In the final scenes, the father rejects all the brutal, material values of his own society and attempts to destroy a dam he is building in order to help his son's tribe survive. The message is that Western people need to stop destroying the rainforests and to re-learn the lost secrets of living in tune with nature which tribal peoples still possess.

Boorman's next film, *Hope and Glory* (1987), was on a much smaller and more personal scale: an autobiographical account of his own childhood during the Second World War. Critics noted, and many were surprised by, the humour, warmth and vitality of his memories of life during the Blitz. But the film's central discourse about nature, cities and suburbs largely escaped attention. The film is in two distinct parts. The first is set in the bland, rootless, history-less London suburb where the family lived from the day Hitler invaded Poland until the night their house burnt down. The second is the period he spent in and around his grandparents' house in the country, a time Boorman depicts as an almost uninterrupted pastoral idyll of cricket games, apple scrumping and messing about on the river: 'That was such an important, healing experience that it left me with a feeling of the magical harmony with nature which I think is the natural condition of man. When I saw that again in the Amazon, it had a very profound effect on me. In *Hope and Glory* I was exploring that in my own life.'

David Puttnam is probably the most influential British film-maker today. He is also president of CPRE and a prominent environmentalist in his own right. Puttnam won Oscars for *Chariots of Fire* and critical acclaim for *The Killing Fields* and *The Mission*. For a year after that he became the first British film-maker ever to head a major Hollywood studio (Columbia). Surprisingly, perhaps, his favourite of the films he has made is the much smaller-scale *Local Hero*, which was written and directed by another important figure in the green film business, Bill Forsyth. *Local Hero* is a gentle and startlingly wise comedy. An eccentric Texan oil billionaire (Burt Lancaster) wants to buy the whole village so it can be turned into an oil refinery complex. The villagers are keen to take the money, but the deal is blocked when a tough old beachcomber (who happens to own a critical stretch of the foreshore) holds out for a very different set of values.

How does Puttnam see the future of green films?

> I think green themes can be more effectively handled in the sub-text of a film than in the main thrust of a story. *Local Hero* is the closest I've ever got to being able to make a green film, and I'm very proud of it. I've spoken about *Local Hero* to audiences who've been moved and affected by it, but who never saw it as green. In the work I'm doing now, it's likely that I'll look for opportunities to give the films I produce a green twist, like bowling a googly, rather than attempting to drive home an 'explicit message'. In the long term, the ability of writers, directors and TV producers to weave environmental issues into their work will be more valuable than having a lot of preachy films which no one wants to watch. For instance, I'm working on a film about Chernobyl which will fail miserably if it's perceived to be solely about the dangers of radioactivity. In order to get it made, let alone give it a chance to succeed, it has to work well as a story about characters with whom the audience can identify; the struggle between differing personalities and so on. That's the way the film industry works and anyone who's thoughtful knows it.

But he stresses that attention to green issues is intimately connected to market forces and economic imperatives:

> In the end, it all comes down to economics. Some films with green concerns or environmentally sensitive characters are the result of something more cynical. When a producer is looking for a sympathetic character in a film, he tends to give them the attributes which one or two newspaper leader articles that week indicate are of the moment. If that means

the character is shown to care about the environment, it's a simple example of cultural expediency. People in the industry are trained to pick up on media ideas that happen to be fashionable.

Concern will finally coalesce around issues that are perceived as *real*. Chernobyl was real because it affected people in their daily lives. But the ozone layer will be seen as a purely theoretical issue until its deterioration is seen to have a perceptible effect. The destruction of the rainforests will almost certainly remain a theoretical issue until people realize that our climate is irreversibly changing.

TV and Radio

A similar sort of process, showing the same kind of aesthetic and commercial tensions, has been under way in television. Issues that would today be labelled 'green' surfaced periodically throughout the 1970s. The first and most important of the TV dramas with an explicitly ecological message was the BBC's *Doomwatch* thriller series, which attracted average audiences of 10 million people in 1970 and 1971. As the series title implied, it was never an excessively cheerful show, but it was completely in tune with the prevailing notions of ecological doom and gloom at that time. Global annihilation continued to be a recurring theme elsewhere. The BBC's *Survivors*, scripted by Terry Nation, the man who created *Dr Who* and produced *Doomwatch*, was based on the idea that 98% of the world's population had been wiped out by a particularly vicious flu virus. It ran for three years from 1975.

But alternative life-styles were also featured, more notably in *The Good Life*, a warm-hearted comedy series about self-sufficiency in Surbiton, which became one of the most popular programmes of the decade. It was regularly watched by between 16 and 18 million people and was reported to be the Queen's favourite show. In it, an ecologically-inclined suburban couple, Tom and Barbara Good (Richard Briers and Felicity Kendal), opt out of the rat race and attempt to create an ecologically pure and sustainable, independent life-style. *The Good Life* satirized as well as popularized these aspirations. The Goods were portrayed as lovable if somewhat eccentric, an image which probably helped to reinforce stereotypes about Greens eating lentils and wearing Fair Isle sweaters. The programme's success owed

120

much to its acting and its skill as a comedy of middle-class manners, as the Goods' values clashed with those of their snobbish and materialistic neighbours. Yet the Goods clearly had the better of things: they were poorer, but happier and more fulfilled.

Apocalyptic themes began to surface more regularly in the early 1980s as anxiety over the deployment of cruise, Pershing and SS-20 missiles of the period filtered through to TV drama. In 1965, the BBC had made, and then banned, Peter Watkins's terrifying *The War Game*, the first TV film to depict the horrific and terminal consequences of nuclear war. Nearly twenty years later, two landmark television films finally broke TV drama's nuclear taboo. ITV's screening of the American-made *The Day After* in December 1983 came at a critical time, when the peace movement was at its most influential. The film generated considerable political heat; for instance, the day after *The Day After* was shown, the Secretary of State for Defence, Michael Heseltine, demanded a ministerial 'right of reply' to the film and rushed from one TV studio to another to denounce it as a piece of anti-nuclear propaganda.

The other major film was the BBC's *Threads*, shown in 1984, depicting the effects of a nuclear attack on Sheffield. Apart from that, a flood of programmes, ranging from debates and documentaries to black comedies like London Weekend's *Whoops Apocalypse* all concentrated on the threat of nuclear annihilation.

The most striking of all the nuclear dramas was Troy Kennedy Martin's *Edge of Darkness*, a complex and overtly green thriller which the BBC broadcast twice in quick succession at the end of 1985. The series was the BBC's most admired thriller of the early 1980s (despite the fact that *Daily Express* columnist George Gale saw it as a piece of propaganda designed 'to make the world safe for Soviet expansion and prepare the way for a world communist dictatorship'[2]), but the attention which its dazzling style rightly received tended to obscure its central green content. At a cursory glance, the series looked to be a conventional, if superior, conspiracy thriller in which a Yorkshire policeman, Detective Inspector Ronnie Craven (Bob Peck), pursues the mysterious agents who murdered his daughter. But these conventional elements were only vehicles for a much more ambitious study of deeper, darker and more controversial issues: the power of the British nuclear establishment (portrayed for the first time in a TV drama as an utterly undemocratic and sinister state-within-a-state) and the 'Star Warrior philosophy' behind President Reagan's Strategic Defence Initiative (SDI).

121

Edge of Darkness was not originally conceived as a piece of deliberate green consciousness-raising. In 1982, Jonathan Powell, the newly appointed head of the BBC's Drama Series and Serials department, wanted to start his reign with something exceptional to restore some of the BBC's dramatic reputation, which had recently been somewhat eclipsed by Granada's award-grabbing series, *Brideshead Revisited*. Powell's objective in going to the creator of the influential 1960s police series, *Z Cars*, was to produce a piece of adventurous television, not a green tract. The nuclear, ecological and secrecy themes only came together in the author's mind during his research:

> The BBC Series department ought to be a place for the continuation of the nineteenth-century novel and the tradition of Dickens: tackling important social questions with big stories and lots of emotion. That's what *Edge of Darkness* was always going to be. I wanted to do something to make people more aware, but without banging any drums. Explicit consciousness-raising tends to be a rather old-fashioned way of writing television, and it's counter-productive because audiences are pretty sophisticated and they know when they're being preached at. I also wanted to counteract the kind of very reactionary, right-wing series which had dominated television pretty well since the 1960s. The department had been churning out middle-of-the-road period costume dramas and pieces which paid lip service to social questions, but where authority was never questioned and the police were always right.

Even more unusual than the political orientation was the way the series adopted an explicitly deep green perspective to explore the prospects for the long-term survival of the planet. Six years earlier, J. E. Lovelock, an eminent British scientist who had worked for NASA in the 1970s on techniques for finding life on Mars, had published his now famous book *Gaia: a New Look at Life on Earth*. He argued that all the myriad life-forms on earth, in their totality, constitute a kind of global super-organism (named 'Gaia' after the Greek goddess of the earth) which regulates the biosphere in such a way as to optimize conditions for life. In the event of a planetary catastrophe, such as a collision with a giant meteor or a major nuclear war, Gaia would respond (by producing new species, for example) and life would survive.

Kennedy Martin was profoundly affected by the book. In *Edge of Darkness*, Gaia becomes the name of a radical ecological group fighting nuclear power in general and a private company secretly manufacturing plutonium for use in 'Star Wars' laser weapons in particular. By the end, Craven speaks for nature and the planet. His faith in the police force, the Government, in 'the system' and all its values, has been shredded and replaced by a new-found loyalty to Gaia. His physical being is overwhelmed by radiation sickness, but even as he awaits death he proclaims his certainty that Gaia will defend herself by spawning carpets of new black flowers to absorb more radiation from the sun, which in turn will thaw the polar ice caps, flood Europe and destroy the nuclear menace. The final scene bears out this hope. Alone in the Scottish mountains, Craven screams his daughter's name and vanishes. But the first black blooms have already emerged into a landscape of melting snow. In an early draft, the ending was even bolder. Kennedy Martin explains: 'I saw Craven as the original "Green Man". At the end, I wanted him to turn into a tree. Very slowly, over a period of a thousand years, he'd have become a gnarled, nuclear-blasted oak on a devastated plain in a post-nuclear world. But Bob Peck wasn't having any of it. He said: "I'm not turning into a fucking tree!" He thought it was all a bit much.'

As it was, some Lovelock supporters were still scandalized by the treatment of his theory in *Edge of Darkness*. Gaia Books Ltd, a green publishing house backed by several academic ecologists, primly obliged the BBC to broadcast a statement dissociating their name from the series. Lovelock himself told the *Mail on Sunday*: 'Scientifically, it's infinitely less credible than *Dr Who*.' He conceded that the series was 'damned good entertainment', but he objected to Kennedy Martin's notion that Gaia could anticipate and take preventive action to stop mankind perpetrating global biocide. The planet's life-support systems, says Lovelock, could manage disaster only *after* it had happened.

Kennedy Martin is unapologetic.:

> I used the concept of Gaia in a poetic, metaphorical way. But suddenly people were screaming that my idea of it was a terrible distortion, as if Gaia was a religion. There was no church yet, but I was being accused of heresy! I think of Lovelock as the Green Movement's Rousseau, so I was trying to give him all the credit. I know he meant his hypothesis to be a dry, scientific thing, but it also works on a very powerful ideological, poetic and emotional level. It's very easy to turn it into a religion. As a Green, one gets so tired of being *against*

123

things: against nuclear energy, the destruction of the rain-forests, pesticides and so on. But, if you can feel that you're *for* the planet, that gives you a wonderful feeling and makes you much braver. There was the most incredible spirit when we were making the film. The shooting lasted about six months. All the people involved had the feeling they were part of something much bigger than themselves. They completely accepted the idea of Gaia without really going into it. I'm not sure Lovelock has thought enough about the way human beings are also part of Gaia. Other species have special attributes. We have our intelligence and imagination. I like to think of the Green Movement as part of a 'Gaian' response to the planet's problems.

After winning critical acclaim for *Edge of Darkness*, Kennedy Martin moved to Hollywood. He considers himself to be part of a much wider greening process going on in both America and Britain, and argues that the 1990s will see the emergence of a dominant green perspective in film, television and drama.

In the 1960s, we had Class and the politics of the Left. Young writers like David Mercer and Dennis Potter, whose fathers had been miners, were writing about different aspects of socialism. Feminism was the big thing in the 1970s. In the 1990s, the perspective is going to be green. The general trend is in that direction. In the next few years, we're going to see a lot more drama exploring all these ideas. There has been a huge change in values and assumptions. Views which were considered quite odd a few years ago, like being a vegetarian, are taken for granted now.

Things will only begin to get really interesting when you start getting debates *inside* the subject, in the way that now we're getting post-feminist debates.

But Jonathan Powell, who moved on to become head of BBC drama and, later, controller of BBC 1, believes green TV drama is still in its infancy: 'In the loosest sense, TV drama is slightly more aware than it used to be. There are certainly not as many jokes and stereotypes as there used to be. But, much as I'd like it to be otherwise, I couldn't say that it was really becoming *substantially* more committed to green issues.'

Nevertheless, mainstream TV drama programmes have undoubtedly begun to reflect green sensibilities, albeit at a less ambitious level than *Edge of Darkness*. A storyline in the yuppy-ish BBC soap, *Howard's Way*, for example, included a clash between good environmentalists and greedy property developers. Yorkshire's *Emmerdale Farm* fictionalized the 1987 controversy about NIREX plans to bury low-level nuclear waste with a long-running saga about proposals to site a radioactive dump in the farmers' back yard. Nuclear waste plans also formed the backdrop to Yorkshire's comedy thriller, *The Beiderbecke Tapes*, adapted by Alan Plater from his own novel and broadcast in December 1987. In it, two comprehensive school teachers, Jill and Trevor (played by Barbara Flynn and James Bolam), are drawn into a battle of wits with M15 heavies over a secret tape about plans for a nuclear dump in the Yorkshire Dales. A green perspective is woven into a deliciously observed social comedy. Trevor's home is demolished to make way for a motorway. Jill is a resourceful, radical but not dogmatic ecology-minded feminist and partial vegetarian who refuses to buy non-biodegradable loo rolls. The couple live together, eat healthy foods, have an equal relationship and take an interest in community politics. Their banter and something of their life-style is reminiscent of Tom and Barbara in *The Good Life* more than ten years earlier. But while the Goods were distinctly eccentric figures of fun, people like Jill and Trevor have become part of a cultural mainstream.

Another important dramatist, G. F. Newman, best known for his TV exposés of corruption in the legal system (*Law and Order*) and of malpractice and widespread incompetence in the NHS (*The Nation's Health*), has now also undertaken a journey towards green themes. In the 1970s, Newman ate red meat and wrote about police corruption. By the late 1980s, he had become a passionate vegan and was working on a major eco-thriller series for the BBC about environmental damage caused by modern farming methods. The series, provisionally entitled *A Bitter Harvest* (also commissioned by Jonathan Powell), is to be produced by Tony Garnett and broadcast some time in 1989. Newman's sense of outrage over injustice and corruption has not altered, but his world view has widened to encompass concerns which a few years earlier he knows he would have considered cranky. He has come to see the poisoning of our land and water, the destruction of our landscape and gross over-production of food through intensive farming as critical issues which intimately affect all our lives:

125

The planet lives and breathes. It's not a dead dumping ground for our waste. You can't harm the planet without harming yourself. We've got to try to sound a few alarm bells and alert people to the fact that we are harming large tracts of land through chemical-intensive farming. The media is scattering information about this kind of thing everywhere, but not everyone wants to pick it up. It will come. Fifteen years ago, when I started writing about police corruption, I was looked at very strangely. People didn't even like the idea that there were just a few bad apples. Now we can talk about the whole barrel being rotten. The people who are talking about greening are still in the vanguard now. It hasn't been absorbed into everyone's consciousness yet because people resist and they're lazy. But if you tell them there are about 3,500 chemicals, drugs and pesticides in animal fat, then they've got to do something about it, even if it's only to stop eating the stuff.

But Newman has no illusions about these changes coming about for reasons of compassion and humanity. Change is much more likely to be self-interested, in that people basically don't want to poison themselves. He is encouraged by the fact that there are 4 million vegetarians in the UK today; twenty years ago, there were just a few:

If writers can help people find their centre, to explore their own fears and anxieties, that would be a great benefit. If you get your personal psychology and emotions right, I think your politics comes right too. I don't really think that's happening though. Most concerns seem to be materialistic ones, which militate *against* recognizing the problems of our finite world and environment. But if I wasn't an optimist, I suppose I wouldn't be writing to try to raise people's consciousness to bring about change.

Soap opera producers, on both television and radio, have long been aware of their power to go in for a spot of subtle consciousness-raising. But new soaps like *Eastenders* and *Brookside* still have a long way to go before they can claim to rival *The Archers*. From its earliest days, Britain's longest-running soap opera has consciously (and sometimes rather too self-consciously for some people's taste) worked in information, guidance and specific warnings of interest to the agricultural community. There are few livestock diseases that Ambridge has missed out on during its time, and the *Archers'* 6.5 million regular listeners probably know as much about agricultural rust by now as they do about most human ailments.

Liz Rigbey, the editor of the programme since 1986, feels she is permanently balancing on a tightrope when it comes to getting the right mix of human interest and agricultural concern.

> Contrary to most people's expectations, I have to spend much of my time battling to keep in the agricultural and rural stuff. The programme has four scriptwriters and an agricultural adviser [Tony Parkin]. The scriptwriters at the moment are basically urban types who have absolutely no difficulty stirring in the human interest, but sometimes need to be persuaded to take up at least one of the fifteen or so agricultural stories we come up with every month. If anything, I have to rein in their green sympathies!

Part of the *Archers'* brief has always been to reflect controversial current issues. But in farming, such issues usually refer to policy proposals emanating (or failing to emanate) from the Ministry of Agriculture, or to the National Farmers Union spluttering with rage at the latest assault from the Greens. Not exactly the stuff of riveting drama on radio, or anywhere else, with the sole and wonderful exception of *Yes, Minister*. Equally, being a drama and not a documentary means that the time-honoured BBC line on neutrality and objectivity can be an impediment. For instance, when a storyline indicated hostility if not outright opposition to the possible use of Bovine Somatotrophin (a highly controversial growth hormone used to increase milk production which is being tested secretly on a few selected dairy herds in Britain), the farming establishment didn't like it one little bit, and were quick to let Liz Rigbey know that they didn't like it:

> Both myself and Tony Parkin are heavily lobbied by all and sundry. Some of the animal rights charities are absolutely relentless. We also get endless complaints from organic farmers. But Pat and Tony [two *Archers* characters who have gone organic] have done a lot to publicize both the potential and the problems of organic farming.

But what about Mick of Zodiac Organics (an outrageously stereotyped throw-back from the late 1960s with earrings, Spanish leather boots and a tendency to say things like, 'If you want to know what to plant, man, just smell the earth')? Liz Rigbey shows no contrition:

'Are you saying such types don't exist?' They do, of course, but most organic dealers today are very different and much more businesslike. This was in fact borne out by the anguish of Pat and Tony when Zodiac Organics went bust. 'Should have stuck with the co-op,' says Pat to Tony. And so they should – just another gently infiltrated little message for all organic farmers.

But no characters in *The Archers* have caused more aggravation to environmentalists than the Snells, the intensive, know-it-all, greener-than-green incomers from the big city. They epitomize everything that's awful about narrow-minded, pull-up-the-drawbridge conservationists: having snuggled themselves down in Ambridge, they're damned if anyone else is going to join them there. That means no new houses, no new businesses, indeed no change at all to the Ambridge fabric. These tireless defenders of Britain's natural heritage have rapidly become comic characters, but since all *Archers* fanatics see themselves as part of Ambridge, the Snells are the ones they just love to hate! In this, as in many other instances, *The Archers* provides a peculiarly perceptive slice of life. If Ambridge *wasn't* going a little green at the edges, the cynics would certainly be asking whether there was any substance at all to the claims of the Green Movement.

Theatre

With such a rich crop of green activity in broadcast drama, the dearth of similar themes on the stage seems surprising. But one has to look long and hard for any signs of a contemporary greening of the English theatre. There is no self-defining green drama to match the work of social reformers like John Galsworthy or George Bernard Shaw in the early part of the century, or of the 'angry young men' of the 1950s. Greens may claim that their concerns are at least as significant and universally relevant as anything in Galsworthy's *Strife*, Shaw's *Man and Superman*, Osborne's *Look Back In Anger* or Arthur Miller's *Death of a Salesman*. But this perception has so far signally failed to strike a similar chord with contemporary dramatists.

Among influential directors, Jonathan Miller, artistic director of the Old Vic, is probably not alone in viewing the very idea of green theatre with evident distaste: 'It really doesn't interest me. I don't like didactic or manifesto theatre of any sort because it tends to be rather heavy-handed, like the theatre you used to get on the side of the road on CND marches.'

Fay Weldon, one of the few writers who *has* tried to bring explicitly green themes to the stage, takes a different view:

I don't write to save the world and I don't write propaganda. I just set out what preoccupies and interests me. You can't tell people how to react and you certainly can't have characters just standing around saying how dreadful everything is. But fiction is a much better form for communicating than documentary, because it is the only way to make people feel it affects them personally. As a writer, you always try to hold a mirror to society, to deal with the preoccupations of the time. But you also try to be a bit ahead of everyone else. People like me who were brought up in television have it bred into our bones that what we do has to be socially useful. We can pose and define problems, but we can't get bills passed in Parliament.

Her play *The Hole in the Top of the World*, first seen at the Orange Tree Theatre in Richmond in 1987, examines some of the social, cultural and emotional implications of impending eco-disaster. The play follows a stormy relationship between radical leftist and fiercely feminist Simone and her sexist scientist husband, Matt. Matt is a child of the Bomb, who as a boy made coffee for scientists on the Manhattan Project and later lost his virginity amid the ruins of Hiroshima. In the 1960s, in which the play opens, he boastfully proclaims his faith in scientific progress. By the mid-1980s, the couple have divorced and Matt's world has changed: he is a climatologist monitoring the growing hole in the ozone layer from an Antarctic research station, where he lives with an ambitious young woman scientist. The play explores everything from linguistics and gender to motherhood and growing old. But the spectre of ecological ruin, made explicit by monologues about the consequences of the global 'greenhouse effect' and the thinning of the ozone layer, provides a steadily darkening backdrop which makes the characters' other concerns begin to seem increasingly irrelevant. In the end, Matt and Simone, who had been sharing her life with a transvestite, camomile-tea-swilling parody of a New Man, reunite in order to grow old and die together. But the causes they believed in have been rendered redundant, their faith dissipated as fatefully as the ozone itself. Weldon explains:

129

A couple of years ago, if you talked about what was happening to the ozone layer, most people thought you were making it up. Now they know it's true. The play isn't just about the hole over Antarctica, but about all the theories which now have to be discarded because they are drifting out of the hole. We used to think that Marxism or feminism held the answers to all our problems. We thought, 'If only we can get rid of racism, change capitalism and educate people, everything will be different.' But now we know those hopes and aspirations left out something fundamental. They failed because they failed to take account of the earth we walk on. Without the earth, we have nothing. Our Utopian concepts are flying out of the sky. So we have to rethink all our ideas in a new framework.

The pace of environmental destruction which now threatens our lives and health has become much more extreme, so art will reflect this. I expect it to grow gently, like the way feminism impinged on us over a period of twenty years. But people are still much more interested in sex, murder and passion. At the moment, green concern in the arts is a kind of luxury item.

She is willing to categorize herself as a Green, but with qualifications: 'Actually, I'm rather suspicious of some parts of the Green Movement, because it seems to me that if they had to choose between seals and people, they'd choose the seals! There's a danger in being simple-minded.' She also loathes 'middle-class greens being self-congratulatory and saying: "See, see! We told you so!" It's really off-putting: élitist and boring with fascist overtones. It's not the whole truth, either. If everyone had a job and everyone was living by choice rather than necessity, I'm sure the entire country would be saying things about the environment. But they don't.'

Weldon is a prolific writer, and her work has increasingly reflected green concerns. The sub-plot of her TV series and novel *Heart of the Country*, for example, is a protest against farmers who put nitrates and chemicals in food: 'The country is not the rural idyll city people think it is; it is the source of poison.' She is also writing a television series for the BBC (working title: *Green Fingers*) about a clash between a gardener and a nuclear power plant. She describes it as 'a kind of ecological thriller about the conflict between the organic and the inorganic world, between atomic particles and whole, living

130

organisms'. Meanwhile, she has no doubts that ecological matters demand our urgent and complete attention.

Perhaps the most important work for the theatre with a green theme yet seen in Britain was a nuclear play written by a Russian – *Sarcophagus*, succinctly described by the *Guardian* as 'unquestionably the most important play in London' in 1987. This powerful play is about the immediate aftermath of the Chernobyl disaster, as seen through the eyes of its victims as they rapidly succumb to radiation sickness, and is all the more remarkable for having been written by Vladimir Gubaryev, the science editor of *Pravda*. It was performed to enormous acclaim in at least ten regional theatres in the USSR before moving to the West.

Gubaryev was one of the first to start sending back on-the-spot reports from Chernobyl, and was horrified by what he learned. He is *not* opposed to nuclear power itself, but to the corruption, secrecy, arrogance and incompetence that characterize nuclear industries the world over: 'We physicists thought we knew all about the atomic devil. Well, I'm sorry, but we didn't. We thought it could never happen here.' It was to dispel exactly that complacency that he wrote *Sarcophagus*:

> There is no concealing the fact: there are people who think it is time to forget about Chernobyl on the grounds that more important matters are claiming their attention. Worse still, there are also people who are trying to cover up the truth about Chernobyl – indeed, to lie about it. Lies, however, are only needed by those who can't do their jobs properly, who need to hide their own incompetence and cowardice. There is only one way of avoiding a repetition of Chernobyl: to tell the truth about what happened, to make the most painstaking analysis of the causes of the tragedy – and not let the culprits get away with it. For only the cleansing truth will show us the way into the future . . .

A stunning performance by Nicholas Woodeson as Bessmertny, the survivor of an earlier radiation 'incident' and long-suffering guinea-pig of the radiation unit in which the play is set, heightens the pathos of Chernobyl's victims, traumatized, uncomprehending, angry, disbelieving or resigned as they individually are.

'The plot of this play was born in Chernobyl,' says Gubaryev. 'How could I convey to people what I had seen and experienced? How could I enable everyone to feel the pain lodged in my very soul? It seemed to me that this was only possible in the theatre, where the audience always becomes a participant in the action – provided, of course, that the play is frank and honest.'³ *Sarcophagus* was indeed a startlingly frank and honest play, thus making possible an even more powerful contrast with the manifest lack of such attributes in the nuclear industry itself.

CHAPTER SIX

We're All Environmentalists Now

'We're all environmentalists now' has become one of the favoured catch-phrases of many leading industrialists in the late 1980s. They'd better be. The Brundtland Report pointed out that the world manufactures seven times more goods today than it did in 1950, and that current styles of development 'draw too heavily, too quickly on already overdrawn environmental resource accounts to be affordable far into the future without bankrupting those accounts. They may show profits on the balance sheets of *our* generation, but our children will inherit the losses.'[1] So, if we are not all environmentalists now, we are basically up that sewage-ridden creek without a paddle.

It is one thing to come out with such populist sentiments, and quite another to persuade people to put them into practice, as David Puttnam discovered when he addressed the 1987 Annual Conference of the Confederation of British Industry (CBI).

Speaking to the sombre-suited gathering as a fellow businessman as well as an environmentalist, Puttnam made a moderate and conciliatory speech. He referred to the rapid growth of public concern about the environment and called for environmentalists and industrialists to put aside their long-standing mutual suspicions and work together. 'If we get our attitudes right, the burgeoning public pressure for an improved environment can also become the source of new and limitless opportunities for industry,' he promised. 'Chernobyl, the Sandoz pollution of the Rhine, or acid rain, all tell us the same thing: we live and die together. This is every bit as true of industry as it is of us as a species. You read the same newspapers and watch the same television programmes chronicling the destruction of tropical rainforests and the spreading of desert as I do. Nearer home, you are every bit as aware of public concern for Green Belts and our countryside.' He urged industry not to ignore public emotion about the environment: 'Remember what is at stake – nothing less than each individual's sense of where they stand in relation to nature and the rest of creation. Under-estimate this dimension of the environmental phenomenon at your peril. If it is not respected, I promise you it will bite back.'[2]

He also cited the potential of Britain's existing £2.2 billion a year pollution control industry and the estimated £50 billion overseas market, arguing that industry would benefit from exploring new industries which had a commitment to the environment built into them. He may not have been aware that it was in just these terms that William Waldegrave, as Minister for the Environment, had patiently but with an increasing note of urgency directed his message to Britain's industrialists.

His audience was duly attentive and far from hostile until about half-way through the speech, when Puttnam came to the subject of Britain's expanding nuclear industry, which the CBI has always supported. He dared to refer to the fact that the CEGB chairman, Lord Marshall, had recently confessed that nuclear power in Britain had *never* made a profit, in thirty years. He also mentioned Industry Secretary Cecil Parkinson's admission that Britain already had enough plutonium to last 500 years, 'while he continues to finance at large cost the development of a fast breeder reactor whose only advantage is to produce *more* plutonium. That makes Dounreay the most expensive job creation project in history.' A small section of the audience applauded the speech loudly. But most of the listeners responded with cool politeness or even hostility.

'I certainly got a more polite and genuinely warmer reception from them than an industrialist would have received from a green audience! But when I got on to the subject of the nuclear industry, and told them what Lord Marshall and Cecil Parkinson had said, there was an audible gasp. I think they thought I was lying,' said Puttnam later. Sacred cows should not be slaughtered at such ceremonial occasions, and certainly not in the presence of the high priests.

Such an encounter provides an accurate portrait of the ambivalent attitudes in industry to the message of the Greens. A handful of industrialists are actively seeking to ameliorate or fundamentally transform the nature of their business's impact on the environment. Others are prepared to take on board only a small portion of the green message, and have learned, as have their agricultural contemporaries, to turn on the 'Greenspeak' as and when required in the most convincing manner. Some still react with barely veiled hostility. Despite the efforts of some environmentalists to 'talk up' the extent to which things have begun to change, British industry remains for the most part lacking both in the imagination necessary to seize hold of new opportunities and in the determination genuinely to clean up their act rather than just clean up their image. The exceptions to this, however important they may be, remain exceptional.

Environmental Regulation

For the foreseeable future, therefore, we're stuck with what we've got. Very little, if any, of the *theoretical* work of green economics has begun to penetrate mainstream industrial and economic thinking. Industries do not pollute because they are intrinsically wicked, but because it is more profitable for them not to worry about it. This is not a function of the scale of any enterprise, but of the extent to which it can get away with 'externalizing' its environmental costs by passing them on to its neighbours or consumers. Conceptually, there is no difference between a multinational chemical company which pumps effluent into a river and a part-time car mechanic who ruins his neighbours' Sunday afternoon by hammering door panels. Both are 'externalizing' instead of spending more on their production so as not to damage the environment.

This is a fundamental fault of our present economic system, which cannot measure the true value of an unpoisoned or unspoiled environment. Indeed, many of the planet's most alarming ecological problems are simply invisible when looked at through the distorting mirrors of what still passes for economic 'wisdom'. Market-fixated, growth-obsessed economics has no conceptual tools for measuring either the immediate ecological impact or the costs to future generations of, say, the destruction of the tropical rainforests. Accountants are not trained to take account of the possibility of large increases in the numbers of people dying of skin cancer as they monitor the financial health of the companies which make the chemicals which destroy the ozone layer.

In all countries, laws controlling industrial emissions aim to strike a balance between the quality of the environment and the interests of industry. In Britain, it is usually industry which decides where the line is to be drawn. For the most part, British pollution regulations give industry an easier ride than do those of other countries in Northern Europe. With the exception of cases where support for industry will clearly damage the Government politically, Government usually gives industrialists the first and last say on the matter, with a little bit of lip-service consultation with the environmentalists in between. 'Generally speaking, the Government accepts industry's

135

most reactionary arguments all along the line. I'm convinced that even the limited action we've seen on acid rain came about because of a CEGB initiative rather than from Government pressure,' says David Cope, current Director of the UK Centre for Economic and Environmental Development (CEED).

CEED was established in 1984 (as one of the very few practical outcomes of the World Conservation Strategy of the early 1980s) with the specific task of 'reconciling the needs of business *and* industry with the overriding imperative of conserving our irreplaceable natural resources'. The idea is to establish a new, productive partnership between industry and the environment, particularly in terms of the integration of economic and environmental policy at the national and local level.

One of the problems for CEED and other genuinely concerned industrialists is the patchy and piecemeal nature of environmental legislation in Britain, and the extent to which we are all operating within an inadequate regulatory framework. Such legislation has a long pedigree (the first anti-coal burning laws, for example, date back as far as the thirteenth century and the reign of Edward I!), but in recent times there have been three major pieces of legislation: the Public Health Act (1936), the Clean Air Act (1956) and the Control of Pollution Act (1974), each of which spawned a confusing multitude of different inspectorates, all with different powers, to police industry's worst excesses.

The Clean Air Act, passed after the murderous London smog of December 1952 killed about 4,000 people, is generally credited for cleaning up the worst effects of coal-burning. The Act spoke of the 'natural desire of the public to enjoy clean air', but, at the same time, gave equal weight to industrialists' reluctance to spend money on anti-pollution measures which would eat into profits. In particular, the Act's insistence on the use of high chimney stacks merely served to spread pollution further afield and store up problems such as acid rain for the future.

The 1974 Control of Pollution Act was an attempt to update public health legislation. But it did nothing to sort out the ramshackle administrative structure. Almost every pollution hazard still had its own inspectorate: one for hazardous wastes, one for industrial air pollution, one for radio-chemical pollution and so on. In the case of water, the water boards which handled sewage remained precisely the same ones who were responsible for controlling the problem of sewage pollution. In theory, the Act gave individuals the power to prosecute polluters for the first time, but it was thirteen years before the first private action was brought, when an angling club successfully prosecuted the Thames Water Authority over pollution in the River Thames.

In April 1987, the Government finally set up a unified pollution inspectorate (HMIP) within the Department of the Environment after a protracted bout of infighting. HMIP had long been one of the favoured projects of William Waldegrave, and was supported with surprising enthusiasm by the CBI as well as by environmental organizations. On the other hand, it was strenuously opposed by both Lord Young and Lord Marshall (the 'Dark Lords' as they are irreverently known both inside and outside the DoE!) on the grounds that any increased regulation would impose further bureaucratic and regulatory burdens on industry. Their rearguard action eventually came to nothing, as much through the support of the CBI as anything else.

This is by no means the only occasion on which Lord Young has completely misjudged the mood in industry. His address to the 1987 Annual Dinner of the Chemical Industries Association, in which he made his usual call for lifting the burden of regulation and relaxing environmental controls, was met with overt hostility. Some brave spirits even had the temerity to boo the Dark Lord, behaviour unheard of on such occasions. But the point is a simple one: the larger, more respectable chemical companies positively welcome a coherent regulatory framework, for without it their less conscientious competitors and the out-and-out cowboys of the chemical industry can undercut them simply by disregarding their environmental responsibilities.

HMIP brings together all the pollution inspectorates under two chief inspectors (one for Radioactive Substances and one for Air, Water and Wastes). One of its main roles is to establish an integrated approach to the control of pollution, and two case studies to investigate this kind of 'Best Practicable Environmental Option' were announced in October 1987. But in this, as in so many other things, HMIP is seriously weakened by chronic under-staffing and under-funding. The Government has also done it no favours by deciding to establish a new National Rivers Authority to monitor and regulate the work of the Water Authorities once they are privatized, thus creating a further highly damaging division of regulatory responsibilities. It also lacks the teeth to ensure that regulations are observed, and all too often is obliged to depend on *persuading* industry to co-operate. In December 1987, Mr Rodney Perriman, Chief Inspector for Air and Water Wastes, complained that the existing pollution laws were a 'hotchpotch' and urged the Government to give the inspectorate stronger powers.

Despite such disappointments, most environmentalists would readily agree that HMIP represents a distinct improvement on what we had before, and if it is now able to fight its corner to ensure proper funding, proper staffing and a proper statutory back-up, then it may live up to the hopes which William Waldegrave had for it when it was first set up:

> I am very aware that this is a quite small acorn planted so far, but part of the strategy in setting up HMIP was to bring about an outriding and powerful backer for the Department of the Environment within the Whitehall family. I strongly believe that there is a real need in this country for a self-motivating inspectorate which would have the confidence institutionally to behave in a way that would sometimes be inconvenient to Government and to industry. Obviously in our constitution, any government organization has ultimately to be subject to Parliament, but the more it can operate at arm's length, the more independent it can be, and the more effective it will be in achieving tighter regulations. That, of course, is not quite the same thing as the Environmental Protection Agency in America: our constitution makes it impossible to replicate that kind of independent agency here in the UK.

Which is a great pity, since the extensive powers of the Environmental Protection Agency in the United States ensure that industry faces much tighter controls. Industrialists there have to cope with two sets of anti-pollution legislation, at the state and federal level, and the EPA has a comprehensive regional structure as well as a large federal organization in Washington. Cope enthuses: 'It's a different ballgame! The Americans *and* West Germans have very demanding and restrictive local regulations which we don't have. There's so much more energy around; it's a much more dynamic situation. Our local authorities play a terribly limited role; the only way to get more dynamism into our system is to have much greater local control.'

It is considerably more difficult, for example, to get permission for a new landfill site in the USA or West Germany than it is in Britain. In both countries, an applicant faces powerful local controls and fierce local debate. As a result, developers need to be more environmentally sophisticated and prepared to enter into a more overt bargaining process in negotiating with their opponents. The 1981 Resource Conservation Recovery Act obliges US producers to clean up their wastes from the past, which has kept the whole issue of waste clean-up much more in the public eye. In addition, American civil law gives individuals greater scope than we have in this country to take action against businesses whose pollution infringes their rights as citizens. Limits on industry are clearly defined, and it is a good deal easier to take action against third-party companies with whom one has no direct contractual relationship. As a result, successful legal action by individuals has played an important part in forcing American industry as a whole to clean up its act.

With such a disadvantageous legislative and regulatory framework, an awful lot depends on public opinion. And here Cope sees a real glimmer of hope:

> Public opinion is the most effective sanction against companies who cause pollution. The fear of a public humiliation is very powerful, even against the likes of ICI and the CEGB. Nirex, for example, made ICI a very attractive offer to store nuclear waste at ICI's plant at Billingham, but ICI decided they just couldn't face the public acrimony, so they said no. At the end of the day, even the CEGB will try to go along with public opinion rather than forever fight it. No company wants to be permanently cast as environmentally uncaring and villainous.

Industry's Response

But to what extent can we really rely on industrialists to get any greener over the next decade? Throughout the 1970s, industrialists adopted knee-jerk hostility in an attempt to slow the advance of environmentalism. Taking care of the environment would cost too much money and involve the loss of jobs, they argued. In the 1980s that hostility has gradually softened, but many industrialists still see the Green Movement as a malign political force which they like to imagine (as it saves them having to think too much) comes from the militant Left. Others are worried that paying more attention, and hard cash, to the environment will damage their competitiveness in international markets. And still others fear that 'giving in' to environmentalists now would be to open up a Pandora's Box of unreasonable demands for environmental extremists, fondly referred to by some as 'the Flat Earth Society'.

Protagonists on both sides of the debate loosely and impressionistically refer to good and bad practice as and when it suits their needs – there is more than enough of both going on to substantiate both claim and counter-claim. However, environmentalists today are much better at acknowledging and enthusiastically encouraging the good practice. The Pollution Abatement Technology Awards, for instance, are now widely publicized, and the companies which receive these awards (whether they be multinational companies like BP or ICI, or much smaller operations like British Earthworm Technologies!) receive considerable benefits from this kind of favourable coverage. Books like *Healthy Profits: Business Success and the Green Factor*, by Steve Robinson, and *The Green Capitalists*, by John Elkington and Tom Burke (of which more later), enthusiastically dish out the accolades and promote the idea that industry itself is now an increasingly important source of information, technology and other resources needed for sustainable development.

Examples of good practice like the 3P Programme (Pollution Prevention Pays) of the 3M multinational company are rightly trotted out on every available occasion, for they are indeed impressive:

> With 1,528 projects implemented under their 3P Programme by the end of 1984, the company calculated that it had saved itself $235,000,000 by delaying or eliminating the need for add-on pollution control equipment, by saving on raw material, energy and operating costs, and by retaining sales of products which might otherwise have had to be taken off the market as environmentally unacceptable. Equally important, the cumulative impact of 3M's manufacturing activities on the environment between 1975 and 1984 was reduced by the elimination of 98,000 tonnes of air pollutants, 10,500 tonnes of water pollutants, 1,444,000,000 gallons of waste water, and just over 150,000 tonnes of sludges and solid wastes.[3]

Perhaps the company with the best reputation in this area is IBM. At the company's request, CEED examined IBM's UK policies in 1985 to assess the extent to which they conformed to the concept of sustainable development. IBM's ecological track record is certainly impressive. Since 1973, as a matter of policy, the company's management has been required 'to be continuously on guard against adversely affecting the environment and to seek ways to conserve natural resources.' The company has energetically pursued these commitments. It has its own environmental inspectorate and strives to meet or exceed all government environmental regulations. It devotes considerable effort to reducing pollution and providing good environmental quality in its manufacturing, research centres and offices. The buildings themselves are equipped with computer systems for reducing waste and optimizing resources at every stage of activity, from design efficiency through to good relations with its neighbours. None the less, it is interesting to point out that the CEED report also noted that although these policies were generally in line with sustainable development, 'clearly an open-ended objective of continued rapid growth cannot be sustained indefinitely'.

Despite such caveats, the approach of companies like IBM is greatly to be welcomed, for it does indeed add up to a substantial and lasting change of attitude. If nothing else, environmentalists can now claim an outright victory in having made it impossible for today's market leaders to maintain that lead at the expense of the environment. To that extent, we are indeed 'all environmentalists today'.

But (and the 'buts' are never far away when you are dealing with industry!) many of these industrial environmentalists are reluctant converts. The immediate reaction of certain sectors of British industry is still to fight first, and to give in later only after a prolonged struggle. British Leyland, for instance, has long resisted the introduction of any kind of catalytic converter technology to reduce vehicle emissions: they lobbied the DoE as intensively as anyone had ever lobbied them before, predicting all kinds of dire economic woes if they had to adopt any new technology. Meanwhile, their international competitors saw which way the wind was blowing, invested heavily in appropriate research and development, and, now that the EEC has finally agreed on its Vehicle Emissions Directive, must be enjoying the sight of British Leyland/Austin Rover floundering around with their out-of-date ideas and out-of-date technology. It is not just a theoretical advantage that they have gained: at the end of 1987, Land Rover lost a multi-million pound order from the Swiss Army simply because they could not meet Swiss air pollution control standards.

Such stubborn defenders of the environmentally unacceptable are likely to become a thing of the past quite quickly. 'A generational change is taking place,' says David Cope:

141

Over the next ten years we will see people who grew up in the 1960s move into real positions of power. They will be much more alive to new kinds of product which are not damaging to the environment, and sincerely interested in concepts of sustainability. We are seeing an interesting convergence and a meeting of minds between certain far-sighted industrialists and some of the more accommodating members of the environmental lobby who do not see environmental and industrial objectives as being fundamentally incompatible.

That is good news, but *less* accommodating environmentalists still have a few questions that will need answering. What, for instance, of the problem of 'double standards', which leaves many Third World countries the victims of technologies or products that are banned or strictly controlled in the developed world? Since the decision to move to lead-free petrol in Europe, Associated Octel, in the best tradition of multinational companies, has done its best to promote its lead-based anti-knocking products even more energetically overseas in order to compensate for lost sales in Europe. The same is true of the tobacco industry which is now ruthlessly expanding its Third World sales, in the full knowledge that the lives of millions will be blighted as a direct consequence of taking up smoking. Pesticides banned in some developed countries for health and environmental reasons are exported in large volumes to the Third World. According to estimates by the US Accounting Office, about 30% of US pesticide exports were not registered for use in the United States: of these, 20% had been officially cancelled or suspended for health or environmental reasons.

Elsewhere, the export of hazardous industries to Third World countries, who are usually only too pleased to see investment *at any price*, goes on apace. Mike Flux, ICI's Environment Adviser, justifies industry's double standards in the following manner:

Immense problems exist for any international corporation attempting to conduct its business acceptably in a multiplicity of societies having different value systems. It is a monumental arrogance for those in the Environmental Movement to advocate application of one particular set of values throughout the world. They ignore the fact that not only do value systems vary, but that they vary for valid and fundamental reasons.[4]

This is a rather sophisticated variation on the 'life-is-cheap-over-there' theory of development in the Third World. Value systems may indeed vary, but by and large, human emotions at the death or disabling of a loved one do not.

Less accommodating environmentalists are also asking uncomfortable questions about industry's sincerity closer to home. To what extent are we dealing with a public relations exercise rather than any profound shift in emphasis? Much of what is happening is extremely defensive: the huge financial penalties of an environmental disaster are bad enough for the company involved (though they are usually mitigated by insurance cover), but the long-term impact on its image can be much worse. Environmental pragmatists use this fear to put extra pressure on industry, but the danger here is that such pressure encourages companies merely to adopt a positive public relations strategy to enhance their public image. For instance, the chemical industry launched a major campaign in 1986, 'to promote its image as a public benefactor and respectable citizen' and 'to create a far more favourable perception of the industry to counterbalance the efforts of the environment lobby.'[5]

That approach does not always work. Sir John Harvey-Jones, erstwhile Chairman of ICI, acknowledged that: 'You can't advertise your way out of environmental issues. If you spent a lot on advertising, people will say you must be rolling in money – and imagine you must have something to hide. We have got to use a less dramatic, more persistent approach.'[6] A pity he was not on hand to instruct ICI's advertising agency to that effect in 1986, when in response to growing public anxiety about the build-up of nitrates in water supplies they came out with a series of hilarious and utterly fatuous advertisements predicting what would happen if farmers could not go on using more and more of ICI's lovely fertilizers: the cost of an ordinary loaf would soar to around £1.60; cricket pitches on village greens would have to be ploughed up to compensate for lower yields elsewhere . . . etc.

It is hard to think of a more classic example of trying to 'advertise your way out of an environmental issue'. What is more, like many major multinationals, ICI goes in for the production of vast quantities of promotional bumf extolling its efforts to protect the environment. One of these (ICI and the Environmental Challenge) provides an interesting insight into ICI's response to criticism about its production of chlorofluorocarbons (CFCs) and their impact on the ozone layer:

> After eight years of intensive CFC research, ICI published a major review of the results by 1982. It concluded that the

research had 'still not determined whether or not CFCs by themselves, or in combination with other man-made compounds, would have any significant effect on the earth's ozone layer'.

Independent reports in the USA at the beginning of 1984 by NASA and the National Academy of Sciences endorsed earlier findings on the reduced risk of atmospheric ozone depletion. These reports reflect significant advances in scientific understanding, and the EEC has recommended no further legislative action, with a review scheduled for 1985.

Meanwhile, industry continues to support a multi-million dollar research programme which will lead to a better understanding of the impact of human activities on the ozone layer.[7]

As we all know, the science about the ozone layer has moved on considerably since then, and there is no longer any doubt whatsoever that it is primarily CFCs which are responsible for the thinning out of the ozone. But such flatulent PR piffle reveals a much more serious problem: the exploitation of scientific uncertainty to justify continuing inaction on major environmental issues.

ICI has indeed invested many millions of pounds over the last few years in finding substitutes for the use of CFCs, but at the same time they have also been lobbying the British Government to discourage them from supporting international initiatives to move rapidly towards phasing out CFC production. The simple fact is that the US Government (on such 'doubtful' evidence) banned the use of CFCs in aerosols back in 1978, and sinced then, DuPont and Dow Chemicals (ICI's major US competitors in this area) have both agreed to phase out the use of CFCs altogether. If they could do it, why couldn't ICI?

'Where is the Pile of Bodies?'

Fear of higher costs and lower profits through a loss of competitive edge obviously plays a large part in causing scientific inertia over environmental problems. So too does the fact that environmental problems exported to someone else's forest or fishing grounds seem less urgent than those on Britain's doorstep – out of sight, out of mind. But there are also deeper structural reasons for British scientists' taking an exceptionally hard line. Fred Pearce, author of a book about acid rain and news editor of *New Scientist*, blames a combination of innate conservatism, macho values and 'jobs-for-the-boys'. From school chemistry labs to industry boardrooms, he argues, science remains an overwhelmingly male world:

I remember at school there was always a macho atmosphere in the labs, a feeling that it was tough to handle dangerous substances nonchalantly. It was very common for people to chuck mercury or sulphuric acid around out of sheer bravado. You see the same cavalier attitude to safety and pollutants in factories and work-places, whether it's men refusing to wear hard hats on a building site or being careless with dioxin in a chemical plant. There has always been a woeful failure to pay attention to things that are obviously hazardous in the wider environment.

For a variety of reasons, Britain *continues* to be known as the 'Dirty Man of Europe'. Faced with demands for action to clean up sulphur dioxide emissions from power stations, radioactive discharges from Sellafield and many other hazards, British scientists adopt a uniquely obstructive line of argument. This approach might best be described as the 'Where is the pile of bodies?' philosophy of environmental management.

Our scientists are willing to call for curbs on our polluting industries *only* when certain stringent criteria have been met. Firstly, the landscape must be strewn with corpses. Secondly, these corpses must be proved beyond even unreasonable doubt to have been killed by exposure to a specifically *British* pollutant. Until a direct and incontrovertible relationship of cause and effect can be established between a named industrial process and a particular pattern of death, disease or environmental damage, Britain invariably refuses to do anything about it.

In the rest of Northern Europe, the importance of taking preventive action is now widely accepted; in Britain, the 'precautionary principle' was virtually unheard of until Prince Charles made his widely-publicized speech at the North Sea Summit in November 1987: 'If science has taught us anything, it is that the environment is full of uncertainty. It makes no sense to test it to destruction. While we wait for the doctor's diagnosis, the patient may easily die!' This authoritative intervention (which some believe was set up behind the scenes by Martin Holdgate, the DoE's own chief scientist at that time, who despaired of ever persuading Nicholas Ridley, Secretary of State for the Environment, to soften his opposition to precautionary

145

safeguards – and Ridley was certainly sufficiently angry throughout the summit to justify such a hypothesis!) undoubtedly helped to persuade the British delegation to support all sorts of important new measures to protect the North Sea.

But the Brits wouldn't budge on the question of dumping sewage sludge in the North Sea (35% of our sewage wastes are disposed of in this way). This sewage sludge contains high levels of potentially dangerous heavy metals, which are almost certainly linked to the highly disturbing and previously unknown patterns of disease which have started to appear in fish in the North Sea. European scientists agree that they cannot pinpoint precisely what is going wrong, but they argue that cumulative damage is clearly taking place and that this must be linked to the general build-up of pollutants in the North Sea, *including* those coming from Britain's annual contribution of 5 million tonnes of raw sewage. Even when faced with these arguments, British scientists see no 'scientific' reason to stop dumping until such time as *conclusive evidence* is presented which proves that *specific fish diseases* are linked *directly* to *our* sewage.

At one level, the public probably still cherishes the notion inherited from a more trusting age that scientists are bold seekers after the truth, pursuing objective knowledge for its own sake and the betterment of humanity. Science can certainly be good (i.e. accurate) or bad (inaccurate), but it is *never* neutral or purely objective. It must always be seen in its institutional and political context. The crucial questions which scientists try to answer are not the ones they might ask themselves, but the ones they are asked to answer by their employers – industry, the government or science departments in universities. Scientists primarily (and increasingly) serve the interests of those employers.

A notorious example of this syndrome has been the attitude of the CEGB to the problem of acid rain. For many years, the CEGB totally refused to accept that emissions of sulphur dioxide and nitrogen oxides from its power stations could be contributing significantly to the death of the forests, lakes and rivers of Scandinavia and Northern Europe. Faced with a mass of circumstantial scientific evidence against this position, the Government responded by commissioning a five-year, £5 million research programme, the main objective of which was to prove that acidification problems were caused by anything other than CEGB emissions! European scientists, particularly in Scandinavia, were baffled by this attitude, and saw the research programme as a gigantic con-trick. Fred Pearce tries to explain why such attitudes persist:

> The CEGB is almost a kind of freemasonry. Whenever you talk to people who work for the CEGB, you get a sense of their intense, almost missionary zeal to generate electricity. It stems, I think, from the CEGB having enormous and isolated power stations which function as self-contained communities. It's a very powerful and pervasively influential organization which commands intense loyalties, not least among its scientists. The CEGB employs very good scientists, pays them well and gets its money's worth. Look at the way they argued with the Scandinavians over acid rain. The Scandinavians had acid lakes and rivers and saw our power stations as the main source of that acidification. But the CEGB hoped to find other reasons, so their scientists said: 'We don't know the *exact* chemistry of what's happening in the soil or inside the fish.' Scientifically, they were quite right, but the point is that the CEGB's interests are served by this process of trying to reach a higher level of certainty. I'm not suggesting that scientists who work for CEGB do bad science or fix results. On the contrary, they're usually very good and honest scientists who like their work to be interesting. But there is a problem endemic to all organisations, especially large ones: they are unlikely to promote research that is inherently self-damaging.

Such concerted prevarication ensures exactly the kind of delay the CEGB wants. Though they may well have been instrumental, eventually, in helping to persuade the Government to introduce a £600 million programme of Flue Gas Desulphurization to reduce sulphur dioxide pollution, the nature and timing of this programme have also been determined by the CEGB's professional prevaricators. Three years will be spent considering design and engineering features before construction begins in 1990, and will then run through until 1997. Even then, the reductions achieved will still not bring the UK into line with the 30% Club (made up of those countries pledged to reduce sulphur dioxide emissions by that percentage, based on 1980 levels, before 1993), let alone with the far more rigorous reductions now widely accepted as necessary throughout Europe.

The work of Forestry Commission experts provides another striking example of the power of institutional factors to blind scientists to the apparently obvious. Fred Pearce continues the story:

> The Forestry Commission admits that Britain's trees don't look terribly well these days. But instead of saying that air pollution and acid rain might have something to do with it, they blame everything else: bugs, fungi, pests, cold winters and windy hillsides. By contrast, if a tree is damaged by frost in West Germany, they'll say ozone and sulphur dioxide pollution made it more vulnerable. If the same thing happens in Britain, a Forestry Commission scientist says: 'Oh yes, frost damage – seen it year after year, nothing's changed.' It's not in the Forestry Commission's interest to take such a line. They ought to be yelling at the CEGB from the rooftops. But they're inhibited by institutional conservatism in a big way. They presumably don't like criticizing another very influential nationalized industry. There's a kind of clubbiness at the top which makes them immensely reluctant to take action. Again, no one wants to rock the boat.

But after three years of often acrimonious debate with Friends of the Earth (whose own survey of beech and yew trees in Britain in 1985 indicated severe levels of damage), the Forestry Commission started to execute a U-turn at the end of 1987. It is interesting to follow the progressive melting of Forestry Commission complacency and inertia over the years:

> *April 1984.* 'There appears to be no threat to British forests of damage similar to that seen in Central Europe.'

> *March 1985.* 'This survey has shown no signs of the damage seen in West Germany, nor any unexpected abnormalities, and this is very reassuring.'

> *June 1986.* 'Results of the most recent Forestry Commission surveys of woodlands show that Britain's trees are in good health.'

> *December 1986.* 'As judged by needle loss, the health of British conifers must now be rated as only moderate . . . the acidity of fog and mist may be sufficiently high to cause direct injury to trees.'

> *December 1987.* 'The extent of crown thinning and discoloration (the two main symptoms of tree die-back) in Britain is similar to that in West Germany.'

The results of their 1987 Forest Health Survey were so worrying that even they are finding it hard to pretend that nothing is actually going on out there. Despite that, the survey is still riddled with all sorts of caveats and cop-outs. They are simply not prepared to say that air pollution is damaging our trees, only that they can *no longer discount the possibility* that air pollution *might* be a factor in any pattern of damage that is occurring.

Such orthodoxy is reinforced at every stage of a scientist's career by the 'peer review' system by which scientists' work is judged. The system involves panels of fellow scientists sitting in judgement on scientific papers and applications for research grants. It is meant to be fair and democratic. But it also favours conformity and works against anyone who holds unconventional opinions. Moreover, the academic balance in Britain's universities is still strongly loaded in favour of physics and chemistry. Ecology as a science is still barely considered respectable, and the inertia against change and the lack of funding for growth make it hard for ecologists and environmentalists to expand their work.

Green Capitalism

So, with an indifferent and reactionary Government, an inadequate regulatory framework and a hidebound scientific establishment, are we really on the threshold of a new age of 'green capitalism'? Such is the basic thesis of John Elkington and Tom Burke in *The Green Capitalists*. They chart the progress made by big business in terms of good environmental practice, and optimistically assert that we are now moving into a phase of 'green growth', which will be achieved by a 'new alliance of industrialists and environmentalists'.[8] They genuinely seem to believe (and adduce many fascinating examples to justify such a belief) that the most enlightened big businesses have now seen the green light and are enthusiastically going for it. The businesses and industries which fall into this category include what used to be called the 'sunrise industries' (such as bio-technology, micro-electronics, recycling and pollution control) as well as many other new 'clean' technologies such as super-conductors, ceramics and fibre-optics.

This particular book makes no attempt whatsoever to provide a balanced environmental audit of some of the companies which it holds up so enthusiastically for our approval. In the interests of not being 'too confrontational', it raises hardly a whimper at the staggering assault that some multinationals are still carrying out on the global environment. And there is no apparent awareness of the extent to which big business has learnt to play the game by perfecting their double act as Dr Jekyll and Mr Hyde. For instance, Shell pumps millions into the environment movement through its Better Britain Campaign and other large sponsorship schemes, but continues to cause considerable harm in the Third World through its export of Aldrin and Dieldrin. And, as we have already seen, ICI is only too happy to take credit for all sorts of exciting, environmentally friendly innovations, whilst at the same time intransigently defending its right to go on destroying the ozone layer through the production of CFCs.

Such companies, and some environmentalists, simply want to have their cake and green it. Without appropriate criteria in this area, few will be able to tell whether a process of nominal 'greening' represents important transitional steps down the right road or mere opportunism. In the long run, can industrial enterprise on the present exploitative growth-oriented model, even with a new improved green streak, really be compatible with the defence of the planet and the life-support systems on which we depend?

These are difficult issues for Greens. From a pragmatic point of view, green capitalism has obvious attractions over 'dirty' capitalism. It is much better for businesses to make their profits without wrecking the environment. But we should not get too carried away by the idea that the new technologies can, by themselves, make the future safe. At the heart of 'green capitalism' lies the notion that nothing is *structurally* wrong with our present industrial way of life, that all we need is a few new fixes and a few filters on the end of industrial discharge pipes. That idea is extremely dangerous, because it is used to vindicate the argument that industry can go on growing – 'sustainably', whatever that may mean in such a context – presumably until the end of time.

Moreover, green capitalism can give exploitative, destructive industrial capitalism a veneer of ecological respectability. That makes it a potent propaganda tool for industrialists anxious to resist deeper change. Green fundamentalists throughout the Western world have therefore got good reason to despair of the way many people in the Green Movement are rushing to embrace the idea of green capitalism. Once Greens convince themselves that it holds the answer to their

150

prayers, they have, in effect, been outmanoeuvred, since all their more trenchant criticisms of the nature of today's society and economy will be blunted or rendered impotent.

Simply mitigating the most damaging effects of pollution does little to help us move forward to an understanding that the only genuinely ecological way of living is to develop industrial activities that do not cause pollution in the first place. The limitations of the 'polluter pays' approach are becoming increasingly clear in the United States, where the anti-pollution business has become a large and powerful sector of industry. Has this made the American economy ecologically sound? Of course not. All that has happened is that some US companies are making a lot of money causing pollution – and then making even more by cleaning up some of the mess. What we really need to develop are systems which tackle the dilemma of industrial externalities, which force and encourage companies to internalize the environmental and ecological costs they currently pass on to the rest of us. The 'polluter pays' concept pays only lip service to this need; by settling for half-way greenhouses of this kind, Greens risk thereby giving up their long-term objectives for marginal improvements in ecologically unacceptable situations.

It has to be acknowledged quite openly that part of the problem is the scientific naïvety of much of the Green Movement. Most industrial questions are highly technical, and few Greens are equipped to deal with them. For example, the 'sunrise industries' are now being touted as the answer to all our problems, just as nuclear energy, pesticides and other 'miracle technologies' were before them. The industry for which the most potent claims are made is bio-technology. Its champions say it offers us unlimited food and freedom from pollution, just for starters.

But these biotechnologies are certain to be owned, exploited and controlled not by individuals or communities, but by multinational corporations. Will such technologies really save the planet? Or will they be the first steps on the road to a brave new world of widespread human genetic engineering and global totalitarianism? Either way, their impact is certain to be enormous. Yet Greens, along with society as a whole, have scarcely begun to recognize, let alone come to terms with, the issue.

Financially speaking, it's important to remember that industry in Britain stands in the same relation to green pressure groups as the Telecom Tower stands to a medium-sized ants' nest. Their economic power makes it possible for big business and industry to buy off protest, or co-opt some of the less threatening green ideas and turn them to their own purposes. In the Spring of 1987, for example, two of Britain's leading green campaigners, Graham Searle, former Executive Director of Friends of the Earth, and George Pritchard, Greenpeace's top anti-nuclear campaigner, said they were joining what the *Observer* called 'the industries that their pressure groups most love to hate'.[9] Mr Searle was to be a £9,600-a-year part-time consultant for the controversial Rechem company, Britain's largest commercial disposers of toxic chemical waste. (Three years earlier, at Bonnybridge in Scotland, a Rechem plant had closed after an unexplained outbreak of birth deformities and other illnesses among local animals and children. The company was cleared by official investigations into allegations that the deformities were linked to the burning of toxic waste in the plant.) Mr Searle defended himself against the charge that he had sold his environmental soul by arguing that he would take the environmental battle inside the Rechem boardroom.

Meanwhile, Mr Pritchard, once one of the most implacable opponents of nuclear waste dumping in Britain, had taken a new job – in the nuclear waste business – helping to develop a scheme for disposing of nuclear waste under the sea bed. Both former activists fiercely denied the suggestion that they were 'watchdogs who had become lapdogs' by accepting such jobs. There is, of course, some merit in the argument that the best way to educate environmentally unenlightened companies is from inside, and few people were better qualified to do that than Searle and Pritchard. Nevertheless, the appointments were clearly seen as a public relations coup for the companies involved and an embarrassment for the environment movement.

The whole question of how environmentalists can be as effective as possible without losing their integrity is bound to become increasingly important throughout the next few years. It is interesting in this context that Shell's forecasters see two main groups of environmentalists emerging: the ideologists (taking a line similar to the 'fundamentalist' faction in Die Grünen) and the pragmatists. Given the diversity of the Green Movement in the UK, the two are likely to be complementary rather than mutually exclusive, but to a certain extent this depends on what happens to employment patterns within the UK over the next ten to twenty years. If conventional full-time jobs become increasingly inaccessible, then calls to 'deregulate' and relax environmental regulations will grow. But so too will pressure to start thinking about the nature and distribution of *work* in a completely different way.

CHAPTER SEVEN

Green Works

One of the most significant strands of contemporary green thinking relates to the future of work. This strand has been woven together by a rather eclectic amalgam of neo-Luddites and green techno-freaks, of latter-day laid-back hippies and those for whom the puritan work ethic still works, of radical visionaries and those grafting away to cobble together initiatives for good work within the existing system. It is fairly astonishing that anything should have emerged from such a rich melting pot, but it has. Given the erosion of confidence in the ability of the conventional economy to go on generating new jobs, let alone to provide full employment, this is one area where the Greens are confidently expecting that their ideas will become increasingly attractive. To understand that sense of confidence, it is necessary to go back a bit in history.

The Industrial Revolution was the start of employment as we know it today. A working day of fixed hours became the norm: forcibly divorced from the land, people became unable to support themselves with self-grown food. The wage, not bread, became the staff of life. Before that, work had been thought since the Middle Ages to be good for the soul, as a down payment on the afterlife, and work then embraced every category of work, from the merchant selling silks and spices to the woman stirring the pot with a child at each breast. But as families were herded together round factories, only paid employment came to be thought of as proper work. Women were now 'supported' by the 'breadwinner', and the long, unpaid hours they put into child-rearing, cooking and houseworking were (and still are) thought of as contributing less to society than the waged work undertaken away from the home by their husbands. Unpaid work outside the home came to be called 'voluntary' work, undertaken outside 'normal working hours'.

In an age of increasing mass unemployment, work, in this conventional, narrow sense, has become a highly desirable item, and as Ann Barr and Peter York pointed out in their article 'Just the Job' (the *Observer*, 8 November 1987), the term 'workaholic', hitherto signifying a kind of illness, has taken on a chic allure. For green economists, the next step, which they believe has already been taken by many, is to widen our concepts of work to include *all* those activities which sustain and enrich our lives. The springboard for this progression is to accept that the days of full conventional employment are over.

There are statistics from various sources to support this idea, whatever the politicians might tell us during election campaigns. The 1987 annual report on the economy and employment published by the University of Warwick's Institute for Employment Research, for instance, concludes that economic growth *will* bring unemployment down in Britain, but only to 2.5 million by the end of 1995, by which time 28% of employees will work part-time.

Barry Sherman's book, *Working at Leisure*, comes up with some fairly startling predictions. He estimates that by around 1990 there will be just 19.7 million in employment, a decrease of 1.217 million (5.8%) on the 1984 total of 20.846 million. By 1995 that will be down to 18.1 million, and by around 2010 there will be an estimated 14.8 million with jobs, a decrease of 29% on the 1984 figure.[1] Those figures reflect the progressive introduction of new technologies, eventually leading to the adoption of machines with artificial intelligence.

Current Initiatives

There are very few people in Britain who would be prepared to thank Mrs Thatcher and the Conservative government of the 1980s for creating mass unemployment, and the widespread disaffection which has stemmed from it. If, however, we were able to look back from some unspecified future time in which the majority of people have what Professor Charles Handy calls 'portfolios' of work, consisting of some paid employment, freelancing, voluntary work and gift work (including housework), then mass unemployment may, after all, be seen to have had a proverbial silver lining. Such an outlook in no way attempts to belittle the enormous personal suffering and cumulative social decay caused by unemployment, but it does seek to make the most of the opportunity that is there for expanding the concept of work beyond mere cash transactions in the formal economy.

In fact, according to some green thinkers, the Conservative Government has been all but irrelevant to the growth of mass unemployment. As the green economist James Robertson says: 'The breakdown of the mixed economy consensus from 1950 to 1975 was going to happen anyway. It's very unfortunate that it is possible for many people now to think that this is all just due to the Thatcher government. That is a cloud of misunderstanding which means that people don't perceive what is really happening.' Most politicians, he says, are still trying to operate old models, in different ways, according to their particular ideology. As John Prescott, who used to be the Labour Party's employment spokesman, revealingly declared after his party's 1987 General Election campaign: 'Our jobs programme still smacked of full-time jobs for men in manufacturing.'[2] As we saw in Chapter 3, there is little going on to indicate that it won't be exactly the same next time round.

The good news, conceptually and practically, is that unemployment is serving as a stimulus for people to take control of their own lives and start to earn a living in ways that break their dependence on the old 'get a job' *modus operandi*. This is evidenced by the many schemes designed specifically to enable unemployed people to start their own businesses, or become self-employed. Some of these are sponsored by the Government, such as the Enterprise Allowance Scheme, which gives successful applicants, who can raise guarantees for £1,000 capital, £40 a week for a year while their business gets off the ground. The scheme had 270,000 participants between 1983 and 1987.

Other initiatives are run without government support. Organizations like Focus (Forum for Occupational Counselling and Unemployment Services), set up by Bridget Litchfield in 1982, are used by firms making redundancies. There is no particular green ethic at work here, although Focus gives 40% of its profits for 'socially useful purposes' like enterprise agencies. Although many of the people assisted do become self-employed, many are simply advised on how best to get another conventional job. Business for this and other 'outplacement' agencies is growing by 40% a year.

Another scheme, called Head Start, is designed to help the long-term unemployed set up their own businesses, and works in conjunction with the National Association for the Care and Resettlement of Offenders (Nacro) and the Industrial Society. A pilot scheme in 1987 in Nacro's community programme in Birmingham resulted in nine new businesses being set up, ranging from landscape gardening to antique furniture restoration. Also in Birmingham, the Birmingham Unemployment Resources Network (BURN, set up in 1981) assists new initiatives and provides a forum for the pooling of information. The BURN directory lists 1,500 such initiatives, and BURN has spawned a network of similar groups around the country, such as Instant Muscle, an umbrella organization which offers advice and support to young unemployed people setting themselves up in business.

There are a number of credit unions, such as the one run by the Birmingham Settlement, which encourage people to save in small amounts, the money being used to fund local projects. The loans have a default rate of under 1%, even though the recipients are usually 'high-risk' projects. The trades union movement, too, despite its generally archaic, fixed view of what constitutes 'work', is making some headway in a limited, ad hoc way. The Trades Union Bank, Unity Trust, has promoted the idea of employees' share-ownership plans (ESOP), and in 1987 put together a plan for an employee buy-out of Leyland trucks.

Moving away from schemes designed specifically for the unemployed, there are a huge number of projects centred on local enterprise and community business, sponsored by central government, local authorities and their enterprise agencies, and to a limited extent by the private sector. All this fits into what we have come to know as the 'enterprise culture'. We have to ask first of all whether this brave new world is contributing towards a greening of work. Working patterns are not necessarily being altered – people still work long hours most days of the week, they still rely, by and large, on the established financial institutions, and are by no means necessarily of a green frame of mind. There is still a huge suspicion of the Starship Enterprise. Labour MP Andrew Smith, who has studied the role of local authorities in creating environmentally-based jobs, does not buy the enterprise package:

> In many instances what is happening is that people are working for far lower wages in self-employment and co-operatives – co-operatives are no strangers to wage-exploitation – than they would be prepared to accept working for a larger company. It seems to be that that's part of the Government's philosophy. That all we need do to cut employment is to cut wages low enough so that everyone's absorbed into the service industries and we go back to a servant-style economy. I've heard it described by one of Mrs Thatcher's former economic advisers as a 'bazaar economy'.

The point about the enterprise culture, by which we basically mean the proliferation of small businesses, is that although there may not be a green ideology behind any of these businesses, at least half of them are run by one person. These people are working for themselves, and, if employing, are much less likely to exploit. They are unlikely to be operating from an exclusively social rationale or profit rationale; they are most likely to be motivated by a fundamental desire to take control of their own lives.

Perhaps more significant, in a green sense, are the 300 Local Enterprise Agencies (LEAs), and the myriad schemes run in conjunction with the private sector, which seems to have developed the glimmerings of a sense of responsibility in the face of the decline of the inner cities during the 1980s. These agencies are locally based, and usually formed as a result of meetings involving the local authority, large companies in the locality, the Chamber of Commerce, and local trades union representatives. They are funded by donations in both cash and kind from a variety of sources and work to provide premises, counselling and, in some cases, start-up finance for small businesses.

The role of the LEAs was examined by a survey of 300 firms helped by 65 enterprise agencies, conducted by Enterprise Dynamics for Business in the Community (BiC). The survey found that small firms are twice as likely to succeed if assisted by an agency. Help was 'crucial' for 20%, and 'useful' for 50%. Significantly, more than half were working alone. *Small Firms and their Environments*, the results of a study by the Small Business Research Unit at Kingston Polytechnic, found an implicit green ethic at work. None of the owner-managers or co-operative members questioned wanted their enterprises to grow into even medium-sized firms, often because they felt they would lose too much of their valued way of life. They did not see themselves as part of the surge for 'job creation', one of the great buzz-phrases of the 1980s. They often ignored their potential share of the £1 billion and more that the government has pushed into the pockets of small businesses since 1980, because they did not want their hands tied by spools of red tape. None the less, another survey of 500 enterprises and 81 agencies carried out by BiC found that only one in six enterprise agency clients fail, compared with one in three small businesses nationally.

One of the most active agencies is the London Enterprise Agency (LEntA). A small random sample of their work shows the energy and variety they bring to bear. They run a design enterprise programme, for example, which takes twenty design graduates a year and helps them formulate and execute a viable business plan. They run workshops, such as 'Build your own business by working from home', and a 'marriage bureau' to link up entrepreneurs and investors, called the Local Investment Networking Company (LINC). Outside London, a huge amount is being done by regional LEAs. In Lancashire, for example, Lancashire Enterprises Ltd, the economic agency of Lancashire County Council, is the biggest industrial landlord in the country, and directly funds almost 3,000 training places. Again, this has no direct green bearing, but it is an example of the regeneration that can and must take place at local level.

The critical issue for any community involved in such initiatives is *control*. Even within the highly centralized systems we have at the moment, it is possible to achieve a lot by setting up community businesses, conducting community appraisal studies and popular planning exercises, seeking ways of setting up local financial institutions (so that local money can be channelled to support local development), and establishing close links with local colleges and polytechnics. But such activities do *not* in themselves protect local communities from central government or multinational decision-making, where there is no necessary loyalty to that community, but only to the business of being more competitive and profitable. The vulnerability of communities, or the local economy as a whole, to the arbitrary decisions of big business moving its resources in and out, almost at will, has been the main stimulus in encouraging people to promote self-reliance in the local community.

Sheffield City Council is one of the most important authorities in this respect. To finance their activities they use Section 137 of the 1972 Local Government Act, which allows a 2p rate to be used on measures to promote the local economy. In 1971, Sheffield had 50% or more of its job in manufacturing; now there are less than 33% in that sector. The 20,000 people still employed in manufacturing are spread among between 400 and 500 firms, and the main aim of the council is to diversify and stabilize this base. They have developed a number of initiatives in conjunction with the polytechnic, particularly in the area of new product development, and are now able to offer advice and practical help with production, marketing and business plan development.

The council is also developing a science park, where a number of high-technology companies can be located, a business management development programme, an enterprise workshop, where new companies can use low rent premises with management guidance on hand, a women's technology centre, the Sheffield Ethnic Minorities Business Development Initiative, and the Sheffield Centre for Product Technology and Technology Research. Sheffield is also one of the pilot areas for a Department of Energy study on the possibilities of developing combined heat and power schemes. Diversification and participation are the names of the game, and Sheffield is learning to play them to very good effect.

For Andrew Smith, this kind of approach provides an essential counterbalance to the furious centralization policy being carried out by the Tory government in the 1980s:

> If the Government was serious and relatively objective about undertaking inner city regeneration, they would realize the importance of a partnership with the local authorities, recognizing the value of democratic input, through the local authority framework and other frameworks. Instead, the local authorities are being deprived of funds which the Government intends to channel through 'quangos'. I can't believe that they can be as responsive and sensitive over community needs as more democratically-based intervention would be.

For James Robertson, however, the financial and power squeeze on local government is not altogether a bad thing:

> I see it to some extent as the destruction of old institutions, and I don't have any tremendous brief for local government as it has been, say, over the last fifteen years. I think local government has been part of the problem as much as a whole lot of our other institutions. Part of the future has to be a revival of genuine participation at the local level, and if one of the routes to that has to be the weakening of existing local government organization, then I wouldn't weep too many tears over that.

Part of the necessary impetus in creating that kind of participation will undoubtedly come from the private sector. It can often be one small, progressive company that gets the ball rolling in its own locality. Bluemay, for example, is a small Wiltshire firm which makes nuts and bolts out of nylon. The company employs twenty-two people, and in 1986 Bluemay spent a quarter of their pre-tax profits of

£75,000 sending each and every one of them on some form of training course. Richard Nash, a production planner with the company, after doing an external training course, set up a community programme called Basil (Bluemay and Schools Industrial Link). Each employee who has been with Bluemay for four years gets an equity stake in the company.

More formalized interventions by the private sector are being made by BiC, whose president is the Prince of Wales. One of their projects is the Finsbury Park Community Trust, founded in 1985 to attract investment to Finsbury Park in North London. A number of neighbourhood community partnerships were launched, promoting jobs and training for the unemployed and supplying contracts for small local firms. One of the community trust members says: 'Community entrepreneurship breaks away from the notion of "them" and "us". It is communities relating to companies as partners.'[3]

It was BiC's Sir Hector Laing, the Chairman of United Biscuits, who was inspired by the Five Per Cent Group in the USA to form a similar group here. The Five Per Cent Group comprises eighty companies who contribute 5% of their pre-tax income to community-based employment projects. It would be a bit too much to expect the same level of enthusiasm in this country, but we do now have the Per Cent Group, which is working towards a half per cent contribution for the top 200 companies. United Biscuits itself gave a full 1% in 1986, which came to £840,000. If this was emulated by their 199 top colleagues, £300 million would be raked in.

It would be good if BiC were able to pay rather closer attention to the World Conservation Strategy (WCS). At its British launch in 1980, the Secretary of State for the Environment at that time, Michael Heseltine, referred to the WCS as: 'a realistic and unemotive restatement of the evidence that conservation of our natural and living resources is essential to the economic and social welfare of society, and is entirely compatible with sustainable development.'[4] Though many businesses have taken up the idea of 'community entrepreneurship', they have yet to embrace the basic principles of WCS. These appeared in the following form in the British response to the WCS: 'To identify those sectors of the economy where economic growth will contribute to sustainable development; to identify those which are inefficient in resource use and obsolete in economic terms; and to develop a coherent approach to a sustainable resource use by increased investment in areas such as energy efficiency and cleaner, low waste technologies.'[5]

When it comes to following up on the specific recommendations of the WCS, bigger companies might like to take a lead from IBM, a company which, as we saw in Chapter 6, seeks to intertwine profitability and social responsibility whenever possible. The company provides, for example, a five-day management course for voluntary organizations, to enable them to use big business methods for charitable purposes. There is also a wide secondment programme through which employees can spend one or two years working in the community. IBM allows those of its employees who work in the community – local government councillors, magistrates, school governors etc. – to take time away from work, recognizing its responsibility to allow these people time to perform their duties effectively. This type of policy, adopted more widely, could be the start of a 'portfolio approach' to work. Andrew Smith, though, remains deeply suspicious of big business: 'It's one thing to be putting in a bit of money which can be written off as a tax-deductible public relations expense. It's another for very large companies significantly to alter their mainline activities.'

Community Programme (CP)

The Left has, of course, been equally suspicious of the Manpower Services Commission (MSC) and its community programme, arguing that it has extended the boundaries of the 'casualization' of labour and the low-wage economy. Many tasks which a few years ago were part of mainstream local authority activity, in the social services or environmental departments, have now become CP schemes employing people for one year only. The CP has also been centralized and undemocratic in its decision-making, issuing directives rather than operating in partnership with the schemes and management agencies.

All of this is perfectly true, but it is also true that a fair amount of good work in improving the environment has been carried out through the CP schemes. At the end of 1987, a quarter of the CP's 12,000 projects were environmentally-based. A report prepared in 1985 for the British Trust for Conservation and Volunteers (BTCV) looked at the scope for volunteer and MSC work in the environment and came to the conclusion that the potential for this type of approach to land management was vast, despite the inherent problems of MSC-associated schemes. Tasks identified included the maintenance, management, improvement and restoration of footpaths, nature conservation sites, woodland management, visitor centres, historic buildings, urban open spaces, canals, ships and railway land.

Following on from that report, Kenneth Baker, then Secretary of State for the Environment, set up UK 2000 under the charismatic leadership of Richard Branson. By any standards, UK 2000 was then, and still is, a unique organism, bringing together three totally separate cultures: the civil service (with representatives from the Department of the Environment and the MSC); the private sector (joining Richard Branson on the board were people like Stephen Brien, Director of BiC, and Ernest Saunders, a dynamic Northern entrepreneur who helped bring Halifax back to life in the mid-1980s); and the voluntary sector, represented by BTCV, the Royal Society for Nature Conservation, the Civic Trust, Keep Britain Tidy Group, Groundwork Foundation, Community Service Volunteers and − as latecomers to the party, once recycling was included as part of UK 2000's brief − Friends of the Earth.

Despite getting off to a dreadful start in 1986 (with Mrs Thatcher, in a convulsion of indignation upon discovering that Israel's streets were cleaner than Britain's, branding it as a 'clean-up operation', which is exactly how the Press has described it from that moment on), UK 2000 has done a good job in terms of new projects and raising support from the private sector. Whether it has always succeeded in raising the *quality* of the work on its many different projects is rather harder to gauge.

So there is no doubt that the use of CP schemes can both initiate new projects and enhance other activities which directly benefit the environment. In Birmingham, for instance, one finds a huge diversity of different schemes. The Urban Wildlife Group has become a large CP managing agency employing more than eighty people, both full- and part-time. They enjoy considerable local support, with over 400 members and 1,000 supporters, and their landscape team helps groups who want to renovate local sites. The group also has a strong educational department which is a resource for local schools, and acts in an advisory capacity to people who wish to renovate plots of derelict land.

The Urban Ecology Group is financed by the Inner City Partnership, and manages a CP project. It too offers advice on improving land, and would like to see community business opportunities developing around such possibilities as allotments, city farms and bio-mass planting.

Friends of the Earth in Birmingham is one of the strongest Friends of the Earth local groups. They have 250 members and have established a firm base in the city centre. The group has a wholefood shop, a draftproofing project with three core workers and an insulation project which employs twenty-four workers in two teams under the auspices of the CP. A recycling project also employs three full-time workers.

From September 1988 onwards, these schemes, the whole of UK 2000, and many other organizations face a very different future when the Community Programme and the Job Training Scheme (launched just before the 1987 General Election, and basically a dismal failure) will be merged in a new Adult Training Scheme which is intended to cater for many more people than the 250,000 currently on CPs. The shift of emphasis away from projects (with specific environmental improvements as the output) to training (preparing people for notional jobs) is not necessarily going to be advantageous from an environmental perspective: there is no end to the dry-stone walls that need to be repaired or the woodlands that need to be restored, but there are not many actual *jobs* in dry-stone walling or woodland management, or indeed in most other environmental activities that are both desirable and necessary even if they do not create 'commercially viable, real jobs'.

Co-Operatives

Yet again, that all-important clash between 'jobs' and 'work' rears its ugly head. There are those who argue that the only way of reconciling what will always remain irreconcilable within a conventional industrial economy is to promote the massive expansion of the Co-operative Movement. As it happens, it is already a fairly expanded movement: the International Co-operative Alliance has affiliates in sixty-five countries, with a combined membership of around 500 million, which makes it the largest socio-economic movement in the world. This includes worker co-ops, retail co-ops, agricultural co-ops, housing co-ops and credit unions. They all have an important role to play in what has been termed 'the alternative economy', but it is principally in worker co-operatives that we find the potential for creating new and greener patterns of working.

The modern phase of the Co-operative Movement in Britain first took a foothold in the 1970s, not so much through the well-publicized but short-lived 'Benn co-ops' at Meriden and the *Scottish Daily News*, but through a series of organizational and legislative changes. The Society for Democratic Integration in Industry, which started out with only five paid-up members, changed its name in 1971 to the Industrial Common Ownership Movement (ICOM), with a funding body, Industrial Common Ownership Finance (ICOF). There were forty-two co-ops in existence by 1975, but the real spur to the movement's growth was the passing of the Industrial Common Ownership Act in 1976. This was a Private Member's Bill selected in the parliamentary ballot, proposed by David Watkins, the Labour MP for Consett. One of its loudest supporters was not Tony Benn, but the far more unlikely figure of one Norman Tebbitt (perhaps he had bicycle co-ops in mind?), who declared in the Commons that 'nothing but good' could come from common ownership.

The Government then set up the Co-operative Development Agency (CDA) in 1978, and this body, armed with the non-profit loan fund set up by the act and the model rules provided by ICOM, created a fertile soil for the movement to blossom in. By the end of the 1970s, 150 co-operatives had been formed, and growth continued in spectacular fashion. By 1985, 900 had been started, and the *National Directory of New Co-operatives and Community Businesses*, published by the CDA in 1986, listed over 1,400. The CDA's annual report estimated a total of 2,000 by the end of 1987. Just as encouraging is the survival rate of new co-ops. Of the 900 formed between 1976 and 1985, for example, 80% were still trading at the end of 1985, a higher proportion than conventional small businesses. Nearly a third are to be found in Greater London, perhaps not surprisingly, but the rest are fairly evenly distributed round the country.[6]

In terms of the greening of work, when we look at the reasons why co-operatives are formed, we can see signs of a new ethic. There are five types of worker co-ops identified by Cornforth and Lewis in their 1985 survey of nearly 600 co-ops:

1. endowed co-operatives, 'given away' by the original owners to their employees;
2. defensive or 'rescue' co-ops, formed by employees out of failed businesses, and 'phoenix' co-ops, formed out of the ashes of a bankrupt company;
3. 'alternative' co-ops, arising out of the counter-culture of the 1960s and 1970s;

4. job creation co-ops, formed either with government money or with CDA support, encouraging the unemployed to start their own businesses;

5. worker-buyout co-ops – there are very few of these so far, although the CDA has received a few enquiries.

The survey found that 90.5% were 'new starts' (that is, alternative and job creation co-ops), 6.5% were defensive or rescue co-ops, and 3% were endowed.[7] Most co-ops are clearly born not out of desperation or as a last resort, but because people have a vision of how they would like their life to be, and in some cases how they would like society to be. Although the Co-operative Movement may well have been stimulated by the climate of recession and mass unemployment, it is clear that there is more at work here than a simple response to the dole queue. The number of co-op workers is a minuscule fraction of the total work-force of the country – at most, 10,000 full-time and part-time workers by the end of 1987 – but if the Co-operative Movement continues to expand at its present rapid rate, we can expect this figure to increase substantially over the next few years.

How much, then, do co-ops contribute to the greening of work? Apart from a large proportion of part-time employees (just under a third of the total), the actual working patterns, democratic control aside, tend not to differ too much from conventional employment. But co-operatives contribute in several ways to the gradually emerging 'alternative economy'. Building co-ops, for example, work primarily for housing co-ops and housing associations, and printing co-ops tend to do much of their work for community groups, voluntary groups and political pressure groups. Many co-ops tend to discriminate positively with their prices in favour of groups such as the unemployed, or organizations to which the co-op is sympathetic. Few co-ops have the sole aim of making money, and often see themselves as providing a service to movements for change, not least the Green Movement itself. Ideologically sympathetic customers are often willing to pay over the odds for goods or services as an act of solidarity. The impact of this strange way of conducting business, which knocks the god profit off its high altar, is minimal as yet, but it is spreading with the fresh crop of co-ops that flowers every year.

It is important to note that the health of the Co-operative Movement is not dependent on the complexion of the party in power. The period of most intense growth has been under the aegis of a Conservative government. (Indeed, it may tendentiously be speculated that a

Labour government might well have channelled most of its resources into creating an artificially sustained climate of full conventional employment. The Labour Party never did have much time for worker co-operatives.)

New Patterns of Work

The growth of the Co-operative Movement would clearly be a big plus in terms of greening today's economy. But visionaries like James Robertson and Charles Handy clearly feel that we should be moving further and faster in both our ideas and our practice. James Robertson, in his books *Future Work* and *The Sane Alternative*, presents us with different possible scenarios for the future. The 'Business as Usual' scenario anticipates the maintenance of the status quo in every field. All our basic concepts will remain the same, and work, together with most other aspects of life and society, will continue to operate much as it does now. This view is fundamentally flawed, as it fails to see history as a continuously developing process. The 'Hyper-Expansionist' scenario sees increasingly sophisticated technology as society's saviour, with 'bigger toys and more important jobs for the boys'. Society would inevitably become polarized between the professionals with the jobs, the big earning power and the influence over policy and events, and the much larger sector living lives of relatively impecunious enforced leisure, dependent on the wealth creators for their bread and beer money. The 'Sane, Humane and Ecological' scenario looks to a change of direction, towards decentralization, the cessation of growth for growth's sake, and a collective determination 'to give top priority to learning to live supportively on this small and crowded planet'.[8]

The other key idea for discussion of the greening of work is Charles Handy's, mentioned earlier, of everyone having a portfolio of work, which he described as 'a mixture of job work, marginal work and gift work'.[9] This equates with what James Robertson calls 'ownwork', and Robertson's own definition of ownwork is as follows:

Ownwork means activity which is purposeful and important, and which people organize and control for themselves. It may be either paid or unpaid. Just as the Lutheran ethic taught that worldly work was more real than withdrawal into the artificial, abstract sphere of ecclesiastical life, so the new work

167

ethic will now teach that to immerse oneself in today's organizational world is to sink into a world of abstractions and turn one's back on real life; and that real life means real experience, and real work means finding ways of acting directly to meet needs – one's own, other people's and, increasingly, the survival needs of the natural world which supports us.[10]

There are already several changes under way which might well promote a context in which this kind of scenario begins to make sense. Part-time working is probably the fastest-spreading change in working habits. Department of Employment figures issued in October 1987 showed that there have been 1.362 million new jobs on offer since March 1983. Of these, 778,000 were part-time. Unfortunately, rather than indicating a move towards portfolio working, this simply suggests that married women were taking on part-time jobs in addition to all the 'gift work' they still have to do around the house.

Flexible working is another development that has positive and negative sides to it. It can be seen at its best in the Goodyear tyre factory in Wolverhampton, where 350 workers do two twelve-hour shifts on Saturday and Sunday and an eight-hour shift every fourth Friday night. They enjoy the same benefits as their weekday counterparts. On the other hand, fast-food supremos McDonald's have all the conditions for their 'flexible' workers weighted in their own favour. Their flexible practices mean that employees may well be rung up on their rest days and asked to come in, without even the incentive of overtime rates. Labour costs at any single outlet must never exceed 15% of sales, so if sales are down workers are laid off and the rest must simply work harder.[11]

It's the same with freelancing. Freelancing varies from the professional person, working mostly from home, to the worker who has no choice and is freelance simply by virtue of having no security, no sick pay and no holiday pay. By this reckoning, the privatized hospital domestics, who come into work one day to find themselves doing the same job for less money and no benefits, are as much freelance as the financial consultant working from a minimalist office with only a word processor, Psion organizer and cappuccino-maker for company. Are the hospital domestics really contributing to the onset of a new work scenario, or is this just the worst kind of affluent, arrogant, pseudo-liberal nonsense? According to James Robertson:

It's sometimes difficult to get across the notion that this is something that can be very good, a liberation of work, getting away from the idea that people have no freedom to choose how to organize and direct and control their working lives, without being dependent on an employer to do it for them. It's difficult to put that across as an exciting opportunity without seeming very complacent about the people who are going to get hurt in that process. Unless we accept that it is happening and organize it in the best possible way, it's going to make things very much worse for those who are suffering from it.

During the 1980s, an increasing number of employees have accepted the idea of job-sharing. Nearly sixty local authorities have schemes, for example, catering for more than 2,000 sharers. There are at least nine job-share registers, mostly London-based. 50% of sharers are parents of young children, while some are on training or academic courses and others easing gently into retirement. The job-share sector is burgeoning, and will continue to do so, as more people come to trade higher income for greater freedom and flexibility. Job-sharing is good for the employer, who generally gets 15% more person-hours per salary, given the handover time.

One of the newest changes in working habits is so-called 'telecommuting' – people working from home, usually on a computer. There are only a few schemes up and running, but these are successful, and for the most part provide satisfaction all around. F International, a computer-programming company, was founded by Steve Shirley, who started out as a freelance programmer in 1962. Her company now has a work-force of over 1,000, and aims, according to its charter, to tap 'the unutilized intellectual energy of individuals and groups unable to work in a conventional environment'. High professional standards and a minimum commitment of twenty hours a week are demanded. According to Francis Kinsman in his book *The Telecommuters*, F International is helping to 'pioneer perhaps the profoundest revolution for working mothers since the pill'.[12]

Skill-swapping centres are an equally hopeful sign of things to come. In his book *Nice Work If You Can Get It*, Guy Dauncey describes one such centre in Cumbria, started by an engineer who was made redundant. After a year and a half, the centre had 370 members sharing ninety-eight skills, with no evaluation of skills, simply a straight swap. The centre is a social nexus, where people can come and chat and drink tea together.

And then there is always the good old 'black economy'! The black economy accounts for an estimated 8.5% of British GNP. In Italy in 1987, when economists decided to include an estimate for their black economy, they suddenly found they had a stronger economy than Britain! Hobbies and sidelines are becoming more central to peoples' incomes – car maintenance, decorating and the like. All this constitutes what Charles Handy calls 'a respectable fringe'. In 1982, he tells us, a survey found that there were 750,000 more people working than officially estimated, most of them in this kind of economic activity.[13]

Many of the practices mentioned have a down-side, and are sometimes an excuse for blatant exploitation. Employers can pick and choose, and with the unions far from being the most popular institution in this country, there are few constraints. But for James Robertson it is a question of *how*, not *whether* transition will come about: 'There is some probability that the powerful people of today will use the transition for their own advantage. It is therefore extremely important for those of us who do not wish that to happen to understand that this progress is taking place, and that we must shape it.'

Indeed we must, but it is hard shaping anything against the grain. And today's grain still runs, blemishes, knots, imperfections and all, down the antediluvian line of 'jobs for all'. It will not be easy making that change, and it is therefore hardly surprising that many environmentalists concentrate on pointing out the easily quantifiable, tangible benefits of more and better jobs being created through caring for the environment rather than despoiling it.

In every major area of environmental concern (agriculture, land use, energy, transport, pollution control, recycling and waste management), it can be, and endlessly has been, demonstrated that the 'best practical environmental option' (i.e. from a green perspective, the option that is best for the environment, and not necessarily best for industry's profitability) is often the best practical employment option.

It is in this respect that the monetarist policies of Mrs Thatcher's Government bite deepest. The dogmatic adherence to a non-interventionist and econometric ideology means that they simply do not want to know about the economic and ecological advantages of low-input/organic farming over chemical-intensive farming, of energy conservation and efficiency over nuclear power and dirty coal, of efficient mass-transit public transport over more cars on more badly maintained roads, let alone want to intervene with any positive action.

170

Even on a 'soft' issue, such as recycling, the Government's policies are wholly negative and anti-environmental. The 1984 *Wealth of Waste* report estimated that Britain was losing around £750 million a year because it was failing to recycle waste material. Each year, industrial refuse amounts to 36 million tonnes of solid waste, and household refuse to 20 million tonnes, an average of half a tonne of debris for every household in the country. This represents wasted resources, wasted energy and a massive storage problem. The potential for employment creation in a fully developed recycling industry is very considerable. But the Government has steered a consistent line in favour of inaction:

> The government fully recognizes the importance of reclamation and recycling, and welcomes the co-operation between industry, central and local government, and other bodies with interests in the area. It looks to industry, in its own enlightened self-interest, to undertake reclamation/recycling where it makes commercial sense to do so. It does not regard such activities as an end in themselves, and consequently has not thought it appropriate to develop a national policy for the sector as a whole.[14]

Blend that kind of studied Government inaction and ambivalence with the morbid fear of mainstream trades unions when it comes to thinking about things in any context other than full-time jobs for full-time men, and green hopes and visions must necessarily be tempered with grey workaday fears.

CHAPTER EIGHT

Life-styles and Profiles

Ideas are one thing; practice is another. There are many theoretical subscribers to the green faith, but the proof of this particular pudding is indisputably in the eating. So is there any statistical evidence that we are on the brink of a revolutionary and historic change in values? Do opinion polls and social research into life-styles and attitudes reflect the coming of a new age?

Christine McNulty believes they do: 'Social changes today appear to be the early phase of a very profound transformation indeed, a change of greater scope than anything since the Renaissance, and perhaps of a similar nature. The fragmentation we see in society is not so much a sign of decay as of a loosening of old associations in preparation for the formation of a fundamentally new social structure.'

McNulty is the Managing Director of Taylor Nelson Applied Features, a consultancy company which has developed an analytical model of British society which cuts across the more familiar divisions of class, income, education and political allegiance. The Taylor Nelson model, based on an annual survey since 1973, reflects British people's changing values, motivations, hopes and beliefs. It points to an extraordinary growth in green values. Faith in technology as a means for providing a culturally rich and fulfilling future is declining, for example. Anti-materialism and environmental concerns are growing. (See Fig. 1)

But the survey and statistics which flow from the model also provide a portrait of deeper structural changes taking place in British society. The population, McNulty argues, is divided into three main groups: *Sustenance-Driven* people, whose main aim in life is simply to get by; *Outer-Directeds*, who spend most of their lives seeking financial success and social status; and, since the 1960s, the *Inner-Directeds*, who believe in personal development and autonomy. They act and think for themselves and many tend towards adopting low consumption life-styles.

McNulty considers the Inner-Directeds to be the most important emerging social group with the brightest green potential: about 36% of the British population now has some kind of Inner-Directed motivation, and the proportion is growing. Most other Western

172

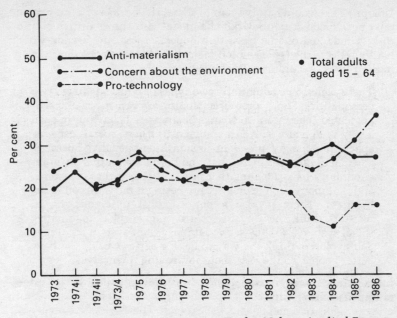

Source: *Taylor Nelson Applied Futures*

industrialized nations are moving in the same direction. But Inner-Directeds are by no means all Greens. Indeed, they are a pretty mixed bunch. Some are interested in caring for things and other people, while others are more interested in their own autonomy. The model reveals various sub-categories. Some are 'experimentalists' – pro-technology, autonomous, hedonistic and invariably un-green; others are 'social resisters', who may well get involved in politics, or the ecology and peace movements, but tend to be rather narrow, intolerant and moralistic about their beliefs. Finally, there are the 'self-explorers', who take an interest in similar political and social issues as the social resisters, but have broader horizons and a more holistic approach to life. Just to confuse things, they also value the vitality and autonomy of the experimentalists!

Politically, Inner-Directeds tend to the right. Before the 1987 election, most of them were split between the Conservatives and the Alliance, and in the end most voted for Mrs Thatcher. (Outer-Directeds are also mainly Tory; Sustenance-Drivens are pretty solidly

Labour.) This would hardly seem to signal the onrush of a 'fundamentally new social structure', but the model also shows British politics to be conducted on the basis of a hopelessly narrow agenda which hardly reflects the issues which many people care about most deeply in their lives. According to McNulty:

> There seem to be potentially two types of political Green, two personalities. Some, the self-explorers, are concerned and self-possessed. They want to change businesses' behaviour in such a way as to really 'solve the problem'. Others, social-resisters, appear to be angry and want to smash and penalize business, particularly big business. I have no hard data on this phenomenon, but I have a feeling that much of this anger is personal, and that many such people are projecting it outwards on to big business. There is also a philosophical difference. Social resisters think the way to get a better world is to improve social systems, so they seek to impose their system on others. Self-explorers think the way to have a better world is to have better people, so they set about improving themselves.

Emerging Inner-Directedness is not the only change in values taking place in Britain:

> It's a lot more complicated than just turning green, though that is a very significant element. The traditional 'working man' is going out of fashion. As he becomes more confident and affluent, he is adopting Outer-Directed values. The inequitable, rigid society which had a place for the unskilled labourer, and kept him in it, is disappearing rapidly. So the numbers of the Sustenance-Driven groups are declining as their members become more Outer-Directed. This explains the dramatic rise in consumer spending and the apparent increase in materialism in British society. As the numbers of the Sustenance-Driven group decline, so their traditional attitudes become more sharply defined. They are the survivors, the guardians of traditional working-class values. For instance, Arthur Scargill can still arouse a good many people with his old-fashioned 'us and them' trade unionism; but fewer than previously because a significant proportion of miners have become Outer-Directed. Yesterday's miner had 'nothing to lose but his chains'; increasingly, today's miner finds that he and his family have a car, house and annual holiday on the

Costa del Sol to lose. As their behaviour during the 1984 strike indicated, many miners have adopted new values.

McNulty calculates that about 4 million people now espouse green values (approximately the same number as the aggregated 'membership' of the Green Movement), or would be very likely to do so if made properly aware of them. She has also noted the 'phasing-in' of new and often radical ideas from the fringe of Inner-Directedness into the mainstream of society. Inner Directeds are trend-setters and confident consumers. Interest in new attitudes to health and food started some years back among some rather extreme Inner-Directeds: 'The health-food freaks, the brown rice and lentil brigade, veggies, joggers, organic-food-onlies, meditators and yoga practitioners. In time, as the very real benefits of these practices became clear, such activities became trendy. When the trendy phase passes, the new ideas are assimilated into the social fabric.'

An altogether more sceptical and less optimistic view of the growth of green principles comes from Bob Worcester, head of the opinion poll giants MORI. Worcester simply does not believe that a major green groundswell is taking place in Britain:

> It's almost non-existent. I know because I've been looking for it since the early 1970s, when I carried out studies for corporate clients like oil, aluminium and tin companies who were being hit by environment pressure groups for the first time. One day, Cadbury Schweppes rang us to say they had just had 600 of their own bottles dumped on their doorstep and wanted to know if they should take it seriously? We did a poll in about ten days and told them: 'Yes, take it seriously. There is a great deal of concern.'

That level of concern was true then and it's there now. But fifteen years on, he has become more cynical about such expressions of environmental concern, and sees little evidence of changing behaviour.

> People are only too willing to say that environmental concerns are really vital to them and their family. They're lovely people, the British: very accommodating and both willing and likely to say nice things and be agreeable. They *are* interested in these things: we know they watch environmental programmes on television; we know there is a thirst for more conservation information in the newspapers. Yet, when we get down to

175

whether it makes any practical differences in their lives or their politics, we find that it's a fairly low priority.

At most, he thinks greening may be affecting 10% of the population. 'The other 90% haven't noticed.'

There remains, he insists, a chasm of difference between worthy green words and even simple green deeds. The issue of lead in petrol offers a good example. A MORI poll in 1982 for the Campaign for Lead Free Air (CLEAR) provided what one would have thought was pretty conclusive evidence of public hostility to the use of lead in petrol: 75% of people questioned said lead was a health hazard; 71% thought it should be banned; and 72% said the government should pass a law to make all petrol in Britain lead-free, even if it made petrol a few pence per gallon more expensive. Yet, six years later, the oil companies have discovered a staggering and almost total lack of interest among the British public regarding lead-free petrol: 'There is a gap between intent and behaviour and the behaviour is disappointing to say the least. The reason is that people think: "Of course, it would be a good thing if there was no lead in petrol and our children would all be healthier. But if I have to have my car adjusted to use it, find a petrol station that provides it and, God forbid, have to pay a penny more for it, even though I said I would, I guess I'd rather not."'

At least people in positions of influence have become more conscious of the potential power of the 'sleeping giant' of ecology and conservation: 'After all, 10% of the population is not an insignificant proportion.' But Worcester believes that a major shift towards greener life-styles and patterns of consumption can only be stimulated by self-interest.

The psychological motivation of the whole body politic is either fear or reward. If things are made socially acceptable and economically sensible, then the bulk of the British people will go along with them. Greens haven't played it like that. Much of the greening that goes on today depends on the degree to which you can successfully frighten people – about the disappearance of the rainforests and so on. But the danger is that this simply produces a feeling of resignation with which people perceive that there is no hope.

Class

Posy Simmonds has been observing and recording the greening of Britain for years without the aid of opinion polls, surveys or statistics. There is nothing scientific about her regular strip in Monday's 'Women's Page' in the *Guardian*. But her cartoons are witty, sophisticated and perceptive, and they capture the complexity and the contradictions of the greening process better than most. Her best-known characters, George and Wendy Weber, are the definitive middle-class armchair radicals: earnest, articulate, socially and ecologically concerned, well-informed about every progressive cause. They live in London and love the countryside. They were avantgarde, prototypical Greens, eating lentils and brown rice back in the 1960s, well before such foods became hippy clichés. They are also wracked with guilt because they know their life-styles don't quite fit their lofty affectations and aspirations.

Her cartoons are unusual for providing not only razor-sharp analyses of muddled, greenish middle-class aspirations and pretensions, but for being hugely affectionate portraits of real people with recognizable foibles. She describes herself as a middle-class green, but is worried that the greening of British society is still overwhelmingly middle-class in character and largely restricted to the South East of England. According to this view, greening seems to have the potential for the perpetuation of class system conflicts by new means, and leaves little room for green politics to play a healing role in the short term:

> When I first started doing these drawings in 1977, I thought I was only writing about people who lived in Hampstead. But from the letters I've received, I know those people now exist anywhere where there's a university, Habitat, Marks and Spencer, Laura Ashley and a good bookshop. They're definitely in places like Exeter, Bristol, Bath, Manchester, Durham, Edinburgh, Leeds and Newcastle, but not much in Liverpool, Blackpool or Glasgow. It still seems to be the rather shrill middle-class voices saying, 'Don't pick the flowers' or 'Gosh! Isn't that a falcon?' when they go to the country. It's quite different when you're actually in the countryside, especially

177

in the North where the shops are full of pretty awful food, tins and packets of white bread.

She considers middle-class bafflement over unhealthy working-class diets to be a form of condescension. In one of her cartoons, a woman witters on about the joys of cheap and healthy eating and imagines members of the working classes as medieval peasants queuing up at supermarket checkouts to pay for basketfuls of curly kale! 'It's not surprising that working-class people don't buy things that middle-class people say are "good for them". The kind of food you buy if you're poor is comforting on a different level. You want sugar and chips and something easy to shut the children up. Why on earth would you buy curly kale? Middle-class people don't have to eat kale. Whenever they feel a bit down, they can pop out and eat crème brulée and drink a spot of Rioja.'

She sees evidence of new patterns of consumption all around:

No one used to worry about wearing furs. Furs are still sold now, but people feel very defensive about wearing them. You sometimes hear them saying: 'It's my granny's.' That's all happened in a very short time. Not many of the people I write about would dare buy a Cuppa Soup. Or, if they did, they'd do it covertly. They'd be terribly ashamed if their friends knew they hadn't made a little broth. All that healthy living stuff is important, too. Being a fit, slim Flora man who goes jogging and doesn't die of a coronary is all part of a greenish way of life. It's still a form of conspicuous consumption focussed on the body, but if you're a thin, taut person twanging with energy instead of a great fat slob dripping with E-numbers, at least you're trying to be more at one with nature.

Most people you ask now only eat white meat. The poor old chicken still gets eaten because I suppose people identify less with chickens than with cows, lambs or little piglets. I remember making a roast and saying, 'What a beautiful joint!' and this friend of mine said, 'What's beautiful about a bit of carrion?' I still eat a bit of meat because my family like it, but I do feel a bit guilty about it. An awful lot of young people, especially girls, have become vegetarians just in the last few years. I'm not sure whether this is overtly feminist, but a lot of greening comes from women. They're usually the ones who care about health, and food and nurturing. They're the ones who tell stories to their children and have to answer all those difficult philosophical questions like 'What happens to bunnies when they die?'

But how much is the espousal of 'natural' furniture, medicine, food and clothing a response to mere fashion? And how much does it signify a genuine shift towards greener values? 'Some of it is fashionable, but most is genuine. Anyway, fashion doesn't grow out of nothing. We first heard that aerosols were bad seven or eight years ago. But now we know there really is a big hole in the ozone layer. People know things are getting worse and they're very worried. That's not fashion and it won't fade away.'

Attitudes to science and technology have changed drastically over the last thirty years. Faith has given way to fear:

In the 1950s, things were pretty dreary. Jelly with Bird's Custard was a real treat and, after rationing ended, Elizabeth David was writing about the joys of lemons. Processed foods were status symbols. Tinned peas were a luxury item at dinner parties. I remember there being tremendous optimism and faith in technology. Nylons and orlon were terribly chic, but no one mentioned they were dreadfully sweaty or that they were hot in the summer and cold in the winter. The petro-chemical industry had a field day.

In the 1960s, we had space-age fashion. Vinyl was modern and exciting. Everything was plastic. In the 1970s, everyone wanted to live like Italian peasants. Habitat sold Italian peasant floor tiles, Italian peasant kitchen chairs, crocks, earthenware and pine. People wanted to live like peasants because peasants were close to 'real things'. Nowadays, the idea of the countryside which people want is that of the squire. They want stuff which looks as if it's come out of a country house and has been in their terribly illustrious family for generations: green wellies, Barbours, Agas, labradors, flat caps, a houseful of butterfly nets, dotty aunts who press flowers in albums. They want to be like the royal family. There's a snobbish element about wanting very good food, as if you had your own free-range chickens running around outside your window and a lovely local baker round the corner making wonderful bread. The good life you buy into is very expensive and has upper-class connotations, but it's been given class and people aspire to it.

179

The issue of class which Posy Simmonds touched on is important in more ways than one. Despite endless discussion in recent years about the old social barriers being broken down, Britain remains one of the most class-ridden and class-obsessed societies in the world. Class is so deeply ingrained in our institutions, politics, literature and humour that people from other countries are still as baffled and amused by the grip it has on us as they ever were. Even if they have lived in Britain for decades, they remain woefully ill-equipped to understand the dynamics of a bewilderingly complex system of power and resentment, suspicion and aspiration that imbues all life from Yorkshire pit villages to the royal family. As Harold Evans, the former *Times* and *Sunday Times* editor who now lives and works in New York, observes:

> Class is the cholesterol in the British body politic. It's a very creative, talented and original country, but class slows every-thing up. Nothing in England can be discussed except in terms of class. I was looking through an article in an English magazine the other day, about who might succeed to some post or other, and all the people were defined in terms of class origins, whether they went to Eton or to grammar school. Nothing was said about their talents or energies or the people they are today. We're all prisoners of this. When I'm in England, I immediately know what milieu I'm in. It's different in the United States, and I find that very exhilarating.

It is hardly surprising, then, that greenery seems to have become irrevocably entangled in the barbed wire of class antagonism by being perceived as being overwhelmingly middle class. Greens are still viewed with suspicion and hostility on the left. Socialist attacks on modern environmentalism have tended to focus almost obsessively on the fact that a lot of green activists are middle-class. This attack sees the Green Movement as élitist and working to defend bourgeois privileges. Hans Magnus Enzensberger, author of *A Critique of Political Ecology*, rejects green claims that we are all in the same boat together as far as the future of 'Spaceship Earth' is concerned. This denies 'the difference between first class and steerage, between the bridge and the engine room'.[1] Greens, by contrast, object to the standard Marxist indifference to ecology and point out that it is usually the poor who suffer the worst effects of environmental degradation. They also argue that unless harsh environmental realities are taken into account, any socialist approach to building a fairer industrial society will be doomed to failure.

Marxist analysis has provided many useful insights into the structure of social and economic relationships. Sadly, it has also stigmatized 'the bourgeoisie' as the mortal enemy of the working class. The legacy of this is that many otherwise intelligent socialists have inherited a deep-rooted paranoia and prejudice on the subject. If their own background happens to be middle-class, they tie themselves in knots of guilt. If they have impeccable working-class credentials, they seem incapable of viewing middle-class people as anything other than agents of class interest.

As it happens, the stereotype of the typical environmental activist as a university-educated middle-class professional is pretty close to the truth. A survey of Friends of the Earth members in 1987, for example, found that the organization drew most of its support from prodigiously well-educated, middle-class professionals. The membership hardly represents a typical cross section of society. No fewer than 87% were found to work in senior managerial, administrative, professional, educational, technical or scientific occupations (more than double the national average). 15% were teachers or lecturers. Doctors, nurses, artists, architects, surveyors, engineers, film-makers and lawyers were also well represented. 70% of members had tertiary level education (compared with a national average of 8%). Conforming pretty closely to the famous self-mocking badge seen on CND demonstrations in the early 1980s ('Well-Meaning *Guardian* Readers Against The Bomb'), about half of them do indeed read the *Guardian* and the *Observer* (national averages 3% and 5% respectively).

This is an overwhelmingly middle-class bunch all right. But whether the Friends of the Earth survey (and other studies which point to a similar profile of environmental activists) demonstrates that Greens are members of the bourgeoisie, in the pejorative Marxist sense, is a different matter entirely. Rather a lot of middle-class people are unequivocally rejecting their chance to become rapacious capitalists. For every middle-class captain of industry and nuclear scientist, there are at least as many social workers and botanists. Even though they may have come from a similar social background, Greens' commitment to low-consumption, non-materialistic lifestyles, and their clear preference for jobs as teachers and artists rather than as sellers of advertising space or yuppies on the financial futures market, doesn't tie in too neatly with the role assigned to them in the Marxist demonology as oppressors of the working class. According to Robyn Eckersley, currently working on a PhD on green politics at the Centre for Environmental Studies in Hobart, Tasmania:

> There is much more in common between the interests of environmentalists and the interests of the workers in an environmentally hazardous industry than there is between environmentalists and the businessmen and financiers who own and control that industry. The élitist argument ought to be turned on its head. Rather than dismissing environmentalism by pointing to the relative affluence of its proponents, I would argue that the more one *can* afford to demonstrate a concern over environmental degradation, by choosing a less wasteful life-style and becoming actively involved in the environmental movement, then the more one *ought* to do so.

She argues that those on the left who are hostile to environmentalism because of its bourgeois character have missed the difference between *class background* and *class interest*: 'This has tended to add to, rather than dispel, ignorance and confusion as to whose interests are being advanced or damaged in the name of environmental reform.'

Harold Evans sees the notion that the working classes are not interested in the environment as an expression of arrogant contempt by middle-class leaders in the Labour Party:

> They have a vision of the working class as proles just waiting to be liberated. You see a similar attitude in the new breed in the Tory Party, the ones with a microchip on their shoulder. They all have a philistine contempt for the environmental movement and for anything they see as 'soft' or 'effete'. They underrate the appreciation which working-class people have for things of beauty and value – you don't actually have to like urban sprawl to be a Labour voter! They think that working-class people live in terraced houses in sooty Lancashire out of choice rather than lack of choice. If you actually live, as I did, in Lancashire in an area desecrated by urban blight, you might discover that you didn't like that kind of environment and squalor. My father and mother loved the countryside and hated to see it eaten up by urban sprawl. These are the people for whom they presume to speak.

Health and Medicine

The question of class also hangs overy the picture of alternative medicine, which is sometimes said, somewhat unfairly, to be the preserve of the middle class. The 1980s have witnessed an unprecedented explosion of interest in alternative medicine. Homeopathy, acupuncture, herbalism, osteopathy and other therapies which all used to be considered 'fringe' medicine are well on their way to becoming part of the lives of the majority. Studies differ as to the precise numbers of people affected by this phenomenon, but they clearly run into millions. The Research Council for Complementary Medicine estimates that 10% of all medical consultations in Britain now take place with alternative practitioners. Others have put the figure as high as a third of the entire population of Britain.[2] Patients have to be highly motivated to go to an alternative practitioner for, unlike the National Health Service, consultations are rarely free and can be expensive. In addition, millions of people are treating themselves according to holistic principles they have heard about – and perhaps sometimes only half understood – from friends, family, magazines, newspapers, TV and radio. Approximately 2,000 health food shops are making healthy profits selling organic foods, vitamins and herbal and homeopathic remedies.

But what lies behind the statistics testifying to the burgeoning interest in the holistic approach to health? There is considerable dissatisfaction with conventional medicine. Orthodox medicine has largely failed to help many patients who suffer from rheumatism, certain kinds of chronic pain, allergies and stress. At a deeper level, holistic principles represent a fundamental challenge to the reductionist view of disease assumed by modern science. Our conventional, science-based medicine tends to view the human body as a machine and offers technical fixes for every affliction. Doctors are trained to see sick people the way a mechanic views a defective car. As an overheating engine is blamed on a leaky radiator, so each illness is attributed to the malfunctioning of a single part or mechanism of the body. Increasing specialization exacerbates the problem. The most esteemed figures in the modern medical profession are the consultants who specialize in treating individual illnesses and parts of the body. This specialization leads some patients to suspect that their doctors are more interested in their disease than in themselves as people. Undoubtedly, one of the most appealing aspects of a visit to an alternative practitioner is that, in contrast to the average three-minute NHS consultation, they may actually devote half an hour listening to their patients. There has also been a growing realization that increased dependence on drugs and the advanced technology of modern medicine may themselves become causes of suffering and disease.

As the alternative, or 'complementary', practitioners have been telling an ever-larger and more receptive audience, there is more to becoming healthy than can be achieved by blitzing the body with chemicals or radical surgery. The aim of an holistic approach is to look at the patient as a whole person rather than as a collection of biological functions. Instead of employing drugs to counteract particular symptoms, holistic doctors take environmental, emotional and psychological factors into account. Thus, for example, while a conventional GP faced with a patient with eczema may prescribe a hydrocortisone cream to make the rash temporarily disappear, a holistic practitioner would look for the root causes of the disease or distress. The treatment is more likely to involve a recommendation to change diet or life-style than a prescription for a drug.

It is a relatively short step to progress from thinking about the body and spirit as a whole to consider the wider environment of which it is part. Among Britain's estimated 30,000 holistic practitioners there is ample evidence of the influence of such implicit linkage. In his book *Holistic Living*, Dr Patrick Pietroni, chairman of the British Holistic Medical Association (BHMA) and a leading figure of the movement, argues that living healthily means more than simply avoiding infections. He makes a clear connection between global environmental degradation and individual health and urges people to take an active interest in green issues specifically in order to feel better:

> As we sow, so we shall reap, and many of the concerns, distresses and epidemics affecting us at this stage of our progress are the direct result of the influence of the environment on us. Just as we need to increase our awareness of the interconnectedness between body, mind and spirit, so we need to understand how each of our actions, from smoking a cigarette to throwing a can of beer away, affects our fellow human beings, some of them many thousands of miles away, others our neighbours in our street . . . Looking after your own environment will help make you aware of the interconnec-

tedness and encourage the balance and harmony necessary for
your individual health.[3]

But how far are this philosophy and these values shared by patients
seeking holistic care? How much is the new passion for holistic
medicine simply a consumer desire for more effective medicine? Dr
Pietroni is cautious: 'Studies suggest there is a trend towards a more
"holistic" acceptance, but my own clinical experience suggests that
many people seek "alternative therapies" as if they were the new
"magic bullet".' But Dr George Lewith, a director of the Centre for
the Study of Complementary Medicine in Southampton and London,
offers a much more radical perspective:

> I don't think the shift towards alternative medicine is consum-
> erist, though that may be part of it. Patients come to us
> because they are unhappy with conventional management and
> fed up with the narrow approach of most GPs. It's not a
> question of fashion. A lot of very sensible, solid middle of the
> road middle- and working-class people are coming to us.
> They're well informed and ask a lot of very shrewd questions.
> They've tried everything and are seeing the disadvantages of
> conventional medicine. People are making a beeline for doc-
> tors with a broad range of skills and experience in complemen-
> tary medicine who are also trained in conventional medicine.
> The demand is growing astronomically.

The rapid growth and popularity of alternative medicine has raised
anxious and suspicious questioning in the medical profession. Are
the 'new' therapies (some of which, like acupuncture, actually predate
modern 'conventional' medicine by many centuries) effective? Are
they safe and properly regulated? Are the practitioners honest healers,
or quacks or charlatans? Part of the orthodox medical establishment
feels its position threatened and has reacted with hostility to the
challenge. In 1983, the most influential doctors' organization, the
British Medical Association (BMA) set up a committee to study
alternative therapies. The initiative for the study was provided not
from the BMA's own ranks but from the BMA's then President,
Prince Charles, a champion of holistic medicine who has done much
to make it popular.

Three years later, the committee delivered its exceptionally hostile
findings, acknowledging the 'interest now taken by all in what, but a
generation ago, was the preoccupation of the few', but launching a

ferocious attack on the usefulness and validity of therapies. The report declared there was no proof that alternative therapies could cure patients. Some were potentially dangerous. Acupuncture was said to be useful for stopping pain 'only in a small number of patients'. There was 'no rational basis' for the theory of homeopathy. Some herbal remedies could cause 'adverse reactions'. Many other therapies were also savagely dismissed. The eminent surgeons and academics who made up the committee said such therapies had 'little in common between them except that they pay little regard to the scientific principles of orthodox medicine, and indeed may contravene them'. It also advanced a quite different explanation for the sudden popularity of alternative medicines, claiming that orthodox medicine was the victim of its own success:

> Because of its remarkable success, orthodox medicine is faced with a hardly rational demand that it should provide instant cures for all diseases, a demand which no system of medicine could meet. There remain conditions for which no effective treatment is available, while in other cases the orthodox medical procedures are distressing ... Misunderstanding of the long-term and painstaking nature of medical research may lead some people to wrongly suspect that nothing is being done about diseases which are at present incurable.[4]

But the BMA report itself ran into serious trouble and was severely criticized for being prejudiced and limited in its approach. The BHMA condemned it as 'hostile and patronizing'. They were angry that the committee's membership had not included GPs or holistic practitioners. In its reply, the BHMA complained: 'Alternative practice is denounced by innuendo. It is criticized from premises which have a limited understanding of science. The possibilities for growth, change and understanding have been squandered to maintain the status quo.'[5] Several conventional doctors also attacked the BMA findings and the report had a rough ride in the Press. 'Well, they would say that, wouldn't they?' was Katharine Whitehorn's view in the *Observer*.[6] In the House of Commons, a backbench Tory MP, William Cash, suggested that the report had been motivated by more than a whiff of self-interest. It was, he said, negative, destructive and prejudiced. He described the BMA as a trade union with a closed shop attitude and said it had 'a vested interest in ensuring the position of its members, including their remuneration'.[7]

The handful of studies carried out among doctors make it clear that other voices in the medical profession are much friendlier to alternative medicine than the BMA. And there is no doubt that the trend towards holism will continue. In 1987 the Royal Society of Medicine (RSM), also at the urging of Prince Charles, organized a more positive investigation in the form of series of colloquia between complementary practitioners and doctors which highlighted the need for increased communication between the two sides. Despite fierce political in-fighting, the RSM report was expected to be considerably more favourable towards complementary medicine than the BMA one. Other straws in the wind also pointed to growing interest in and acceptance of complementary principles. In 1987, Exeter University launched the Centre for Complementary Health Studies, the first of its kind in the Western world, to carry out research into the main alternative therapies and provide a bridge between orthodox and complementary practitioners.

Prince Charles lent yet another helping hand by officially opening the NHS's first holistic general practice, the Marylebone Centre for Healing and Counselling, operating from the renovated crypt of a church near Paddington Station in London. Unlike thousands of other NHS group general practices, the Marylebone Centre offers acupuncture, massage, music and other stress management therapies and lays a greater than usual emphasis on encouraging patients to learn more about their own health.

On the ground, many doctors are also showing professional interest in holistic medicine. One survey of 200 GPs in Avon found that 59% of them referred patients to alternative practitioners, 16% practised a form of alternative medicine and 42% wanted further training in the subject.[8] An earlier study found 86 out of 100 young trainee general practitioners had a positive attitude to alternative medicine.[9]

What of the future? Dr Pietroni predicts further in-fighting in the profession: 'As the alternative practitioners achieve a greater recognition, there is bound to be a backlash. One can anticipate a more determined effort by the medical establishment to discredit these therapies. Several of them do need discrediting anyway.' But Dr Lewith sees a small and increasingly outdated medical establishment fighting a losing battle:

The big career specialists in London want to protect their private practices. They dominate the BMA and most of the policy statements that come through the media. The opposition comes from them, not from doctors in ordinary general

188

practice where there's a very constructive dialogue which is getting progressively better. The orchestrated PR ballyhoo gives the public the impression of great variance and radical difference in the profession. But this noise only comes from a tiny number of academics and private practitioners in the big London hospitals. Complementary medicine will go on growing because that's where the provision of care is needed. Among ordinary GPs the change is already taking place. The bureaucrats at the DHSS like the shift because it offers cheaper health care. This is a health revolution but it is also part of the process of moving away from technology, which is happening in many different disciplines. The lines are drawn slightly differently in each field. Medicine has always mirrored society. As society moves to a different view of technology, so will medicine. The structures will have to be reorganized but that's happening throughout our society.

CHAPTER NINE

Consuming Interests

The willingness of so many people to move towards new approaches to health has important parallels in other areas of our lives. Faced by an extremely depressing political scene in the wake of the 1987 General Election, many Greens have quite simply given up any hope of substantial change through the ordinary political process, at least for the next few years. Instead, they have been casting around for other ways in which to channel their energies. The arena of green consumerism and ethical investment appears to offer excellent opportunities. Green consumers are people who like to spend their money on products they see as healthy and ecologically benign. They aim to both change their own lives and persuade big business and industry to behave better towards the environment. Green consumers also include the green yuppies, or 'guppies', who eat expensive organic food and can be counted on in future to drive their Porsches with catalytic converters and lead-free petrol, as well as millions of potential green consumers from more humble income brackets.

The most successful green capitalist in Britain to date has been Anita Roddick, founder and managing director of Body Shop International PLC, the natural cosmetics company which she launched with her husband Gordon in March 1976 as a single shop in Brighton. The company now employs 3,000 around the world and has stores, many of them on franchise, in thirty-three countries. In 1985, Roddick was voted Businesswoman of the Year, and in 1987 the company was voted Business of the Year.

The Body Shop has earned a reputation for being one of the most environmentally sensitive businesses in the high street. Product packaging is minimal – perfumes, soaps, shampoos, lotions and other body preparations are sold in refillable plastic bottles in several sizes. The shops are also seen as places to educate customers, with details about ingredients on its products and environmental and healthy body books, leaflets, wall charts and window displays. The company devotes considerable resources to education for its own staff. Body Shop literature is printed on recycled paper. The company obtains its natural ingredients like aloe vera, jojoba, cocoa butter, peach kernel, orange, orchid and palm oils, elderflower, hawthorn and soapwort from as close as possible to its sources, which are mainly in the Third World. It refuses to stock products whose manufacture or testing involves cruelty to animals. Since the mid-1980s, it has funded its own homes and workshops in Bangladesh and among refugees in Tibet.

The contrast between Body Shop and the traditional, male-dominated cosmetics industry, based on aggressive selling and chemical perfumes with secret ingredients, could hardly be more striking. Most of the conventional industry, says Roddick, is run on the principle of making women feel dissatisfied with their bodies and then exploiting the insecurities which they themselves have instilled by selling fantasies in the form of highly packaged chemical confections.

There is an unmistakably ecological spirit about the Body Shop now. But it didn't start out that way:

> We didn't come into the business saying we're going to be environmentally sensitive and concerned. Business ideas don't work like that. I was simply in love with the idea of setting up a small shop and selling natural products. I was fascinated by the ingredients, which came from tropical areas. I had already spent a year visiting island communities. It was like an anthropological exercise. I was fascinated by the way people were using herbs, roots, plants on their bodies. Certain things cleansed, polished and protected the skin without having to be formulated into a cream or shampoo. They worked brilliantly and they had been doing so for more than 2,000 years. The environmental thing came out of other values. I had been involved in things like CND, Freedom From Hunger and Shelter, which were all about humanitarian issues. The question of why things in the environment were so screwed up never really occurred to me until I met the people affected.

But it is an uphill slog to provoke and inspire deeper, greener changes in attitudes even amongst Body Shop customers and staff, whose job involves receiving an ecological education. Taking the message to her competitors and the wider world is even harder:

> I am fighting indifference and inertia at every level and it's very difficult to find the trigger to get people excited about the environment. Unfortunately, the people who run most businesses don't care about the environment because they still

191

have the mentality of robber barons. As far as they're concerned, the top and bottom line of business is profit. It isn't. Life would be much easier if all I cared about was making money. But it wouldn't be as much fun. There's much more to my business than bloody moisturizing cream! I can never take a product like that seriously. But I do take very seriously the ingredients we use to make it and the responsibilities that come from the profits you get from selling it: it's a vehicle for getting things changed in our lives.

Roddick has little faith in either the ability or the will of big business to deliver significant environmental change: 'Things like the European Year of the Environment are a lot of whitewash. It's just a few large companies putting a little bit of their money into a PR exercise.' But she does believe in consumer power – 'real change can only come from the ground upwards' – and sees her shops as a force for educating consumers to expect and demand more ecologically benign products and more environmentally sensitive policies from other companies. For instance, 'Body Shop perfumes will carry ingredients' labels years before its rivals to persuade people they have a right to expect such information on *all* products. The language and concepts of "green consumerism" have already arrived. Change will be slow. But it *is* on its way.'

Another leading influence on the green consumer movement in Britain is the author and green activist John Elkington, whose small company SustainAbility was formed to promote green consumerist ideas. In May 1987, SustainAbility and the New Economics Foundation co-hosted a workshop on the green consumer in London which concluded that the time of the 'conscious consumers' had truly arrived, and that their numbers would grow rapidly if they were presented with the right products in a convenient, user-friendly way. A Green Consumer Week in September 1988 was devoted to the idea that it is possible to build a 'consortium of interests' to mobilize 'consumer power' to change present un-green patterns of consumption and promote ecologically-benign products.

In small but highly significant ways, consumer pressure on green issues has proved it can pay off; Friends of the Earth began to move into 'consumer-campaigning' in a big way in 1987. The threat of a boycott campaign was enough to persuade the eight largest aerosol manufacturers to phase out the use of CFCs as fast as possible, thus helping to protect the ozone layer. It prevailed on Coca-Cola to scrap plans to destroy 30,000 acres of tropical rainforest in Belize, and produced a *Good Wood Guide*, designed to encourage people to help save the rainforests by identifying products from sustainably managed forests. Elkington has taken these ideas a stage further by preparing a comprehensive directory with backing from the EEC, industry and the Department of the Environment, as well as a *Green Consumer Guide*.

However, capitalism itself continues to put Greens in a moral dilemma. If consumption is the name of the game, then at least let it be green. But how does that square with the basic green critique of the consumer-driven economy, in which success is measured by quantitative increases in production and consumption, regardless of its impact on the environment? Should we be promoting *any* form of consumerism when the gap between rich North and poor South is inexorably widening? It's a debate that has yet to break in the UK (too many Greens are still reluctant to grasp the nettle of how to win over the world without losing their soul), but Richard North argues that we should not be too hostile to the idea of green capitalism:

> I'm wholly in favour of clean, green consumption. The classic argument is whether we should campaign for fewer cars and more public transport, which was the great cry of the 1970s (and one which I wholly supported as I didn't have a car for years), or do we say, 'The car is here, so let us make it a small, quiet, clean thing?' I have deeply ambivalent attitudes about modern capitalism. In a successful country like Denmark, capitalism can be extremely benign – certainly better than communism. And it might well be market pressures that make the environment a pleasanter and greener place. In fact, I'm not sure that modern environmentalism isn't partly an *expression* of the marketplace. For instance, there is a tremendous demand for owls these days, in that people are prepared to campaign for them, support them with money, buy reserves for them. People are doing this stuff because they like owls and politicians sense this. The thing which 'deep Greens' hate most in all the world is the multinational corporation. But I find it pretty hard to hate multinational corporations because, even in their dealings in the Third World, they are often streets ahead of the small thrusting entrepreneur. For the time being at least, I am a bit romantic about the possibility of people's capitalism.

The Way We Eat

One of the most striking changes in our patterns of consumption has come in relation to the food we choose to eat. The mid- and late 1980s have witnessed an extraordinary and unprecedented increase in vegetarianism, consumption of organic produce and a desire for 'natural' and healthy foods. By no means the whole population is yet affected, but the speed and scale of change has been so rapid in the last few years that it seems we may be witnessing the first phase of a major revolution in our national eating patterns.

There are aspects of the rush towards 'natural' foods which should make us cautious about treating it as a wholly green phenomenon. Organic vegetables and other self-consciously healthy foods are usually expensive – in some cases, up to twice the price of their nitrate- and pesticide-drenched counterparts. Healthy, wholefood eating has also acquired snob value. Writing about the widespread revolt in favour of 'real food' against the kind of tasteless, mass-produced, processed junk foods which had become popular in the 1960s, *The Economist* sneeringly but probably quite accurately distinguished two aspects of the phenomenon:

> The revolt of the Tasties is kin to that of the Healthies, but distinct from it: you can want your daily bread to taste of bread, not preservatives, without wanting it next morning to taste of summer-ripened, natural, free-range mould. Tasties like wholemeal, but they like petits-fours too. They are happy with creamy, stroke-inducing sauces, happy to leave nouvelle cuisine for the birds and the Skinnies and the Aerobores ... The revolt will succeed because it has sound economic precedent. Consumers are doing with food what they did to Ford. The motor car used to be a hand-built, leather-lined Rolls. Then the American miracle of standardized mass production brought it within reach of any family – and those who profited most from the wealth thus created switched back to hand-built, leather-lined Rollses again. So it is with food: bite by bite, Western consumers are becoming rich enough to spurn the cardboard producers.[1]

There is no getting away from the fact that wholewheat pasta or goat's cheese is easier to find in bijou delicatessens in Hampstead than in Blackpool. Nevertheless, espousal of notions of naturalness by the rich in itself denotes a shift, however vague, towards greener values. And there is compelling evidence that the change in eating habits is neither restricted to the middle classes nor likely to be a short-lived phenomenon.

One of the most interesting features of the creation of greener attitudes among food retailers has been the way in which changes have been fuelled by grass-roots pressure and changing demands from a better educated public. Time and again, the food industry has been persuaded to alter its practices – or at least its image – to take account of perceptions of profound shifts in consumer attitudes to food. Alerted to the health hazards of chemical additives by books such as *E for Additives*, and a deluge of health-conscious broadcasting and articles in magazines and newspapers, people have become much better informed about healthier eating. The supermarket chains have been forced to respond. Four main companies we contacted – Waitrose, Tesco's, Sainsbury's and Safeways – said they had changed their policies after public demand and opinion polls indicated that customers were becoming increasingly worried about the health consequences of chemical additives in food. Each of these chains, which overwhelmingly set the tone for food retailing throughout the country, has produced leaflets and booklets for their customers about healthy eating and food labelling policy.

In January 1985, Tesco's, Britain's largest chain with 340 stores, launched a 'healthy eating initiative' after a Gallup poll showed people were concerned about healthy eating and the lack of adequate information on packets. The campaign included putting nutritional information on food, giving away more than 20 million free leaflets about fitness, health and food content. In 1987, the company reported increased sales of wholemeal bread (doubled over two years), pasta, rice and pulses (up 50%), fresh fruit, salad and vegetables (15–20% up in a year) and fruit juice (30%). They were also selling more sunflower margarine, skimmed milk and poultry. As a trial, organic fruit and vegetables had been introduced in only six stores. But more lines were to be introduced in more stores if the experiment succeeded.

Sainsbury's have started selling organic produce in twenty-six stores and promise to increase the range and availability of these foods soon. In addition, growing consumer concern about preservatives, additives and colouring persuaded the company to review its policy in the area. They found that many preservatives had already been removed. Now, says the company, natural herbs and spices have replaced artificial flavours, and artificial colouring has been replaced by counterparts which are either natural or 'nature identical' (i.e. laboratory-created chemical copies of the original). Sainsbury's has also improved its labelling and produced leaflets on healthy eating, vegetarian and vegan, milk- and egg-free foods.

Waitrose, who have also introduced organic foods and additive labelling, report substantially increased interest in fresh foods from fruit and vegetables to fish over the last five years. However, a spokesman for the company told us: 'Only a very small percentage of our customers are specifically interested in what have come to be called health foods, but most are pleased to be able to include them in their purchases from time to time.'

Safeways, the first of the big chains to sell organic produce, also offers free healthy eating leaflets and has improved its policy on additives. Requests by customers and organic farmers persuaded Safeways to introduce organics in a few stores in 1982. By the end of 1987, they were available in all 144 stores, with customers in the North of Britain apparently as eager for natural fruit and veg as those in London and the South East. 'We realized there was a tremendous market,' remembers the company's public affairs officer Tim Hunt. 'There's still a quite small range but demand outstrips our supply. We have to go abroad for a lot of our produce, but British farmers are beginning to realize there's a demand for organic foods and are producing more.' In 1987, organic food accounted for less than 5% of all the fruit and vegetables Safeways sold.

It's a situation that's going to improve in the future. People are becoming more aware of their environment and are telling us what they want, which is more of these products. A few years ago we would never have put recycled paper on our toilet-roll packs because there would have been resistance. Now people are pleased we're doing it. If people contact us, we respond. Sometimes just half a dozen letters is enough because the pure economic fact is that if we can't provide something, people will go somewhere else to shop. The exciting thing is that the customer now knows much more about what he or she is eating.

In June 1985, the company also promised to remove 'all unnecessary ingredients and contentious food additives believed to cause unpleasant reactions' or to replace them with natural additives 'when

196

this is possible' over a period of two or three years.[2] Hunt expects the trend to continue and expand.

Another barometer of the food revolution has been the spectacular growth of vegetarianism. In the 1960s and early 1970s, being a vegetarian was considered distinctly odd – hence the name of London's famous health food restaurant 'Cranks'. Now it is both respectable and commonplace. A Gallup survey commissioned by the Realeat company in March 1987 found 1.7 million pure vegetarians in Britain. That is only 3% of the total population. But the growth rates reflected in the study revealed a more striking picture: a rise of 11% on the previous year and 43% over 1984. Another 2 million people were eating fish but not meat, a rise of 16 per cent over 1986 and 89 per cent over three years. In addition, a third of the population claimed to be eating less meat. The move towards vegetarianism was happening most strongly in the South (79% up on 1984) and among women (twice as likely to be vegetarian than men), students (14%) and children (11%). The older the child, the more likely he or she is not to want to eat meat, and, it seems, children are deciding for themselves not to eat meat. The most commonly cited explanations for change were health (an aim cited more often in the South) and to save money (more in the North). Concern about factory farming methods and other forms of cruelty towards animals has also grown enormously in the last few years. Yet, curiously, the report makes no mention of the undoubtedly significant part which moral and ethical reasons play in persuading people not to eat meat.

Vegetarian restaurants have now sprung up all over the country to cater for the new tastes. And many restaurants which still serve meat now also offer vegetarian dishes. Salads have become a good deal more varied and appetizing than the old British apology for a salad (a slice of tomato and a few soggy lettuce leaves). Even the fast-food giants are getting in on the act. Since the early 1980s, Wimpy, with 400 restaurants around the country, had tried to cater for more health-conscious customers by using lower fat oils and introducing brown bread baps for their burgers. They had also gone out of their way to demonstrate corporate environmental concern by sponsoring groups like Richard Branson's anti-litter campaign UK 2000. Then the company hit on a more radical way of attracting green-minded consumers: the meatless burger. The 'spicy beanburger' (made of kidney beans, green peppers, onions, chillies, carrots and breadcrumbs and served with melted cheese and ketchup) was developed by

Wimpy's senior nutritionist, herself a vegetarian. After laboratory trials, the beanburger hit the streets in October 1986 for a trial run in six selected restaurants. From a green point of view, the company hadn't got it quite right because the new burger was fried in the same fat used for meat and fish. Nevertheless, within a few months it was selling prodigiously all over Britain, mostly to women. The beanburger became Wimpy's most successful new product in years.

Recycling

Recycling is also a growth area. Each year, household refuse amounts to 20 million tons, an average of half a ton of debris for every household in the country. With growing pressure on landfill sites, particularly in the south-east, the Government's efforts to exhort ordinary people to do more, while doing nothing of a practical, concrete kind themselves, are looking increasingly hypocritical.

Mike Newport helps run one of London's most imaginative recycling centres, the Jamestown Centre in Camden Town. He approaches his job with the zeal of a convert, enthusiastically and personally thanking every one of the growing army of people who come to the site to deposit their waste paper, cans, rags, motor oil and bottles. He spreads his message about the virtues of re-using materials in visits to local schools, community groups and libraries. Mike is what one might call a born-again recyclist.

His green conversion occurred in November 1984 on the road to Stonebridge Park in West London, when he started work as a weigh-bridge clerk in a GLC waste transfer station: 'Lorries would come in crammed full of rubbish and just drop their loads on the ground. I'd be standing there looking at about 300 tons of household waste in a huge pile. When you see stuff like that, you also see how much could have been saved because about half of it could have been used again. It was a shock, a real education. It's so daft, you wonder why it's ever been allowed to get that far.'

He believes the growing use of the centre reflects changing attitudes. About 2,000 people a month now take their rubbish there, compared with just 600 in 1986. The number is increasing all the time:

We get all sorts now. When we first started, we depended on people who were active in environmental groups. That was

198

preaching to the converted. But now we get members of the general public who aren't involved and hadn't thought about the issues before. To judge by the newspapers dumped in the centre's waste-paper skip, they include *Daily Express* and *Mirror* as well as *Guardian* and *Observer* readers. They come in cars, by bike or on foot. The groundswell is coming from ordinary people. It is growing, and eventually it will percolate up the system and influence the people at the top who will have to respond and begin to take a more constructive attitude to waste management. It's a way to make the environment a local issue even in an inner city area.

Although the growth of the centre has been impressive, he concedes it is still too small to do anything more than scratch the surface of the problem of a hugely wasteful society:

But it's a good starting point and it's a very good educational vehicle. Every individual who makes the effort to come here is saying something important. We try to recognize that and thank people for coming and talk to everyone who comes in. We've got a long way to go yet, but green politics has come of age and this is part of that. People have said, 'Enough's enough.' Little by little we are moving towards a wider consciousness.

Ethical Investment

If Green consumption on the Roddick/Elkington/North model ('shopping for a better world', as it has been dubbed) became widely adopted, the impact on society would be enormous. But it is still worth stressing that the underlying aim of this green consumerism is to *reform* rather than fundamentally restructure our patterns of consumption. Elkington's dependence on the SDP's ever-so-clever notion of 'green growth' makes it pretty clear that a break from modern capitalism and the present world economic system is not contemplated – and would indeed be most unwelcome.

Burgeoning interest in 'ethical investment' has been another striking manifestation of the desire of an increasingly large number of people to put their money where their morals are, without necessarily pulling the whole system down and starting again. Ethical investors

199

are individuals or institutions who take the trouble *not* to invest in businesses they see as either harmful or immoral. Traditionally, ethical investment has meant avoiding companies with links with South Africa, tobacco, alcohol or the arms trade. But, increasingly, company attitudes towards environmental questions are also playing a part in public perceptions of them as 'ethical' or 'unethical'.

Ethical investment has become big business. The Friends Provident society set the ball rolling in 1984 by setting up its Stewardship Fund in response to complaints that the company had forgotten its Quaker roots. To most people's surprise, the Fund proved to be a huge success, growing by 40% in its first three years, and demonstrating conclusively that money invested in ethical funds could do as well as money invested in conventional (and possibly morally tainted) funds. By early 1988, ten such ethical funds were in the field, competing for a fast growing market, and the major insurance companies were falling over themselves to jump on to the ethical bandwagon. None of these funds are *exclusively* and specifically green, though many have green components, such as opposition to animal experiments, for example.

People not only want to know their money is being used in a relatively 'clean' way, they also like to be more directly involved in the projects in which they're investing. Two of the best examples of organizations subscribing to this principle of 'saver sovereignty' are the Mercury Provident Society, which tries to fit the concerns and interests of potential investors with appropriate projects that come to the society in search of funds, and the Ecology Building Society, which gives loans only to ecologically acceptable and energy-efficient properties.

There is as yet little evidence that any company boycotted by ethical investors has suffered financially from their disdain – with the important exception of Barclays Bank, which was forced to pull out of South Africa by Anti-Apartheid's remorseless campaign. Moreover, there is room for considerable debate – and some cynicism – both about the criteria by which companies are categorized as 'ethical' or 'unethical', and about the ways in which the various funds decide who is good or bad. The charter for N.M. Schroder's Conscience Fund, launched in late 1987, emotively but imprecisely promised to avoid the 'Bad and the Ugly' and only to invest in the 'Good'. A 'validation panel', including David Bellamy as one of its members, and with plans for twice-yearly unit-holders' meetings, are to judge the fund's performance. There will certainly be plenty for the unit-holders to talk about. For example, by what criteria is the 'oppressiveness' of countries' régimes to be measured?

Heather Swailes of the Ethical Investment Research and Investment Service (EIRIS) believes that ethical investors fall into two main categories. Some simply want to avoid having a guilty conscience. Others believe their actions can help to change the world. 'People who think they really can change the world are kidding themselves,' she says. 'Even if every individual investor in the country went ethical, it's the big pension funds and organizations like the Church Commissioners who make the difference. If individuals can start pressurizing those funds, then they could get somewhere.' Meanwhile, she believes that most of the powerful established trust companies 'are in it purely for the money. They saw a jolly good bandwagon rolling and they're now meeting a demand. But the fact that they are doing it proves that ethical investment is not a flavour of the month. In the last three years it has really begun to take off. It's here to stay.'

EIRIS provides research and information to give prospective ethical investors information they need to make choices about which companies to avoid and which are 'safe' to support. There is plenty of room for apparent inconsistency: more than a few individuals who refuse to have anything to do with companies involved in animal experiments have no qualms about putting their money into arms manufacturing. EIRIS researchers do not make too many of their own subjective judgements. Instead, they compile and keep up to date records of the activities of Britain's 630 biggest companies (those listed on the *Financial Times* Share Index), and ask their clients to identify their own concerns on a 'check-list' of potentially offensive activities they want to avoid.

The service was set up in 1983 with grants from church organizations as well as Oxfam and the Rowntree Trust, but has now become successful and busy enough to be self-supporting. Charities, universities, local authorities and trade unions are among the users of the service, and increasingly large numbers of individual investors also approach EIRIS for advice. These range from 'ordinary, middle-of-the-road old ladies' and young professionals who have inherited money for the first time to high-powered City investors. According to Swailes:

> Not long ago, stockbrokers were telling anyone who wanted
> to invest ethically that they were mad. Now they're coming

to us for advice because a growing number of their clients are now asking to put their money into ethical companies. There are still plenty of City people who tut-tut about the whole idea, and are convinced that it's only wild-eyed lefties who want to invest ethically. But since the beginning of 1987, ethical investment has become completely respectable. People are now willing to take personal responsibility for where their money goes and to extend the moral judgements they make in other parts of their lives to their finances.

The concept is much further advanced in the United States. Ethical investment started there during the Vietnam War when churches led a move to boycott companies making napalm. These days it is normal for US pension funds, universities and state funds to include ethical considerations when making investment decisions. An estimated 10% of all the money passing through Wall Street now has some kind of ethical restraint upon it. No one knows precisely how many people or how much money is involved in Britain (though ethical funds account for a fraction of 1% of all investment on the London Stock Exchange) but few doubt that the growth of the last few years will be sustained.

Conceivably, it may also develop into a rather more dynamic, proactive understanding of wealth creation. A very much more radical idea of what green consumerism/ethical investment might amount to has come from Japan. The example of the Seikatsu Club Consumers' Co-operative demonstrates that it is possible to promote these developments not just as another part of the existing order, but as the foundation of a wholly different kind of society based on new patterns of economic and social relations.

The Club was formed by a Tokyo housewife in 1965 with the idea of exploiting the possibilities of bulk-buying to obtain cheaper food for its members. In the 1970s, a profound change took place, when it dramatically widened its horizons to take account of social issues and growing worries about the environment. For example, its members switched from buying synthetic detergents to using ecologically benign soap powders. When they discovered they couldn't buy additive-free milk anywhere in the conventional market, Seikatsu simply set up its own milk processing plant using produce from an organic dairy. The Club has now developed into a major institution, with half a million members, mostly women, throughout Japan. It also wields increasingly powerful financial muscle in the form of large investment funds and an annual turnover of about £160 million.

The basic unit of the Club, which is run according to Gramscian socialist principles, is the autonomous local group – or *han* – made up of up to a dozen families. These *han*s are linked to the local and regional branches which have full-time staff. Since its inception, the Club has moved a long way from concerning itself with basic material goods and services. It has also developed a distinct social ideology based on co-operative principles, a parallel political movement, and a focus for campaigns over environmental protection, women's rights, health, welfare and peace issues. In the 1970s, members tried to influence local politicians to see their point of view. When that failed, they stood for office themselves with the slogan 'political reform from the kitchen'. Their first successful candidate won office in 1979. There are now thirty-one club members in three regional prefectures.

Seikatsu's most intriguing and revolutionary innovation is the way it integrates the roles of the producer, consumer and investor. Club members seek a direct and personal relationship with their producers; for example, they visit their organic farmers to become acquainted with the production process, its problems and ecological impact. At harvest time, they help in the fields. The farmer has a guaranteed market, doesn't have to advertise and knows that everything he produces will be bought, so prices are held at a reasonable level. The buyers get better quality food than is available in the ordinary shops and, unlike most consumers in Western countries, they know precisely where this food comes from. Seikatsu now supports the entire organic movement in Japan, with farmers dealing directly with the *han*s. As its consumer power has grown, so have its ambitions as a movement for social change. In 1986, the Club launched a national campaign with the slogan: 'From Collective Buying to All of Life.'

Green economist Paul Ekins, who has studied the Seikatsu co-ops in detail, believes that Western Greens can learn much from the way such a grass-roots co-op organization with green principles can develop into a powerhouse for alternative economics and politics *in action*, rather than theory. He also argues that such ideologically-directed consumer power could acquire the visionary appeal of early socialism and become a green-print for profound change:

> Socialism is based on theories about the inherent collapse of capitalism and the importance of labour power. The capitalist economy couldn't function without it, and because labour

power could easily be organized in its communities and work-places, it gave the socialists power. But labour power is now finished as a political force because capitalism has been exceedingly successful in dispensing with labour through technology and in co-opting the remaining labour power that really matters. It's also been smart enough to pay just enough to ensure these people are not going to become revolutionaries – where does Thatcher get her support if not from the working classes? In the early years of this century, there was a struggle between two types of socialism: between those who wanted a genuinely socialist economy and those in the trade union movement who wanted to screw the capitalists out of what they could get and increase their wages. They won – and the Labour Party was the result. The Labour Movement capitulated to productivism, and decided to settle for a bigger share of the proceeds of capitalism. The remaining socialists who really wanted to organize the economy in a different sort of way were essentially bought off by the productivists.

Leftists are still calling for an alliance of social movements and labour power, but that's absolute eyewash. It simply won't happen. So, radicals and progressives need a different way of achieving power – and here is a form of *consumer power* which can be organized. The theoretical work has all been done. We know about intermediate technologies and environmental audits, about responsible consumerism, ethical investment and so on. We are more aware of the true costs of productivism. We also have access to more environmentally benign technologies, a greater impetus towards co-operative working, more people who want to be more autonomous at work, and more people who are simply better off. Consumer power, therefore, could add up to something to revitalize the economic vision of the early co-operatives and make that vision economically viable.

Ekins is at pains to distinguish this kind of 'green consumerism' from the older British forms of industrial co-operativism and the 'reactionary' consumer movement of the kind represented by *Which?* magazine:

> I don't see this as simply extending the work of existing movements, because its impulse is essentially green. It is not simply co-operation or consumerism but *building a different*

204

economy, which is what we have to do. The tools to do that are each person's individual spending power – it's the old idea that the pound in your pocket is a vote for the kind of society you live in. People need to get organized locally in order to make real advantages for themselves and also to contribute to a movement for social change – it is a politicized extension of the Tupperware idea! We have to be able to say to people: 'You know that our society leaves a lot to be desired. There are social problems, environmental problems and problems with the quality of goods we buy which affect our health. We can only sort this out if we get ourselves properly organized, because only then can we be sure that the goods we buy are contributing to an environmentally and socially sound way of life.'

CHAPTER TEN

Greens the World Over

The state of the Green Movement in other countries has always been a source of great interest to UK Greens. News from all corners of the world is lapped up with eager enthusiasm, and even the smallest ray of hope tends to be seized on as hard evidence of some international breakthrough. The truth, of course, is that green ideas and practice are filtering through in very different ways in different countries, and that one would have to write a book similar to this for *each* country in order to get the full picture. What follows, therefore, can only be a flying visit, to as many countries as possible, just to get a flavour of what is going on internationally.

The USA

Where better to start than the United States, where a multiplicity of organizations, networks, magazines and periodicals that may be defined as 'vaguely green' have flourished for many years. Much of the written work that has underpinned the development of worldwide green politics and philosophy has been done in the USA. The vision and wisdom of this collected body of work is astonishing, and there is quite clearly a higher level of general awareness about such issues there than in Europe. And yet, rather mysteriously, one cannot yet point to a Green Movement in the USA as coherent as that which is now flourishing in Europe.

One of the main reasons for this is the sheer scale of the operation. Just as in the UK, the range and diversity of the many different groups and individuals involved often militates against the likelihood of any umbrella organization securely establishing the common ground that exists between them. With a mixture of fairly conservative groups (such as the National Audubon Society and the Sierra Club), of progressives (such as Friends of the Earth and Greenpeace), of outright radicals (such as Earth First!) and the usual higgledy-piggledy collection of grass-roots groups doing their own thing out in the boondocks, the US Environment Movement (which is, of course, only part of the Green Movement there, just as it is here) is a classic example of the way such loosely defined movements are often to be found moving in many different directions at the same time.

The ever-green Murray Bookchin, Director of the Institute for Social Ecology in Vermont, and one of the leading proponents for green politics in the USA today, looks at the Green Movement in the following way:

> The Green Movement that is emerging in the United States represents, if not a culminating point, then a very high point in the development of previous movements. What I now detect is the coming together of the new left of the 1960s, the counter-culture, the mid-1960s social ecology movement, the 'Earth Day' environmentalists of the 1970s, the Feminist Movement, and the Anti-nuclear Movement, which was enormously influential at its height. Green at its best (though not at its worst!) represents a kind of re-focussing of some of the most dynamic elements in the US politics over the last twenty-five years. The only real question is the extent to which people identify as Green, with a capital G, and the extent to which they can now *organize* as Greens in a unique political movement.

This business of turning 'green' into 'Green' in the USA has preoccupied activists since the early 1980s. Charlene Spretnak and Fritjof Capra's *Green Politics* is primarily about the history and development of Die Grünen in Germany, but its final chapter still provides the best summary of the different directions that might be followed in the USA:

1 *A Green Network*. The purpose of such a network would be to link existing decentralized groups to make a more co-ordinated input into the political system. Such a network might well develop into a long-term political movement (and possibly even, in the longer term, into a separate Green Party), but the delicate decentralist sensibilities of many of those involved would seem to make this problematic.

2 *A Green Movement*. Charlene Spretnak sees this as a 'national membership organization that would formulate a coherent view and present proposals to the Democrats and Republicans at all levels'. It would not put up candidates of its own, but it would have its own political action committee and paid lobbyists.

207

3 *A Green Caucus*. Such a caucus, concentrating on electoral and legislative strategies, would provide 'green' candidates within both the Democrats and the Republicans. This may look unnecessarily unwieldly to a European, but there is often little option within the USA for moving the argument forward other than to operate within the established parties.

4 *A Green Party*. There are enormous financial, ideological and organizational problems associated with the establishment of any such Green Party in the USA, and the reluctance of most activists to get involved in setting one up may well be justified.

The situation at the moment can be relatively easily described: there are several Green Networks, but no one national membership movement and no (serious) separate Green party. What is more, in contrast to the UK, there has been relatively little infiltration of green ideas into either the Democrats or the Republicans, and they in turn have shown little inclination to co-opt those ideas. The 1988 Presidential Election will no doubt sharpen up whatever green tendencies are there, particularly amongst the Democratic aspirants. There are some who still see Jessie Jackson's 'Rainbow Coalition' as the best hope, even though Jackson has made very little effort to weave a green strand into his rainbow over the last four years.

As regards the emergence of a separate Green Party the experience of various third parties trying to operate within an electoral system which is, if anything, even less advantageous for minority politics than the UK system, has done little to undermine the prevailing wisdom that third parties in the USA are only for extremists, idealists and unwitting masochists. The Citizens' Party, which put up presidential candidates in both 1980 and 1984 on a vaguely green platform, and looked for a while as if it was going to assume the green mantle, has now faded away in all but a few states. However, it is important to point out that the absence of a national political party does not mean to say that there is no green electoral presence in the USA. Local Green Parties (such as in Maine, Newhaven, Vermont, Rhode Island, Lake Superior, Buffalo, North Carolina and several other places) have put up local candidates in various elections, and have gradually seen the green vote building up and up.

All these local parties are also part of the most important nationwide green network in the USA, the Committees of Correspondence, which was founded in August 1984. The Committees of Correspondence was the original name of the network set up by rebellious

Town Meetings to exchange views and co-ordinate the political action that led to the first American Revolution. The Committees stress ten key values: ecological wisdom; grass-roots democracy; personal and social responsibility; non-violence; decentralization; community-based economics; post-patriarchal values; respect for diversity; global responsibility; and sustainability. Their excellent newsletter (*Green Letter*) has done much to spread the word throughout America. The structure which they have developed (and the caution with which they have had to proceed!) reflects both the problem and the potential of organizing anything on a national basis in the USA. Local Committees (which go by a wide variety of names and are engaged in many different kinds of activities) co-ordinate their work through regional confederations, which in turn are co-ordinated on the national level by the Inter-regional Committee of regional delegates.

Brian Tokar's recently published book *The Green Alternative*, which provides the most accessible account to date of green politics within the USA, lays great emphasis on this whole question of decentralization:

> A major hope for Greens everywhere lies in the development of new community-based institutions and experiments in local democracy. Such efforts could begin to create a genuine counter-power to the influence of established institutions. If a few communities in the regions can begin mapping out a more independent course for themselves, they can help others discover how to break the web of dependencies that keep people believing in the present system.[1]

The structure of the Committees of Correspondence complements and sometimes overlaps with that of another important strand in the US Green Movement: the Bio-regionalists. Their emphasis is subtly different from that of many other Greens, as seen in this following statement of general principles agreed at their 1984 Congress:

> Bio-regionalism recognizes, nurtures, sustains and celebrates our local connections with land, plants and animals, rivers, lakes, oceans, the air, families, friends, neighbours, community, native traditions and local systems of production and trade.
>
> It is taking the time to learn the possibilities of place.
>
> It is a mindfulness of local environment, history and com-

209

munity aspirations that can lead to a future of safe and sustainable life.

It is reliance on well-understood and widely used sources of food, power and waste-disposal.

It is secure employment based on supplying a rich diversity of services within the community and prudent surpluses to other regions.

Bio-regionalism is working to satisfy basic needs through local control in schools, health centres and governments.

The Bio-regional Movement seeks to re-create a widely shared sense of regional identity founded upon a renewed critical awareness of and respect for the integrity of our natural ecological communities.

Security begins by acting responsibly at home. Welcome home!

One cannot help but observe that such a statement not only evades most of the nitty-gritty, predominantly urban problems which dominate politics today, but also entirely lacks the international awareness on which the future of green politics depends. Bio-regionalists clearly have very little in common with the abhorrent para-military antics of the many 'survivalist' groups that have sprung up in the USA, but *all* decentralized movements have to beware of the parochialized isolationism that lurks behind many a move to get back to the land. Holing up in the Ozarks is both a challenge and a privilege for a few – and as such something to be welcomed – but it is hardly a solution for the many.

None the less, bio-regionalism certainly appeals to a very powerful streak within the American character. Murray Bookchin explains:

What we are trying to do is to redeem certain aspects of the American Dream. There are, of course, several American Dreams: one is the John Wayne tradition of the cowboy going out to the West and the whole notion of pioneering individualism; another is the immigrant American dream, this being the land of opportunity where the streets are made of gold. But then there is a *third* American dream which is the oldest of the lot, dating back to Puritan times, which stresses community, decentralization, self-sufficiency, mutual aid and face-to-face democracy.

210

Re-interpreting the American Dream is likely to prove an important activity, not just for those still outside the Green Movement, but for those inside it. As we know all too well from our experiences in the UK, there is a thin line between the attractive notion of 'strength through diversity' and the unattractive reality of 'impotence through permanent dissension'. The first ever National Green Gathering ('Building the Green Movement') sponsored by the Committees of Correspondence and held in Amherst, Massachusetts, in July 1987, clearly teetered along that line in a sometimes perilous fashion!

This event has been widely accepted as one of the most important historical moments in the growth of the US Green Movement, a real coming of age from which much is expected to flow. An excellent report of the Gathering was written up by Mark Satin, editor of *New Options* (one of the longest-running, most reliable and entertaining green publications in the USA), which both underlined the significance of what was going on and highlighted some of the important areas of dissension: the 'political/spiritual' and the 'social ecology versus the deep ecology' divides (which are looked at in the next chapter); the degree to which US Greens oppose capitalism (i.e. either opposing it *absolutely* or opposing what is being done today in the name of capitalism); and finally, the 'movement/party split', which in reality is not so much a split (as most US Greens believe they have to learn to function as both a movement and, in time, a party), but rather a question of emphasis:

> Generally, the 'movement' side insisted that things should grow slowly and organically, taking plenty of time to work out appropriate modes of decision-making and an appropriate stance of political and organization work. The Committees of Correspondence are very definitely wedded to this approach – as witness its having spent three years unsuccessfully trying to come up with an appropriate decision-making process for itself, and feeling no great need to apologize.
>
> The 'party' side felt a much stronger sense of urgency – felt that the lessons we needed to learn had already been learned many times over. Jutta Ditfurth, spokesperson for the Executive Committee of Die Grünen, berated the participants because 'nothing will *happen* after this conference', and urged them to get their organizational act together.[2]

211

Most outside commentators are fairly confident that that is exactly what the Green Movement in America is in the process of doing. It is highly unlikely that they will follow the model of Die Grünen; one of the strongest themes to emerge from the first National Gathering was the need to stress their own home-grown traditions and history. And pragmatists have been quick to point out that the easiest way to condemn the whole Green Movement in America to total oblivion would be definitively to declare themselves to be aligned with the forces of the Left!

Germany

It is one thing for the US Greens to follow a different path from that of Die Grünen; it has proved quite another for most European Green Parties, the majority of which have been in thrall, ideologically or financially, to the world's largest, most dynamic and most successful Green Party. This is wholly understandable. From the time they first arrived on the international scene (in the 1979 European Parliamentary elections), Die Grünen have seized hold of the imagination of all those even remotely interested in green matters. They have been a beacon of hope to which many people have turned over the last few years, and have done more than any other organization to establish green politics as a serious and credible alternative to contemporary mainstream politics by integrating an extraordinary diversity of anti-nuclear, feminist, environmental and popular protest movements into a more or less unified party. Their efforts to make democracy work at the grass roots make most other parties look quite undemocratic.

It is therefore not the 'done thing' to criticize Die Grünen too openly, and it is probably no less than blasphemy to suggest that it is high time Greens in other countries stopped genuflecting before them and began to see them for what they really are. Die Grünen do *not* constitute the only model for the development of green politics; they have in many important respects made an appalling mess of things in their own country; and their contribution to the international scene has been almost wholly negative. Their readiness to air differences in public *may* ultimately prove to be a source of strength rather than weakness, but for the time being their schismatic tendencies have reached a new pitch of ferocity. Between the time of writing this book and the time of publication, Die Grünen could quite possibly have split.

212

This may all sound rather dramatic, but it has become an inevitable aspect of green politics in Germany that everything should be done in the most theatrical way possible. Histrionics are absolutely *de rigueur* at Die Grünen conferences. The natural consequence of this has been to emphasize the role of certain high-profile individuals, and often to reduce more constructive internal debate to wholly destructive personal rivalry and hatred. 'The personal is political' is one of the favourite clichés of Die Grünen, yet there is not a single Green Party in Europe that more comprehensively fails to live up to such an aspiration in their lack of respect and concern for each other.

Behind the personalities there is an intensely serious debate about the heart and soul of green politics: to what extent is it possible for Greens to co-operate with the existing system without compromising their basic principles? The debate is crudely but conveniently conveyed through the by now familiar dichotomy between the 'realos' and the 'fundis'. The realos (which is short for 'realists', or 'radical reformers' as some of them prefer to be called) have accepted the need to form coalitions with the SPD at both regional and national level, on the predictable but respectable grounds that politics is indeed the art of the possible. Some of them have also begun to question the party's policy commitments to withdraw from NATO and to close down all nuclear reactors *instantly. All* of them have lost sympathy with those Greens who have actively promoted dialogue with various terrorist groups, and with those who have failed to condemn all violence, even when used as a tactic in the fight against the industrial state.

The 'fundis' (short for 'fundamentalists') are opposed to any coalitions, believe that green politics is essentially an extra-parliamentary process geared to undermining the existing order, and consider any compromise with those fundamental principles to be something akin to 'cleaning the dragon's teeth and wiping away its excrement', in Rudolf Bahro's memorable phrase. Most 'fundis' are either Marxist Greens or rather milder green socialists. Some are 'spiritual fundamentalists'. Bahro himself, who resigned from the Green Party in 1986, remains a spiritual fundamentalist of the deepest green hue, and now has little time for the shenanigans of his erstwhile colleagues.

The 'realos versus the fundis' is of course the same sort of debate, writ much larger, as that between the reformist environmentalists/

green capitalists and the radical/deep Greens in this country. The difference is that in Germany they have power; in the UK we do not. It is made worse for Die Grünen in that the majority of MPs are basically of the realo persuasion (in the full knowledge that various opinion polls have indicated as many as 90% of Die Grünen supporters to be in favour of building coalitions with the SPD), whilst the Party Executive is predominantly fundamentalist in its orientation.

Weaving in and out of that particular dividing line are several others, the most important of which is the Green-Green versus the Red-Green debate. The early history of Die Grünen has ensured that many leftists and Marxists were deeply involved in the party right from the start; the universally recognized slogan about the Greens being 'neither right nor left, but ahead' has long since become irrelevant to the way in which the party projects itself within Germany. The Red-Greens are particularly strong in Hamburg (where one of their spokespersons, Thomas Ebermann, openly describes himself as a communist), and anyone who is not of their persuasion is automatically dismissed as being reactionary and right-wing – precisely the kind of facile sloganeering which green politics initially aspired to avoid.

It is hard to estimate just how much all this internecine strife affects the party's fortunes. Voters seem to have accepted the inherent urge to fight amongst themselves as part of Die Grünen's slow process of outgrowing a belligerent adolescence, and the vote they receive rarely reflects dissatisfaction on that score. At the last Election (and it is important to remember that their vote went up from 5.6%, with twenty-seven MPs, in 1983 to 8.3%, with forty-two MPs, more than half of them women, in 1987), both the SPD and the CDU attacked Die Grünen so forcefully as to render any internal differences all but irrelevant. Here is an example from a typical CDU Election advertisement:

THE SPD INTENDS TO MAKE COMMON CAUSE WITH THESE PEOPLE: the Greens call themselves the Party of Life. They are not.

1 The Greens want to replace nuclear power by coal-powered stations immediately, i.e. to increase air pollution by 1.4 billion tonnes. That is a death sentence for our forests.

2 The Greens want to legalize drug-taking. Thus hundreds of thousands of young people will be led to ruin and destroyed physically and mentally at an early age.

3 The Greens defame our police as a 'civil war army', and want to do away with the police force. Breach of the peace will no longer be punishable. Anarchists and radicals will rampage through our streets plundering and destroying.

4 The Greens believe imprisonment is inhumane and want to abolish prisons. Murderers, sex offenders etc. will then walk around in freedom.

5 The Greens intend to legalize all abortions prior to birth. That is absolutely inhuman.

6 The Greens did not demonstrate against the Soviet Union over Chernobyl, which shows they are not interested in life so much as in crippling our energy supplies.

[Etc., etc.]

The SPD's propaganda was slightly more sophisticated. They are still under a lot of pressure from the Greens, and simply cannot decide whether to treat them as a legitimate (and lasting) political force in their own right, or simply as lapsed SPD voters to be wooed back into the fold. It is as difficult for the SPD to make coalitions with the Greens as it is for the Greens to make coalitions with them; the first Red/Green coalition in Hesse (heartland of the realos) between October 1985 and February 1987 was always strained, and the SPD knew that they were pushing Joschka Fischer (the Greens' Environment Minister in the coalition) and his colleagues too far when they insisted in pressing ahead with the operation of a nuclear fuels factory in Hesse. The green vote went up in the Election which was held immediately after the coalition collapsed, but the SPD's vote fell dramatically, and the CDU/FDP came to power as a direct consequence of this. In Hamburg (heartland of the fundis), the SPD had better luck: when the Greens refused to form a coalition with them, they promptly turned to the FDP as coalition partners.

The future of Die Grünen is very dependent on what the SPD eventually decides to do about them. At the moment the line is that they will not co-operate with them at the national level on any terms. Such categorical statements conceal the extent of the SPD's own vulnerability, which the Greens are sadly unable to exploit on account of their own internal weaknesses. Awareness of this has at long last been reflected in moves currently afoot to end the internal wars. A group of 'neutralos', including as many as twenty of the forty-four MPs, and backed by increasingly strong grass-roots support, have simply declared: 'We are not available for a split.' Their case is a simple one: realos and fundis should easily be able to co-exist and learn to complement rather than seek to conquer one another.

Equally, Die Grünen may genuinely succeed in building a synthesis of Reds and Greens. Writing in the *New Internationalist* in May 1987, Diana Johnston explained the attraction of this to leftist movements elsewhere:

> The unique success of Die Grünen stems from its unique origins: it's the product of an unexpected mating between single issue Greens and militant remnants of the old Left. It is this cross-breeding between cultures that usually refuse to have anything to do with each other that has endowed Die Grünen with exceptional vigour. Greens need the influence of the Left to keep them aware of the social dimension.[3]

Possibly, but such sweet synthesis may not necessarily be the outcome. There has always been a school of thought which sees the long arm of the Marxist Left deeply and *explicitly* at work in Germany to undermine and eventually destroy Die Grünen, and the evidence for that proposition builds day by day. Whether the Green-Greens have enough determination and organizational ability to overcome that malign force is questionable.

And that in turn means that the outlook for the international Green Movement is not as rosy as it might be. One can forgive Die Grünen almost anything (after all, power was just dumped in their laps before they had even begun to work out how to use it), but not the way in which they have either ignored the development of green politics in other countries, or deliberately sought to subvert it with their own hidden agenda.

The two international bodies best placed to co-ordinate and promote green politics in Europe are the Green Alternative European Link (GRAEL), the loose coalition of green, vaguely green and not even remotely green MEPs in the European Parliament, and the European Green Co-ordination, which is now ten years old and on which Green Parties from eleven different countries are represented. Die Grünen have comprehensively messed up both from the word go, and with one or two notable individual exceptions (such as Petra Kelly, who has tirelessly taken the green message to hundreds of international audiences, with or without the permission of the party autocrats), they have hardly bothered to conceal their contempt for other Green Parties. The GRAEL can only be described as a joke. Of the seven MEPs from Germany who make up the largest group in this fraction, only three were actually party members. By virtue of being MEPs, they have a lot of money and a lot of influence, though very little power. Again, with one or two honourable exceptions (such as Jacob von Uexkull, the founder of the Right Livelihood Foundation), they have spent most of the last four years bickering among themselves, making feeble stabs at green politics.

As far as the European Green Co-ordination is concerned, Die Grünen finally deigned to join it in 1987, without making any conditions. Up until then, they had argued strenuously that the Green Co-ordination would have to broaden out to include representatives of various leftist and alternative parties. They nearly destroyed the Co-ordination in 1984 and 1985 by pressing the candidature of a motley coalition of parties in Holland (called the Green Progressive Accord and made up of the Radical Party, the Pacifist Socialist Party and the Communist Party!) in preference to the small (and admittedly very weedy, albeit genuinely green) Green Party. Since then, they have meddled assiduously in the affairs of Green Parties in France, Portugal, Austria, Luxembourg, Spain and who knows elsewhere – and the outcome of their meddling has rarely been positive.

Little wonder, then, that at the Third International Green Congress in Sweden in August 1987, Paul Staes, a Green MEP from Belgium, made a swingeing attack on 'the cultural imperialism and ideological colonialism' of Die Grünen. Sad though it is to have to say it, the Executive Committee of Die Grünen has bullied, brow-beaten and used its muscle against anyone who dares for a moment to question its automatic right to determine the future of green politics throughout Europe. Frankly, the less one knows about this side of Die Grünen, the easier it is to keep that beacon of hope burning brightly for the future.

Western Europe

Hope there is aplenty in the rest of Europe. There are now seven national parliaments with Green MPs. In June 1987, 'green list' candidates in Italy swept to an amazing election triumph, gaining thirteen deputies in the Italian Parliament and one senator with just 2.5% of the vote. The lists were cobbled together by various environmental groups such as Friends of the Earth and the World Wide Fund for Nature (who are both a great deal more progressive and imaginative than in some other parts of the world!) and made hay by

217

concentrating on nuclear power, beach pollution and many other environmental issues which have only recently begun to worry Italians. They did not even have time to constitute themselves as a proper party before the election. The Communists and the Radicals all tried to outflank them by putting well-known environmentalists on their own lists, but to no avail: the Italian Greens were in on their first outing.

Shortly after that, the Swiss voters moved in the same direction, electing nine Green representatives to the Lower House of the Swiss Federal Parliament – though this was actually fewer than had been predicted in the polls. The Swiss model of green politics is just as interesting as anything going on in Germany, but a great deal less histrionic, as is their way, and thus of little interest to the mass media. They even claim the first Green MP ever, Daniel Brelaz, back in 1979. The movement really got under way in the early 1970s, with most activity taking place at the level of the twenty-three cantons, though the Green Party itself was founded in 1983 as a federation of all the different cantonal parties to agree a common national programme. The Greens are well represented in many of the cantons (with twenty-two seats in Zurich and eleven out of eighty seats in Geneva), and have forced the four main parties furiously to green themselves over the last two or three years.

These two relative new-comers add great weight to the work already being done by the most tried and tested of all European Green Parties, Ecolo (French-speaking) and Agalev (Flemish-speaking) in Belgium. Although the appalling linguistic problems in Belgium ensure that there have to be two separate parties, they do work very closely together, not least on radical proposals to resolve their complex linguistic problems. From 1981 onwards, they have both been represented in the upper and lower Houses of Parliament, and in the 1987 Election Agalev won six seats in the Lower House, and five seats in the Upper House, whilst Ecolo took three in each.

But all is not as well here as it should be. Ecolo has been riven by appalling internal strife on whether they should become a 'professional' party (which they did not much want) or remain enthusiastic grass-rooting amateurs (which they did), as a result of which they promptly lost much of their support. Activists acknowledge they simply could not cope with the success they had gained so quickly, but well-meaning amateurs are something of a luxury for Green Parties wherever they may be.

In Austria, the internal debate is just as lively, but much more complicated. As is so often the case, the Green Party there achieved success almost despite itself. Before the November 1986 General Election, there were at least three separate Green Parties, each competing against the others, with the far-left Greens egged on enthusiastically by Die Grünen in Germany. When their joint presidential candidate, Freda Meissner-Blau, won more than 5% in the 1986 Presidential Election (at which the notorious Kurt Waldheim was elected), they suddenly realized that people thought rather more of them than they did themselves. With commendable promptitude, they settled their differences to establish a joint front for the General Election. They proceeded to win 4.8% of the vote, and ended up with eight MPs.

Sara Parkin, International Secretary of the UK Greens and probably the best-informed person anywhere in Europe on the state of the Green Movement in all these different countries (her book *Green Parties* is to be published in autumn 1988), points out that it is really hardly surprising that most UK Greens are a little down in the dumps, looking at those results:

> If anyone doubts that it is only the lack of proportional representation that keeps the Green Party from being elected to Parliament in this country, then just take a look at what has happened in Germany, Italy, Switzerland, Belgium and Austria. However, the electoral disadvantage for Greens in the UK may eventually be compensated for by not having to go through a rather messy adolescence in public. Though we may not win many votes, we are considered to be out in front intellectually by many of our European colleagues, who have not even begun to ask themselves the thorniest of all questions: Where exactly is the natural constituency for the Greens beyond that 5–10% protest vote?

Green Parties are also represented in Finland (with four MPs, who are hoping to organize themselves into an official party in the near future!) and Luxembourg (with two MPs). There are also extremely good prospects of success in Sweden, where Miljopartiet has high hopes of crossing the 4% threshold in the September 1988 election after a steady build-up in their support at the local level. It is interesting to note that their fortunes were greatly enhanced when one of the major polling organizations suddenly started referring to Miljopartiet by name, rather than lumping them in with all the 'others'.

219

This round-up has necessarily concentrated on political parties, but in each of the countries referred to one would expect to find the same sort of diversity of groups and organizations as in the UK – if fewer in number. These organizations sometimes have a major bearing on electoral politics, directly or indirectly, as has happened with startling effect in Iceland. Iceland is the only country in the world where a women's organization has succeeded in gaining significant representation in a national parliament: the Kvennalistinn, or Women's Alliance, was founded in 1983, gained 5.2% of the vote in the General Election that year, and then nearly doubled their vote in the 1987 election to 10.1%. Although the word 'green' is not used once in their programme, it still reads just about as green as green can be.

So much for the successes. To balance these, there are no immediate prospects of success in Holland, where the Green Movement is riven by personality disputes as several small fish in several small ponds defend their tiny percentages (you only need 0.7% of the vote in Holland to get somebody elected!) rather than getting together to break the system wide open. Nor in Spain, where Los Verdes and Los Verdes Alternativos play out a rather different but equally sad game; nor in Portugal, despite the presence of two MPs who call themselves 'green' (but were elected on the Communist Party list), a Democratic Green Group which has the blessing of Die Grünen (always a worrying sign), and an anarchistically inclined Monarchist Party (which is apparently as green as anything else on offer at the moment).

Nor, lastly, in France, which remains a matter of complete bafflement to the whole European Green Movement. A profound streak of 1960s eco-fatalism, coupled with a predilection for sitting around in Gauloise-filled rooms using Marxist dialectics to discuss the theoretical possibilities of a green breakthrough in a post-structuralist world, cannot alone account for their all but invisible profile. Despite real success in the last two Presidential Elections (Brice Lalonde, the 1981 presidential candidate, who has in fact done as much to mess up green politics in France as he has to promote it, gained just over 1 million votes in that election, but then allowed the momentum of that wonderful success to slip slowly and sadly away), the French Green Movement has never managed to establish itself in the eyes of the French voter. This is all the more extraordinary in that all four major parties in France, right and left, are solidly in favour of both nuclear power and the French independent nuclear deterrent. Even Chernobyl made little immediate difference in France, although

Antoine Waechter, the 1988 presidential candidate, and a regional councillor for the Greens in Alsace, has at last begun to tap into a latent sense of anti-nuclear opposition that can no longer be ignored.

Eastern Europe

The difficulties faced by the Green Movement in France are really small beer compared to those of any budding Greens in Eastern Europe. To be a committed environmentalist in most Eastern European countries is, by definition, to be a subversive, not in the cosy kind of way of polite English subversives, but subversive as in ripe for beating and locking up. (In East Germany, for instance, several leading Greens and anti-nuclear activists were arrested in November 1987, and the Protestant Church, which for some time had been giving them shelter, particularly in East Berlin, was warned to steer clear of any further trouble.) Not only are conditions tougher, but most environmental problems are much more serious in Eastern Europe. In their anxiety to catch up with capitalism, they have simply not bothered with even the minimalist environmental controls and regulations that are now commonplace in Western Europe. The scale of devastation, particularly to their forests and rivers, beggars belief.

The harsh approach of the authorities in Eastern Europe has meant that the few Greens there are have had to adopt different tactics. More often than not, academic ecologists are in the forefront of any movement, and base their campaign on strictly scientific and economic critiques of what is happening. The Greens in Hungary (collectively known as the Blues, as in the Blue Danube!) have been involved for the last few years in a major campaign against a scheme to divert the Danube along the Hungarian/Czechoslovak border in order to build two hydro-electric power stations. The Danube Circle, made up largely of academics and professionals, has led the campaign and has succeeded in attracting widespread international attention, much to the embarrassment of the Hungarian Government. Although the Blues are downcast at their failure to stop the scheme, their efforts have done more to spread environmental awareness than they have realized; this would seem to be recognized even by the Hungarian Government, which appointed the first-ever East European Minister for the Environment in January 1988.

The same sort of pattern is going on in Bulgaria and Czechoslovakia. In Yugoslavia, however, it is very different. A burgeoning Green

Movement has emerged in the Republic of Slovenia, and has already notched up some very significant successes, such as forcing the central Government to abandon plans for a nuclear reactor on the Dalmatian coast – would that we had been so lucky at Sizewell. The centre of activity here is the *official* Organization of Slovenian Youth, which has basically been taken over by the Greens, thus making it very difficult for the Government to come down too heavily against them. They have also been mightily boosted by Chernobyl, which has had a deeper and more lasting impact on Eastern Europe than on some Western European countries.

That is certainly the case in Poland, where there is now a wide diversity of organizations getting increasingly involved in ecological issues. The 'Ecology Club' (a body largely made up of academics but with considerable grass-roots experience) is now a full member of Friends of the Earth International, and hosted the 1988 Friends of the Earth International Conference. They have been particularly involved in air pollution and acid rain campaigning; 40% of Poland's forests are simply not regenerating any more, and medieval towns like Cracow are literally falling to pieces.

Solidarity brought an end to censorship on ecological issues, and since 1981 there has been far more information available on a whole range of environmental issues than in most other Eastern European countries. The Ecology Club benefited enormously from its close links with Solidarity, as did Freedom and Peace, which is probably the most radical organization in Eastern Europe, with at least seven established groups and many thousands of supporters. Having started life as a group of people involved in human rights and conscientious objection, it is now able to make genuinely deep green links between social and ecological issues.

The Gorbachev era, with its ringing declarations of 'Glasnost' and 'Perestroika', has brought great hope to many environmentalists in Eastern European countries who see in the growing awareness of green issues a new opportunity for establishing international solidarity and thus breaking the East/West divide. Things are even beginning to move in the USSR itself, with hopeful signs of new groups springing up all over the place now that the political permafrost has begun to thaw out. In January 1988, the youth newspaper *Komsomolskaya Pravda* reported that construction of a nuclear power station at Krasnodar in the Caucasus had been brought to a halt as a direct result of public protest. Chernobyl has clearly set off a 'chain reaction'

222

in Russia itself, despite the official policy of pressing ahead with a massive expansion of the nuclear industry.[4]

The South

At the 1986 Friends of the Earth International Conference in Penang, members of Sahabat Alam (Friends of the Earth in Malaysia, or SAM for short) were quick to point out that our somewhat simplistic distinction between 'light green' (i.e. old-fashioned environmental reformism) and 'dark green' (i.e. the politics of radical, holistic transformation) was largely irrelevant as far as environmental Non-Governmental Organizations (NGOs) were concerned. They are dark green of necessity, in that 'the environment' is an almost meaningless concept in the South if it is abstracted from a broader social and political context. Transnational corporations, international trade relations and high technology are now the dominant forces shaping their environment, obliging many countries to use their best land for cash crops rather than for local food production, and to export their natural resources at prices which are clearly beneficial to the already rich.

It is for this reason that the prevailing Western model of environmental reformism means little to a group like SAM in Malaysia. In a country where the Prime Minister is calling for an increase in population from 17 to 50 million so as to create a market for its rapidly industrializing production process, in which the rainforests of peninsular Malaysia will have completely disappeared by 1990, and where opposition to the role of transnational agro-chemical companies is interpreted as a deeply subversive attack on the national interests of Malaysia itself, to be worrying one's head about 'an optimum balance of natural resource uses' is seen as something of a luxury.

SAM's position is now even more perilous after Prime Minister Mahathir imposed emergency legislation in October 1987, ostensibly to crack down on those parties stirring up racial unrest. Several leading environmentalists were swept up in the same net, which is pretty ironic, as SAM and its sister organization, the Consumers Association of Penang, are model examples of multi-racial policies in practice. Among those arrested was Harrison Ngau, SAM's representative in Sarawak, who had been helping to co-ordinate the blockade of logging camps in Sarawak by the Penan and other tribal people. Though Ngau has since been released (into 'house arrest'), some of

223

his colleagues are still in detention centres, and many Penan tribes-people will be tried on trumped-up charges towards the end of 1988. SAM's activities will be even more carefully controlled than before; those newspapers that have not now been shut down will be 'advised' not to cover any of their activities. It's not easy being green in countries such as Malaysia.

Non-violent struggle against the oppression of those who claim to be acting in the name of progress is the hallmark of NGOs throughout the Third World. There is no more inspiring example of this than the Chipko Movement of Northern India. Chipko's political and spiritual roots reach deep down into India's history and culture, but today's generation of 'tree-huggers' (which is what 'Chipko' actually means) first became involved in their non-violent techniques of resistance in 1973, when women villagers protested against the commercial exploitation of a stand of ash trees by embracing the trees to prevent them being felled.

Sunderlal Bahaguna takes up the story:

> The message was taken from village to village by footmarchers. The main demands were replacing the contract system of forest exploitation with forest labour co-operatives. A ban on felling of trees in certain sensitive areas was added later. The Government reacted with the traditional weapons of the establishment – fear and greed – and came forward to crush the movement. But the women boldly challenged the old slogan of forestry management – 'What do the forests bear? Resin, timber and foreign exchange' – by putting in its place, 'What do the forests bear? Soil, water and pure air, which are the basis of life.' They had to pay a hefty price for this in the shape of police repression and arrests. This continued for two years. But repression strengthens a non-violent movement. The two alternative weapons which Gandhi suggested – fearlessness against fear, and selflessness against greed – became more effective with continuous use during these struggles.[5]

They gradually won both the ecological argument and the campaign for a wholly different pattern of development in the Himalayan foothills. The protests in Uttar Pradesh achieved a major victory in 1986 with a fifteen-year ban on any green-felling in the Himalayan forests of that state. Since then, the movement has spread through all India.

Chipko's demands are simply stated:

1 All remaining natural forests should be preserved.

2 Water should be declared the main product of forests, besides oxygen and soil.

3 Monoculture forests should be converted into mixed forests, with priority being given to food, fodder, fuel, fertilizer and fibre trees for self-sufficiency in basic community needs.

4 Community control should be established over the forests so as to get the right balance between development and environment.

The Chipko Movement has had an enormous influence both within India itself (there are now literally hundreds of environmental organizations of one kind or another in India, and green awareness is much more widespread owing to the inspired work of people like Anil Agarwal, who is said to have the sympathetic ear of Rajiv Gandhi himself – though one would not actually know it from the way in which conventional 'development' policies are still so ardently advocated and practised throughout India) and within the wider international community. The award of the 1987 Alternative Nobel Prize to the Chipko Movement was widely acclaimed.

How long will it be before these non-violent Ghandian tactics become the only way left to put an end to the destruction of the world's forests? In Brazil, environmentalists face a massive uphill struggle as the forests of Amazonia are destroyed at the rate of 100,000 square kilometres every year, and all in the name of progress. The impassioned pleas of José Lutzenburger and other leading Greens make more impact internationally than they do on a hopelessly recalcitrant Brazilian Government. But again, Brazilian NGOs are growing in both numbers and influence, and have recently been joined in their struggles by a new Partido Verde, led by some of the urban guerrillas of the late 1960s.

Further north, in Central America, one of the real highpoints of green hopes for the future is to be found in Nicaragua.

Since the Sandanistas kicked out President Somoza from Nicaragua in 1979, a comprehensive programme of eco-development has been put in place which may well provide a model for the whole of that troubled region. Pioneered by the Nicaraguan Institute for Natural Resources and the Environment (IRENA), the Sandanistas have mounted massive reafforestation and soil rehabilitation schemes, developed one of the world's largest geo-thermal plants (producing 25% of the nation's electricity) using a series of wells buried deep in

225

a volcano on the shores of Lake Managua, diversified food production away from cash crops and cattle for export to the US hamburger market into self-sufficiency based on 'fruits, roots and tubers', co-ordinated a major integrated pest management project to reduce the use of pesticides on its cotton crops, and carried out a nationwide education programme to inform people about the links between environment and development in their country. As Lorenzo Cardenal, Director of the National Parks Association, puts it: 'Our revolution is recovering the link between the people and nature. Rational use of our material resources is a fundamental part of our new society. In Nicaragua, we consider that conservation, far from being in contradiction with development, plays a key role within it.'[6]

And all this in the face of massive pressure from the US-funded Contras, who have done their best at every turn to destroy successful environmental projects and impede moves towards such innovative forms of economic progress. You would think with the blood of the 40,000 people killed in this war since 1979 on his conscience, even President Reagan would have had enough; but until only recently he persisted in going back to Congress for more dollars to dole out more death year after year.

The Pacific

The United States, of course, considers Nicaragua to be in its own back yard, and therefore fair game. But it is not at all averse to throwing its extremely un-green weight around wheresoever it pleases, as witnessed by its efforts to bully and intimidate New Zealand into reversing its stand on nuclear weapons. In June 1987, after a long and successful campaign within New Zealand, the Labour Government confirmed its anti-nuclear stance by passing the Nuclear Free Zone Act. This legislation makes New Zealand and its territorial waters a Nuclear Free Zone, ensures that nuclear weapons shall not be stationed or deployed in New Zealand and bans foreign ships and aircraft unless the authorities are satisfied that no nuclear weapons are on board. (Nuclear-powered ships are included in this ban.)

The US Government had done everything in its power to put pressure on Prime Minister Lange, ensuring that they were kicked out of the ANZUS Defence Pact, and threatening very damaging trade sanctions. Despite this, the Labour party and the people of New Zealand (who were deeply angered by US tactics) stuck to their metaphorical guns and the Labour Government was resoundingly re-elected in August 1987. This has provided an enormous inspiration to peace movements all around the world.

But not, unfortunately, to Bob Hawke, Australia's Prime Minister and someone by whom green activists in Australia once set great store. Indeed, he got off to a good start when elected in March 1983 by taking the issue of the proposed Franklin Dam in Tasmania to the High Court, which decided that the Federal Government *could* overrule the Tasmanian state government as the whole area was covered under the World Heritage Convention. The Federal Government has also (so far) come down on the side of the 'greenies' in their defence of the remaining rainforests in Queensland and the huge Kakadu national park in the Northern Territories. But from the moment he reversed the Labour Party's policy on exporting uranium to France, Bob Hawke has been revealed in his true political colours as a good old-fashioned opportunist, and there are grave fears that he will yield to pressure from the mining industry to allow both exploration and development within the national parks.

His strategy of moving the Labour Party well to the right so as to lock out the conservative opposition has left an enormous vacuum in the political landscape, which augurs well for the Green Movement in Australia. Exactly how they fill it remains a matter of intense speculation. Despite a couple of excellent 'Getting Together' conferences in 1986 and 1987, Australian Greens are as diffuse and diverse as anywhere in the world. There are more than 1,000 environmental groups, with membership exceeding 500,000, some of which (such as the Wilderness Society, which led the extremely successful campaign to save the Franklin River from hydro-electric development) are extremely influential. Beyond them, there is as yet no nationally organized Green Party, although there are Green Parties in Brisbane and Sidney, and two Green Independents in Tasmania (the only state in Australia which has proportional representation, which gives them real hope of achieving a balance of power at the next State Election).

The Peace Movement is not as influential now as it once used to be, and has not succeeded in persuading Bob Hawke to curb the powers of his American allies and their nuclear empire. The Nuclear Disarmament Party (NDP) first erupted on to the scene in 1983, when the Peace Movement was at the height of its influence, but promptly fell to pieces after concerted infiltration from the Socialist Workers Party. The NDP still holds two seats in the Senate, and works closely there with the progressive and increasingly greenish Democratic Party, whom some now see as the best option for establishing a major green presence on the political scene.

For that and other reasons, many people remain sceptical about setting up a separate Green Party, and prefer a more decentralized, networking model. Even Bob Brown, one of the Tasmanian Independents and the leading light of the whole Australian Green Movement, is not sure that the time is yet ripe. A new organization was launched late in 1987, bringing together Bob Brown, the NDP and several disillusioned refugees from the Labour Party, but the name they have chosen, 'The Rainbow Alliance', hardly fills one with confidence; very poetic, but politically insubstantial.

Australia and New Zealand certainly have an important role to play helping peace and environmental organizations throughout the Pacific. For here too the USA has cast its evil shadow over the lives of thousands of Pacific Islanders. In 1947, the USA was entrusted with the administration of Micronesia, on behalf of the United Nations. Far from carrying out this trust, it has used the islands of Micronesia to test its nuclear weapons technology and expand its strategic military presence. From the time it exploded its first H-bomb, code-named Bravo, on the Island of Bikini, the suffering of the people of Rongelap and other Marshall Islanders has been appalling. Together with the French, who are hanging on with grim and bloody determination to their nuclear testing facilities on Muroroa, the USA is gradually turning a Pacific paradise into a nuclear hell-hole.

The Japanese were keen to get in on the act too, when they came up with a proposal in 1985 to dump their nuclear waste in the sea just off the Marianas Islands. Concerted international pressure put paid to that particular effort, but the Japanese continue to see the Pacific as a convenient back yard to 'externalize' the costs of their nuclear power programme. It therefore remains a matter of enormous international concern that the Green Movement in Japan has never been very strong. People there have only recently begun to wake up to some of the very considerable environmental costs that they will now have to pay for their phenomenal industrial progress. Worse still, Japan has ruthlessly plundered the Pacific Basin for the raw materials they needed to fuel their ongoing industrial revolution. For example, by importing vast quantities of raw logs from countries like Malaysia, Indonesia and the Philippines, it is the Japanese who have gained the real economic benefit from the processing of the logs, whilst leaving their trading partners to pick up the bill for the untold ecological devastation caused by so much indiscriminate logging.

Sustainable Development

The world economy abounds with similar examples of ecologically insane trading relationships. Such a concerted assault on people's life-support systems is literally unsustainable. This rather obvious conclusion was powerfully represented in *Our Common Future*, the official report of the World Commission on Environment Development set up by the United Nations General Assembly in 1983 under the Chairmanship of Mrs Brundtland, the Prime Minister of Norway. As we saw in Chapter 2, its specific brief was to assess the links between development policies and their impact on the environment, and to propose alternative patterns of development for the future.

The Brundtland Report is an important document, and were any of its conclusions and recommendations to be taken up in a big way, the world would be a much better place for it. The central notion of the report is 'sustainable development' – which has now become the latest in a series of trendy buzz-phrases. As it happens, the idea of sustainable development was first put on the map about twenty years ago by Barbara Ward, one of the founders of the International Institute for Environment and Development. Since its foundation in 1971, no organization has done more to get some genuinely radical and progressive thinking into the whole development debate, and they were significantly involved in the drafting of the Brundtland Report. But not significantly enough; ironically, the Brundtland Report does more than its fair share to devalue sustainability as a useful concept through its complete lack of intellectual rigour. On the one hand, it bewails the devastating impact of conventional, growth-driven development policies on the environment of many Third World countries. On the other, it advocates *accelerated* rates of growth in the world economy and especially in the Third World in order to relieve the poverty. It attempts to bridge this divide by piously hoping that the growth process will be appropriately tempered: 'it will have to change radically in terms of the *quality* of development'.

It was, apparently, deemed to be politically unacceptable from the start to criticize, let alone sacrifice, that sacred cow of *economic growth at all costs*. But such a cop-out still leaves *all* the hard questions to be asked. It may well be true that 'our most urgent task

229

today is to persuade nations of the need to return to multi-lateralism after a decade and a half of a standstill or even a deterioration in global co-operation'; but how does one square that with another equally compelling truth to be discerned between the lines of the Brundtland Report, that the developed world has little serious intention of sharing its wealth more equitably with those at the bottom of the pile?

The specific policy proposals at the end of the report are disturbingly thin and insubstantial. Even the wholly justifiable recommendations for significantly increased funding and institutional support for the United Nations Environment Programme are muted and curiously unenthusiastic. The truth is that the United Nations is not even remotely geared up to cope with the challenge of the Brundtland Report. The United Nations Development Programme is still committed to large-scale capital-intensive projects. The United Nations Environment Programme itself is desperately under-funded and almost completely marginalized in the constant process of power-broking that goes on all the time within the UN. And the Food and Agriculture Organization is not only hopelessly inefficient and bureaucratic, but represents a significant threat to the environment through its criminally irresponsible promotion of large-scale, chemical intensive cash cropping.

Non-Governmental Organizations have found it enormously difficult to establish any kind of toe-hold within the UN system, and have tended to concentrate their efforts on other multi-lateral agencies. Since the early 1980s the number one target has been the World Bank, and there are clear signs that this concerted pressure is now beginning to pay off. The pressure has been most intense in the United States, where a powerful combination of established politicians (concerned about the misuse of the US contribution to the World Bank) and extremely professional environmental organizations has ensured that even a body as remote, powerful and seemingly unaccountable as the World Bank has had to answer its critics in public.

The most impassioned criticism of all has come through the pages of the *Ecologist*, which has produced one devastating edition after another exposing the World Bank for what it really is: an insensitive and incompetent perpetrator of environmental destruction on an unprecedented scale. There are three main thrusts behind Teddy Goldsmith's (editor of the *Ecologist*) criticism: that the World Bank

230

is obsessed with major projects (such as large dams, road building and mega-industrial projects like the Grande Carajas project in Brazil which will transform an area the size of England and France combined into an industrial zone); that the World Bank is oblivious of the rights or interests of indigenous tribal peoples, and that their fine words in this area are just so many worthless lies; that the World Bank lends money only to projects that make money, and that this 'monetization' of raw materials and communities the world over has caused massive environmental degradation. In a letter to Barber Conable, the President of the World Bank, Goldsmith summed it up like this:

> The only way to avoid the terrible destruction caused by the development schemes that your Bank has so irresponsibly financed over the last forty years is simply to stop financing them. There is no alternative. It is not as if these schemes were needed to combat poverty or to improve the welfare of Third World peoples; they are not. Such projects only satisfy the short-term financial and political interests of a small group of bankers, bureaucrats, industrialists, engineers and politicians. The short-term interests and needs of such a group are totally incompatible with the long-term interests and needs of an increasingly impoverished humanity.[7]

This analysis is confirmed by the latest report to the Club of Rome, *The Barefoot Revolution*, by Bertrand Schneider, which was published in February 1988. The report is based on the results of surveys of ninety-three small-scale development projects, from which he concludes that today's new generation of NGOs, operating at the grass roots, are bringing hope to thousands of the world's poorest people in rural areas. It is this 'barefoot revolution' that is now radically changing the whole concept of development, and the report calls on governments and financial institutions to recognize this by funding NGOs as fully-fledged agents of appropriate, ecological and sustainable development.[8]

It may just be that even the World Bank has begun to get the message. Slowly, like a massive oil tanker, lost in the fog, leaking and heading for the rocks, the World Bank is beginning to turn – as a direct result of international pressure at the highest level. In January 1988, it created the new post of Director for Environment, thus reinforcing initiatives taken over preceding years to appoint a senior economist to advise on sustainable development and to create an environment department within each of the regional divisions. Such structural changes may just be mere window-dressing, and one has to remember that some of the old guard within the Bank would dearly love this 'imposed environmentalism' to fall flat on its face. But the Bank's determination to make loans conditional on promises of environmental protection has to be seen as a real step forward.

The 'internationalization' of environmental campaigns and protection measures has provided environmentalists with a whole new range of campaigning and lobbying opportunities. This has had a particular impact on organizations which are part of wider international networks, such as Greenpeace, the World Wide Fund for Nature and Friends of the Earth. Over the last few years, all of these organizations have gradually directed more and more resources into international work. If it is not possible to change Government policy by frontal assault, then one has to find ways of getting in behind it, and using the greater concern and awareness of other European countries or the wider international community to off-set the indifference and apathy of our own Government.

What is more, such an approach reflects the very nature of the ecological crisis we are now up against, which is overwhelmingly 'transboundary' rather than nation-specific. It is unlikely that we shall find any lasting solutions to today's environmental problems unless they are international. It may even be that the very gravity of these problems serves as the catalyst for a qualitatively different kind of international co-operation based on a much more profound perception of our responsibilities as citizens of Planet Earth. International consultant Norman Myers, who is one of the most forthright commentators on the state of the global environment, sees a new window of opportunity:

> What can nations do to meet the new challenges? Primarily, they can recognize that the many emergent forms of environmental impoverishment and resource degradation constitute a distinctive category of international problems, unlike anything in the past. To this extent, environmentalism helps to articulate the shared interests of nations: confrontation must give way to co-operation.[9]

Realization of the true nature of our environmental problems may, according to this highly optimistic outlook, thus open the way for a new era of internationalism.

CHAPTER ELEVEN
Spirits of the Earth

Though latter-day Greens go to enormous (and often quite dishonest) lengths to avoid the doom and gloom of their 1970s forebears, it is really very difficult to sit down and envisage a series of exclusively political strategies to save the world. Our current industrial way of life is too far gone. It is not a question of nearing the abyss; we daily look down into it, if we choose to open our eyes, and millions are already at the bottom of it. We cannot turn away from that dark side. Despite all the doughty campaigners out there hard at work, the hydra-headed monster of industrialism has, frankly, slipped its leash. We will not tame it again. It is not so much decapitation that we should be aiming at as the decommissioning of the entire monster.

It is therefore hardly surprising that so many people in the Green Movement have now begun to pay more and more attention to the spiritual dimension of what it is that makes us green. In *Breaking Through*, Walter and Dorothy Schwarz put it this way:

> Human-scale thinking must have spiritual content. If we are to move from partial, fragmented, compartmentalized living towards completeness and holistic living, we have to put back what our dominant industrial-materialist-scientific world view leaves out. That omitted area is what we mean by spiritual.
>
> In that sense, the spiritual is not identified with any actual religion, nor confined to religious sentiments; it includes the intuitive, non-measurable, the aesthetic, the caring and the loving. All these aspects of our consciousness have been progressively relegated in our world to the domain of the private, subjective, even secret world of the individual. The loss is immense, almost impossible to comprehend or define.[1]

1987 marked the tenth anniversary of Fritz Schumacher's death. As in so many other things, Schumacher led the way by synthesizing his political, economic and spiritual concerns. His chapter on Buddhist economics in *Small is Beautiful* remains one of the classics for budding Greens. His last book, *A Guide for the Perplexed*, was published posthumously, and is seen by many as an expression of the sense of homecoming which he felt after finally converting to Catholicism just before his death. Throughout his life Schumacher consistently appealed for some kind of 'metaphysical reconstruction', and it is partly a sign of his influence that few writers on green matters since then have failed to deal with the spiritual dimension in one way or another, if only, though rarely, to disparage and belittle the importance of this aspect of the Green Movement.

The Second International Green Congress in 1985 in Dover was opened by the Bishop of Lewes, Father Peter, with these uncompromising words: 'I must say this to you: you haven't got a hope in a million years of changing anything by political methods unless you concentrate on changing attitudes, changing thought-forms deep, deep down in society, or at least understanding the need to do this. Unless this is expressed, a political party is simply a wonderful sort of spanner which fits no bolt.'[2] Some commentators believe that the numbers of people giving greater prominence to their spiritual concerns is increasing rapidly, though there is little statistical or polling evidence to back that up. Indeed, almost all churches would still reluctantly acknowledge 'a gradual decline in the formal expression of faith'. Whatever the actual numbers involved, one can still discern today an enormous need for some kind of spiritual fulfilment and spiritual meaning, a need to look beyond some of the material confines within which most of our life is pitched. It is difficult to pin down, dogmatize that kind of feeling, try and classify it, try and pigeon-hole it by putting a bit of pretentious polysyllabic nomenclature to it, and it just blows away. Theologians don't like that, of course, but this kind of spiritual yearning is not so much an intellectual abstraction as a powerfully felt gut-feeling, a metaphorical throb of the heart.

Neil Evernden explains the relevance of this for environmentalists:

> For although they seldom recognize it, environmentalists are protesting not at the stripping of natural resources, but the stripping of earthly meaning. I have suggested elsewhere that environmentalism, like romanticism in a previous century, actually constitutes a defence of value. I am now asserting an even more fundamental role for environmentalism, namely the defence of meaning. We call people 'environmentalists' because they are moved to defend what we call the environ-

ment; but at the bottom, their action is actually a defence of the cosmos, not of scenery.[3]

Deep Ecology

It is precisely that kind of perception that so many environmentalists have been grafting on to their single issue campaigning or their political involvement, and that is now loosely referred to by many as 'Deep Ecology'. The term 'Deep Ecology' was coined by Arne Naess, a Norwegian philosopher, back in 1973, in an attempt to go beyond the factual level of ecology as a science to a deeper level of self-awareness and 'Earth wisdom'. Since then, a lot of work has been done developing the concept of Deep Ecology, particularly by Bill Devall and George Sessions in the USA and by Warwick Fox in Australia. In 1984 Naess and Sessions summarized the principles of Deep Ecology as follows:

1 The well-being and flourishing of non-human life on Earth have value in themselves, independent of the usefulness of the non-human world for human purposes.

2 Richness and diversity of life-forms contribute to the realization of these values and are also values in themselves.

3 Humans have no right to reduce this richness and diversity except to satisfy *vital* needs.

4 The flourishing of human life and cultures is compatible with a substantial decrease of the human population. The flourishing of non-human life requires such a decrease.

5 Present human interference with the non-human world is excessive, and the situation is rapidly worsening.

6 Policies must therefore be changed. These policies affect basic economic, technological and ideological structures. The resulting state of affairs would be deeply different from the present.

7 The ideological change is mainly that of appreciating *life quality* rather than adhering to an increasingly higher standard of living.

8 Those who subscribe to the foregoing points have an obligation either directly or indirectly to try to implement the necessary changes.[4]

Deep Ecology imposes quite a challenge to concerned environmentalists with its emphasis both on personal growth, and on 'the need to see beyond our narrow contemporary and cultural assumptions and values to achieve an identification which goes beyond humanity to include the non-human world'.[5] The inspirational quality of such an approach (which leading Deep Ecologists would be the first to agree cannot be fully grasped intellectually but is ultimately experiential) is enormous, and the Deep Ecology Movement is gaining in influence year by year, particularly in America.

That in turn has triggered off a backlash from those who have become increasingly suspicious of what it stands for. The National Gathering of US Greens in Amherst in June 1987 became the forum for an extraordinary confrontation between the protagonists of Deep/Spiritual Ecology and those of Social Ecology. The catalyst for this was a devastating paper to the Gathering from Murray Bookchin, in which he set up a stark polarity between Deep Ecology and Social Ecology:

> The greatest difference that is now emerging in the so-called 'Ecology Movement' today is between a vague, formless, self-contradictory, invertebrate thing called 'Deep Ecology', and a long-developing, coherent, socially-oriented body of ideas that is best called Social Ecology. Deep Ecology has parachuted into our midst quite recently from the sun-belt's bizarre mix of Hollywood and Disneyland, re-born Christianity, spiced homilies from Taoism, Buddhism, spirituality and so on and so forth. Social Ecology draws its inspiration from outstanding radical de-centralist thinkers like Peter Kropotkin, William Morris, Paul Goodman, to mention a few, amongst others, who have advanced a serious challenge to the present society with its vast, hierarchical, sexist, class-ruled, status apparatus and militaristic history. Let us face these differences bluntly. Deep Ecology, despite all its social rhetoric, has virtually no real sense that our ecological problems have their ultimate roots in society and in social problems. It preaches a gospel of a kind of original sin that accurses a vague species called humanity, as though people of colour are equatable with whites, women with men, the Third World with the First, the poor with the rich, and the exploited with the exploiters.[6]

It is worth looking in some detail at exactly what bugs Bookchin, for there is no doubt that this is going to become an increasingly important debate over the next few years.

THE INDIVIDUAL VERSUS SOCIETY

Deep Ecology tends to put the emphasis on the individual to take up his or her responsibility as citizens of Planet Earth. Social Ecology emphasizes the role of society:

> We do not say that people are responsible for the economic crisis: we say that a social order based on profit, accumulation, grow-or-die capitalism is responsible; a market system which makes it possible for people to become self-sufficient, or to decentralize, is responsible. And we do not hold all people equally responsible for these systems: we don't believe blacks are in the same position as whites, we don't believe women are in the same position as men.[7]

It is not difficult to bridge that divide: taken to extremes, both positions (blaming it all on society or all on the individual) are equally ridiculous. They *have* to be combined for any Green Movement to be effective.

POPULATION

The fourth cardinal principle of Deep Ecology is the real bone of contention here, providing opportunities for yet another over-heated reworking of that hoary old issue of population. Bookchin and his disciples have accused the Deep Ecologists of being 'neo-Malthusians', largely on the evidence of a pretty zany interview between Bill Devall and David Foreman (who is widely known to hold more than his fair share of off-the-wall views: i.e. 'Put the Earth first in *all* decisions, even ahead of human welfare if necessary') in which the latter apparently said that no more emergency food aid should be shipped out to Ethiopia and that nature should be permitted to take its course.

Such comments are indeed the hallmark of a rather nasty, callous strain of eco-populism, and there is a very thin line between this and outright eco-fascism. But that does not mean to say that all Deep Ecologists should suddenly stop campaigning, responsibly, humanely and intelligently, for a long-term decrease in the population, whilst acknowledging at the same time that this is as much a problem for the North as for the South.

This is obviously not the place to go more deeply into the population debate, but those who go on arguing that it is *all* about the distribution of the world's wealth, and that numbers of people simply do not come into it, just do not understand what is happening in

237

Africa, and many other developing countries. The ecological concept of 'carrying capacity' is not one that can be dismissed by reference to the standard redistribution blarny. This particular storm in a condom will, unfortunately, run and run. Equally, if Deep Ecologists don't understand that probably the single most important factor in reducing population growth is the degree of control that women have over their own bodies (and that this depends largely on the provision of appropriate education and health-care facilities), then their influence in this area will indeed be highly questionable.

ANTHROPOCENTRIC VERSUS BIOCENTRIC

Though much harder to get worked up about than the population question, this is actually just as important. A critical aspect of the Deep Ecologists' approach is to question the anthropocentric (exclusively human-centred) way of looking at the world, and to promote a more biocentric (life-centred) philosophy, emphasizing the fact that we are just one strand in the enormous complex web of life.

Any philosophical approach which seeks to interpret the relationship between humankind and the rest of life on Earth more sensitively and less arrogantly than either scientific materialism or even the most benign form of humanism have managed to do up until now must be a good thing. Such an approach can, of course, be taken to extremes, and that tiny minority of Deep Ecologists who argue from a position of 'biological egalitarianism' (i.e. all organisms have equal rights, so that in principle a dandelion, let alone an AIDS virus, would be seen to have as much intrinsic value as a human being) are really a bit dotty.

Even the question of closer identification with the non-human world is problematic. It does not seem to help all that much to be told that we should be 'thinking like a mountain'. It is pretentious to suppose that we will think in any other way than as human beings, however close to nature we may be or however respectful of the rights of other creatures we may be. In this context, Bookchin distinguishes usefully between *first nature* (meaning primeval, non-human nature) and *second nature* (the specifically human development of life on Earth, uniquely endowed with cerebral and conceptual capacities which inevitably oblige us to take on a stewardship role). We comprehensively intervene in first nature in a way that sets us apart, even as we acknowledge our interdependence.

But 'the recognition of value inherent in all living nature' is an important part of an emerging green spirituality. It stems from the deep ecological awareness that nature and the self are one. And, as Fritjof Capra has pointed out, 'this is also the very core of spiritual awareness. Indeed, when the concept of the human spirit is understood as the mode of consciousness in which the individual feels connected to the cosmos as a whole, it becomes clear that ecological awareness is spiritual in its deepest essence, and that the new ecological ethics is grounded in spirituality.[8]

SPIRITUALITY

The attempt to establish a rigid polarity between Deep Ecology and Social Ecology is in fact a front for something much more problematic. What really bothers Bookchin is what he refers to as 'eco-lala', by which he means: 'all that nebulous nature-worship with its suspicious bouquet of wood-sprites and fertility rites, its animist, shamanistic figures and post-industrial paganism'

Bookchin's own description of Social Ecology is revealing:

> Social Ecology is neither 'deep', 'tall', 'fat', nor 'thick'. It is *social*. It does not fall back on incantations, sutras, flow diagrams or spiritual vagaries. It is avowedly *rational*. It does not try to regale metaphorical forms of spiritual mechanism and crude biologism with Taoist, Buddhist, Christian or shamanistic eco-lala. It is a coherent form of naturalism that looks to evolution and biosphere, not to deities in the sky or under the earth, for quasi-religious and supernaturalistic explanations of natural and social phenomena.[9]

What we find here is an old-fashioned hatred of anything supernatural, anything that seeks to transcend a solidly scientific explanation of life on Earth. He dismisses each and every one of those who believe that there *is* a spiritual dimension as 'flaky spiritualists'.

In his highly perceptive review of the National Gathering, Mark Satin explained it this way:

> The conflict was between Greens coming out of a leftist perspective who still shared many of the anti-capitalist and confrontational assumptions of that perspective, and Greens coming out of a holistic or 'new age' perspective who sought to bring together the best of all the traditional political 'isms' and whose approach is healing rather than confrontational.
>
> The hectoring, polemical, super-intellectual style of argument of many of the leftist Greens was anathema to many of

the new-age Greens. Bookchin began his first speech with a statement to the effect that he did not mean to hurt anyone's feelings; but plenty of people were convinced his speech was meant to drum them out of the Green Movement.[10]

The same sort of row is common in Germany, where one of the deepest-seated divisions is the difference between those who see themselves on the ex-Marxist Left, and those who feel themselves to be inspired by a more visionary, spiritual understanding of what it is to be green. The leftists claim that the whole spiritual bit merely confuses and muddies their limpid green water – especially in Germany. After all, they say, just consider how successfully Hitler manipulated pre-Christian, Teutonic myths in order to corrupt a whole generation of young German people.

None would deny such a danger. Too many people claim to speak with the voice of religion whose politics are utterly and totally abhorrent. But despite that difficulty, most Greens in this country would still insist that without some understanding of the spiritual dimension, it will always be a rather lifeless, insipid shade of green that we are dealing with.

One hesitates to speak on behalf of 'most Greens' on so sensitive a question, and the more specifically one pins down any interpretation of the spiritual dimension, the more likely one is to produce divergence rather than convergence. The Green Movement must therefore remain open on this question, enthusiastically embracing a pluralistic green ecumenism, despite all the risks entailed therein. For many, this seems to be an unforgivable weakness, indicating a lack of intellectual rigour, even a lack of spiritual integrity. After all, if one takes pluralism too far, so that the spiritual dimension of the Green Movement becomes *almost* all things to *almost* all people, is there actually anything of lasting value to be found at the heart of such a concept? For others, this openness, this rejection of dogma, is a precondition for any genuine metaphysical reconstruction.

The first thing is to understand that politics and spirituality are *not* separate. They are, if anything, two sides of the same coin. As Gandhi said: 'I claim that human mind or human society is not divided into water-tight compartments, called social, political, religious. All act and react upon another. I do not believe that the spiritual law works on a field of its own. On the contrary, it expresses itself only through the ordinary activities of life. It thus affects the economic, the social and the political fields.'[11]

What's more, no one is proposing a gleaming, brand new, ecologically pure religion. No one is summoning people to genuflect at the altar of Gaia, or to abandon all that has provided spiritual or transcendental meaning up until now. To propose any such spiritual artefact would be a meaningless and arrogant exercise. The essential component of this is therefore to promote ecological wisdom in *all* existing religious and spiritual traditions, by drawing out the teaching practices already inherent in those traditions. It is, of course, a different procedure that is called for with each tradition.

Christianity

As regards Christianity, there has been a pretty lively debate for some years now about whether or not Christianity is itself partly responsible for the ecological mess that we're in. Ever since 1967, when the American historian Lynn White launched his famous attack on the Judaeo-Christian tradition, referring to it as 'the most anthropocentric religion the world has ever seen' and blaming literally all the horrors of modern civilization on that tradition, there has been an intense debate amongst theologians about the extent to which one can pin the blame on Christianity for what has gone wrong with our world.

Lynn White asserted quite simply that we shall continue to see a worsening ecological crisis until we reject that central Christian axiom that 'nature has no reason but to serve man', and that science and technology today are 'so tinctured with orthodox Christian arrogance towards nature' that no solution for our ecological crisis can be expected from them alone. This is no mere academic argument! This is an extremely important debate about the whole future of Christianity in the late twentieth century, which revolves around an important (and, this time, quite genuine) polarity.

On the one hand, there is the theory that God created man 'in the image of God', and gave us 'dominion over all the fish of the sea, the birds of the heaven, all the wild beasts and all the reptiles that crawl upon the Earth'. It is precisely the confusion between 'dominion' and 'domination' that has provided Christianity with a licence for participating, often with uncommon enthusiasm, in the wholesale exploitation of the Earth, eliminating a sense of reverence for God's creation and suppressing any residual hint of pagan or animist traditions. (Christians hang on to the Harvest Festival, but only just!)

In a book called *Continuous Harmony*, Wendell Berry puts this very clearly in perspective:

> Perhaps the greatest disaster of human history is one that happened to religion, that is the division between the holy and the world, the taking out of the Creator from creation. If God was not in the world, then quite obviously the world was a thing of inferior importance or of no importance at all. Those who were disposed to exploit it were thus free to do so, and this split in public attitudes was inevitably mirrored in the lives of individuals. A man could aspire to heaven with his mind and his heart while destroying the Earth and his fellow man with his hands.[12]

That, then, is one side of the debate: Christianity, by taking the divine out of all that is earthly and lodging it in some distant and comprehensively male God-head, has managed only to endorse and indeed accelerate the pattern of ecological destruction that we now see.

Against that, there is a very different interpretation, based on the understanding that 'the Earth is the Lord's and the fullness thereof'. All we have actually been given is the *stewardship*, not the *control*, of that creation. Here, of course, the whole concept of ecological interdependence finds an important biblical resonance in the covenant that God made with Noah after the Flood: 'This is a sign I am giving you for all ages to come, of the covenant between Me and you and *every living creature with you*.'

That text, in the ninth chapter of Genesis, underpins the progressive Christian concept of stewardship. It has been taken up throughout the years by many people who found in it the absolute essence of their Christianity.

The figure most often mentioned here is St Benedict of Norcia, the sixth-century saint who set up a series of monasteries, and was the first to encourage monks to get stuck in to some proper manual labour, to shape and manage the environment in order to make the best and most sustainable use of God's wealth. Their monastic life helped monks to establish close contact with the natural world through daily and seasonal rituals. (It is interesting that the current writings of Rudolf Bahro show a clear reflection of that Benedictine concept of community and the sustainable stewardship of the Earth.)

It is, of course, the figure of St Francis of Assisi that is held up as the most appropriate patron saint of ecology. His approach was a different kettle of fish altogether: much more loving, much more contemplative, much more to do with reverencing creation rather than managing it. One finds in him no will to dominate, but rather a sense of joy and wonder at our participation in a miracle.

That understanding of the relationship between the planet and its creator is, of course, very close to the sense of spiritual fellowship of many American Indians and other so-called 'primitive' peoples. But you do not necessarily have to live out in the wild to share such an understanding. Consider the words of Archbishop William Temple: 'The treatment of the Earth by man the exploiter is not only imprudent, it is sacrilegious. We are not likely to correct our hideous mistakes in this realm unless we recover the mystical sense of our oneness with nature. Many people think this is fantastic. I think it is fundamental to our sanity.'[13] Now that would be a suitably radical starting point for all Christians!

While this intense debate has been going on, the Church of England itself, with one or two notable exceptions, has been sitting back and twiddling its thumbs. In 1970, the Board of Social Responsibility produced a document called *Man in his Living Environment*. This was a weighty and very academic document, and did little to get the message out into the parishes where such documents either sink or swim. That must have been quite a disappointment to Hugh Montefiore, the Bishop of Birmingham, and Chair of the Board of Social Responsibility, who was very much in the vanguard of those trying to get the Church of England more involved in environmental issues. It was at his instigation that Barbara Ward was invited to address the 1978 Lambeth Conference. People were deeply impressed by what she had to say, but, as so often, nothing came of it. Thus few people were surprised when the Board of Social Responsibility's next initiative in this area (*Our Responsibility for the Living Environment*, published in 1986) still did little more than scratch the surface of the enormously complex problems we now face.

One of the most interesting recent developments has been the setting up of the 'Church and Conservation Project', to assist with the training of clergy in rural areas and to provide a forum for agricultural chaplains. It is supported by the Nature Conservancy Council, the WWF, the Royal Agricultural Society of England and the Ernest Cook Trust. Eve Dennis, the Project Officer, explains her hopes:

'What on earth has religion got to do with conservation?' was
the queston most frequently asked when I was preparing to
take up this new work.

The crux of the matter is whether or not one believes that
the world of man, plant and animal is part of God's creation
in our search for an ethical basis for our work in conserving
the earth and the fullness thereof.

The barometer is set fair for a new environmental revolution
where men and women of faith have a hope for a future world
that is more nearly as God intended it to be – a habitation
more fit for man, plant and animal alike in the generations to
come.[14]

And things are certainly stirring elsewhere. Hugh Montefiore
recalls how things have changed: 'In those early days I found myself
virtually alone when questions on the environment came up. Now, it
is commonplace to find both clergy and lay people making this a
priority.' This is confirmed by Walter Schwarz, the *Guardian*'s
religious correspondent, who is particularly impressed by the spate of
new initiatives being taken by the Church in the inner cities,
following on from the publication of *Faith in the Cities*. He cites as
an example the work of the Industrial Chaplaincy, which may not
call itself green, but which is pursuing exactly the same kind of ideas
referred to in Chapter 7.

Montefiore's mantle as 'Green Bishop' has now been taken over by
David Jenkins, the Bishop of Durham. His acerbic comments at the
time of the Stock Exchange crash in 1987 (that its 'victims' should
expect no better in an immoral world where 'very many people do
not have the means to live anything like a human life as enjoyed by
those who, at the moment, live off living beyond their means')
contrasted strongly with those of the Archbishop of Canterbury, who
merely suggested that investors 'should not panic'!

Jenkins's important address at St James's Church in Piccadilly, in
November 1987, made clear the extent of his concern:

I believe that the apocalyptic pressures upon us can and should
be read and responded to as the pressure of the Judgement of
God. We are collectively and comprehensively failing in the
love of our neighbour. We are blasphemously, conceitedly and
indifferently failing in our stewardship of the earth, and we
are worshipping and giving ourselves up to greed, consumption

244

and sensuality. These are the perennial, simple and basic sins against the great commandments.

There is no future in the twenty-first century based on nineteenth-century nostalgias about either market powers or workers' powers. To refuse to acknowledge and to face the queston is not to be practical, but to be promoting a fools' paradise which will become more and more an idiots' hell. Moreover, answers are appearing, and there is already a vast network of so far small but influential groups throughout the world who are wrestling with these things. Some of the Schumacher suggestions are very down-to-earth, and perfectly practicable – once there is sufficient political will. Nothing but our own obtuseness and self-serving ignorance requires us to insist on going on as we are and thus heading for destruction.[15]

The main message here is a simple one: that no church will have any relevance whatsoever to what is going on on this planet until it wakes up to what is actually happening to the planet and commits itself, from top to bottom, to presenting a different set of values, rather than try to mitigate the damage accruing from our current values.

Happily, a new theology is emerging to meet that challenge. People like Thomas Berry, Matthew Fox and Sean MacDonagh are now beginning to develop a different way of looking at the Christian religion, a different way of drawing out those inherently rich ecological traditions that are already there. Sean MacDonagh, whose book *To Care for the Earth* can be strongly recommended as one of the most accessible representations of this new theology, says this:

Rather than acting as a parasite, human beings must now assume their proper function as the head and mind of Gaia, and thereby optimize the conditions necessary for life on Earth. We carry within ourselves, and every life-form carries within itself, a unique manifestation of the ultimate mystery of life. And understood in this way, each reality in the story, from the hydrogen atom onwards, has its own unique value, irrespective of its usefulness to human beings.[16]

Metaphysical Reconstruction

Though this section has dealt in some detail with what is happening in the Anglican Christian Church, the same drawing out of inherent ecological wisdom is going on in all the major faiths. Some have more drawing out to do than others, as the suppression that has gone on over the centuries has often been intense. Only Buddhism can make any real claim to being permeated through and through with ecological awareness and guidance about 'right livelihood'.

On this ecumenical front, one of the most exciting initiatives for years has been the WWF's Network on Conservation and Religion. They celebrated their twenty-fifth anniversary in 1986 with an inspirational Interfaith Ceremony in Assisi, bringing together representatives of the world's five great religions (Buddhism, Christianity, Hinduism, Islam, Judaism) both to draw attention to global ecological problems and to celebrate what it was in their own religions which allowed them to glorify the miracle of creation.

This was followed up in October 1987 with a startlingly original Harvest Festival Service in Winchester Cathedral to launch a new inter-faith initiative appropriately designated the Rainbow Covenant. The conventional Harvest procession was halted in its tracks by these far from conventional words from the Dean:

> Come no further. Your offering is not acceptable in the sight of God. Nor is it acceptable in the sight of God's creation from whom you have taken it. Jesus said, 'If you are bringing your offering to the altar, and there remember that your brother has something against you, leave your offering there before the altar, go and be reconciled with your brother first, and then come back and present your offering.
>
> St Francis has taught us to see all creation in terms of brothers and sisters under God. We who have destroyed so much of Sister Earth, wasted so many of God's gifts, and slain so many of our brothers and sisters in creation, have no right to bring these gifts to the altar. There is a time for rejoicing and for offerings, but there is also a time for repenting of our destruction of God's creation.[17]

The Harvest Festival is, of course, one of those crucial bridges between contemporary Christianity and the pagan or animist past.

246

When it comes to ways of encouraging people to reconnect with the Earth, this deeper spring may be just as important as any formal Church liturgy. Pitched at its simplest level, we no longer sing the song of the Earth. There is no longer harmony between us and the rest of creation. There is concrete between, and technological super-abundance, and the discords of distorted reason. Though indisputedly dominant, mankind is no longer at home on this planet. Likewise, few people are at harmony within themselves. A crude, consumer-driven culture prevails, in which the spirit is denied and the arts are rejected or reduced to a privileged enclave for the few. Our children are set fair to inherit a cultural, spiritual and ecological wasteland.

Any metaphysical reconstruction must therefore start with the Earth itself. As Blake had it:

> To see a World in a Grain of Sand,
> And a Heaven in a Wild Flower,
> Hold Infinity in the palm of your hand,
> And Eternity in an hour.

In order to be at home in the world, we must be fully of it, experiencing it *directly* as mud between our toes, as the rough bark on a tree, as the song of the world awakening every morning. The Earth speaks to something in each and every person, even when we are imprisoned by concrete and steel. In that dialogue lies a form of celebration as primitively powerful as anything to be found in our anaemic, emaciated culture.

Learning how to reconnect with ourselves and with the Earth, and then learning how to celebrate that reconnection, is a very personal thing. It can also be very confusing. The New Age movement, for instance, covers a multitude of networks, communities, individuals, tendencies and gurus which it is almost impossible to sort out. All one can incontrovertibly claim is that many thousands in the UK have found in New Age thinking and teaching a sense of hope and meaning that has eluded them elsewhere.

That hopefulness takes many different forms. 17 August 1987 saw the Harmonic Convergence, where people the world over gathered at sacred centres (like Lake Titicaca in Peru, Ayers Rock in Australia, Mount Fuji in Japan and Glastonbury Tor here in Britain) to welcome that 'coming of the age of Aquarius'. John Vidal of the *Guardian* summed up these New Age seekers in the following way:

In political terms, the seers, prophets, spiritualists and star-gazers who have been meeting to usher in a supposed awakening of energy in the Earth, are really the religious wing of the new thinking which has been steadily working its way through the developed countries over the last twenty years. The New Age tag has only been recently applied to this very broad church, so as to focus attention on the whole revolution of ideas which has been taking place and which has been largely ignored by the media, derided by the establishment or scoffed at when touched upon by the likes of Prince Charles.

The religious side – the holistic world view – is only now beginning to surface, and at its margins is totally incomprehensible to the outsider, with its own vocabulary, symbols and myths. People are turning every which way to make some meaning of the world, but if there is a consensus, it is in the view that we are all part of the whole, and if you want to change the whole, you have to start on yourself.[18]

This sense of psychic as well as physical interconnectedness (which is basically what 'holistic' thinking is all about) is what has inspired Sir George Trevelyan, the most eminent New Ager, since his 'conversion' in 1942 at a lecture by one of Rudolf Steiner's students. He recently published a book called *Summons to a High Crusade*, a collection of his talks to the Findhorn Foundation over the last decade, in which he explains his vision of the human race on the point of assuming its true cosmic role:

In spiritual and even physical terms, something is happening which is polarizing humanity into two different levels. There are those who are lifting to the light and are being prepared to set aside ego, will and desire and who are taking part in dedicating life to wholeness. And there are those who, through free will, are stopping it happening.

On its highest level, it is a vast cosmic battlefield. In spiritual terms the forces of good and evil are locked in a fight to the finish for man's soul; the fallen angels are out to capture the divine being, and will take us over unless we wake up and volunteer.[19]

Not all New Agers go along with this kind of extra-terrestrial supernaturalism. David Spangler, another of Findhorn's mentors, sees the New Age as a way of being rather than a future event.

248

The current media attention may so identify the idea of a new age with a form of yuppie exploration of psychic and self-centred life-styles, that the very image will lose its transformative currency. This would be a shame, but it would not alter anything. The real transformation occurring in our society will continue. The New Age has little to do with prophecy or the imagination of a new world, but everything to do with the imagination to see our world in new ways that can empower us towards compassionate, transformative actions and attitudes. If we remember this, then we can forget the new age of channels, crystals and charisma, and get on with discovering and co-creating a harmonious world that will nourish and empower ourselves and our children.[20]

With or without the psychic exploration, it is exactly this kind of stuff which gives a lot of Greens the screaming ab-dabs. 'Here we are,' they reason, 'striving to establish the credibility and viability of the green alternative, and all you can do is to frolic around, usually naked, getting your spirit in tune with the planet's ley-lines. With friends of the Earth like you, who needs enemies?'

Gaia

That certainly is the reasoning of Jim Lovelock, whose by now famous book, *Gaia: a New Look at Life on Earth*, raises the fascinating idea that the Earth 'constitutes a single system, made and managed to their own convenience by living organisms. We all know that life here is only made possible because of the right balance of gases in the atmosphere. But what we do not realize is that this balance is maintained *not* by chance, but by the very process of life itself.'

The proportion of oxygen in the atmosphere, for instance, bears out the idea that life's chemistry is hard at work. Oxygen is highly volatile. Too much or too little would be disastrous. Too much and everything flammable burns; too little and life chokes. What, then, has kept it at just the right level for millions of years over widely fluctuating circumstances? How is it that the balance of oxygen and methane 'inexplicably' remains constant? How is it that the temperature at the surface of the Earth has been maintained at a comfortable level for billions of years (give or take the odd Ice Age in the Polar

249

regions!) despite the fact that the heat reaching us from the sun has increased by as much as 40%?

The biosphere (by which we mean all living matter, whether in the oceans, the forests or the soil) is made up of billions and billions of separate organisms. Lovelock's breathtaking hypothesis is that all these organisms, in their totality, combine together as one self-regulating system to maintain just the right conditions for life to flourish. That is to say, the Earth controls its own environment!

As is so often the case, the scientific establishment initially huffed and puffed and pooh-poohed Lovelock's idea. Since then, more and more of them have come to accept not only the scientific concept of the Gaia hypothesis, but also its basic wisdom. Many of the biosphere's natural cycles and processes – ocean currents, climatic patterns, and the recycling of energy and nutrients between the sun, water, air and soil – act as the hypothesis predicts.

Gaia, of course, was the Greek Goddess of the Earth. One cannot help but be struck by the way in which Lovelock's hypothesis is so clearly linked to an older and once universal philosophy that experienced the Earth as a divine being, a Mother Earth: 'The Earth is a Goddess and she teaches justice to those who can learn, for the better she is served, the more good things she gives in return.' Xenophon's words express the belief of the ancient Greeks that they were the children of the Earth, and that the Earth was an animate, living organism with a 'natural law' which rewarded those who protected her and struck down those who harmed her.

But as far as Jim Lovelock himself is concerned, his hypothesis is strictly scientific, and not to be adulterated by the metaphysical meanderings of a bunch of latter-day hippies. Hugh Montefiore, who well understands Lovelock's need not to be seen as a mystic if he is to retain his pre-eminence amongst his scientific colleagues, none the less sees something quite different in the Gaia hypothesis – neither pure science nor a pretext for pantheism:

> I fail to see how this whole system could sort of happen by chance, by hazard. How can those 'inexplicable' balances of the environment be maintained in any kind of random way? The fundamental theological truth for a Christian is that the world is indeed a living thing: the whole of the spirit of God is at work within it, and everything has intrinsic value of itself. I believe there *are* hierarchies of value, with humankind at the top (by virtue of being able to feel, think and worship),

but all things have intrinsic value precisely because they are part of the stream of life in which the spirit of God has caused them to evolve into what they are.

So there you have it: a trinity of Gaias – scientific, pantheistic and Christian! Perhaps Jim Lovelock now wishes he had given his hypothesis some tediously predictable scientific title, but that would, in fact, have been very sad. For those who find his ideas both scientifically and intellectually compelling, and yet feel quite at home with the spiritual dimension of the Green Movement, one can only feel a sense of delight that the concept of Gaia has been so powerfully re-released into the world, and not particularly concerned about how people chose to interpret it. As we have heard, the Green Movement is indeed a broad church!

John Stewart Collis, one of the least well-known but most important visionaries of the Green Movement, put it this way back in 1972:

> This is now regarded as a very irreligious age. But perhaps it only means that the mind is moving from one state to another. The next stage is not a belief in many gods. It is not a belief in one God. It is not a belief at all – not a conception in the intellect. It is an extension of the consciousness so that we may *feel* God, or, if you will, an experience of harmony, an intonation of the Divine which will link us again with animism, the experience of unity lost and the in-break of self-consciousness.[21]

It is crucially important not to make too much of a mystery out of this because the whole point is that there is no mystery to it. To relate to the Earth in this way is natural, ordinary and theoretically accessible to everybody. The spiritual can and often should be utterly mundane. The problem, of course, is that fewer and fewer people have access to the Earth in that way, either because they are imprisoned in their urban hell, or because they are bound by the equally demonic constraints of conventional education, religion or politics.

Richard North, who counts himself as a 'spiritual environmentalist', draws a very clear link between the desire to break through those constraints and the religious impulse that is to be seen in so many people today:

> An awful lot of us just need to worship something. But in order to be able to worship, you have to be able to find

251

something outside of yourself – and better than yourself. God is a construct for that. So is nature. We are all falling in love with the environment as an extension to and in lieu of having fallen out of love with God. As it happens, it makes for a pretty deficient religion, but as an object of worship, nature takes some beating.

There remains amongst all green sceptics one final and widespread suspicion: that to be spiritual means to 'drop out', to disappear narcissistically inwards, devoting one's life to meditation and non-specific navel-gazing. There *is* a time and a place, and even, on occasion, a critical need for such contemplative practice, as *part* of one's spirituality, but it seems clear to me that too exclusive an emphasis on the unworldly, on withdrawal from this grotty industrial culture of ours, has merely reinforced the parody of spirituality as a morally superior way of dropping out. Greens themselves must share some of the responsibility for the suffocation of the spirit by continuing in this way to perpetuate the meaningless divide between our political and spiritual concerns.

Just think for a moment of those who have not had their lives warped by such crude reductionism. Think, for example, of the Penan people in the forests of Sarawak, even now defending their forests against the assault of the logging companies, hemmed in by the corruption of Malaysian politicians and by the rapacity of those who see their forests as no more than a convenient resource to be converted into instant money. For the Penan, and for all tribal people in similar situations, the forest is both a home and a livelihood, and the source of all that provides meaning in their culture and their religion. Their decision to defend the forest, therefore, is as much spiritual as it is political. The same is true of the Chipko movement in India and of indigenous peoples throughout the world for whom contact and dependence on the Earth remains a living, vibrant reality.

For Greens today, this is an international community of which they feel an active part. In the USA, the history and culture of the North American Indians now plays an enormously important role in shaping the deeper and more spiritual aspects of the Green Movement. The same is true of the Aborigines in Australia and the Maoris in New Zealand. These connections are not just about providing us with a series of inspirational texts (of which there are many) which show us what living in harmony with the environment is all about;

they provide as powerful and compelling a call to *action* as anything written anywhere in any green manifesto.

That is why so many Greens believe that salvation lies in opening our spirit to the presence of the divine in the world, acknowledging joyfully a sense of wonder and humility before the miracle of creation, and *then* going out and taking action to put things right, inspired by that vision.

CHAPTER TWELVE

Hopes and Fears

Of hopes and fears we have encountered many in the course of conducting the interviews for this book. The fears are never far away, automatic almost, as if the uttering of them might just manage to ward off the evil they anticipate; the hopes are deeper down, needing to be coaxed out, shame-faced even, as if the uttering of *them* were somehow peculiar or laughable.

It is not easy to be both hopeful *and* realistic as a Green. Jeremy Seabrook has written of one of the least-recognized consequences of the Thatcher revolution, namely the 'privatization of *social hope*':

> The electoral decay of Labourism in Britain and of socialism more generally in the Western world is not, as the Labour Party prefers to believe, a result of the distortions of the media, real though these undoubtedly are. It has far more to do with the waning of faith, the decline of collective hope vested in those political formations. Hope, having been virtually eclipsed in the public domain, reappears the more powerfully in the lives of individuals.
>
> The loss of faith in socialism has been accompanied by a growing faith in the power of money. There are no secular societies in the world: all must be cemented by some deeply shared and unifying belief. Indeed, the vigour, dynamism and energy of the market economy make it the most conspicuous and inescapable feature of our lives. It commands our reverence as nothing else can. When Mrs Thatcher utters her incantatory phrases about the 'creation of wealth', these sound like readings from the Book of Genesis. Small wonder that these processes have laid hold of both the imagination and the homeless faith of the majority of people in the Western World.

The erosion of social hope, and the increasing dominance of faith in materialistic individualism, are the twin characteristics of a society which seems to be beyond conventional healing. They are also the source of both green fears and green hopes.

The way most of us in the Western world live now poses a fundamental threat to the planet and to our ability to survive. If we fail to restructure our economies, to re-evaluate our social and economic relations, we will be in grave danger. To ask an individual to change his or her life and, in the process, to abandon some of their most cherished assumptions and beliefs overnight – even with good reason – is a tall order. To persuade the entire population of the planet to do likewise, and to do it, historically speaking, virtually overnight, is a colossal undertaking. So what makes the Greens think they can achieve such an undertaking?

There are several stages in the process of responding constructively to our modern crisis. The essential first step is to be prepared to listen to and accept the worrying information we now possess about the irreparable damage the human race is inflicting on the planet, instead of trying to reinterpret the information to make it fit in with our existing hopes and expectations. In some ways, this step is the hardest of all to take. People are formidably well-equipped subconsciously to screen out information which threatens their view of themselves or the world. Psychologists call this mechanism 'denial'.

There are many varieties of 'denial' at work today, many strategies for avoiding knowledge about the perilous state of the planet's life-support systems. We can absolve ourselves of personal responsibility or involvement on the basis that, as *individuals*, we are powerless to make a difference. Those who are rich and comfortable enough may delude themselves that nothing is essentially wrong with the world, and that even if there is, their wealth will shield them from the worst. And there are many who believe that we have only to look to technology, which partly got us into our ecological mess in the first place, to get us out of it as well. It is not only scientists and technocrats who believe that human ingenuity, if not unlimited, is nevertheless so great that it can indefinitely fend off eco-catastrophe.

The technocrats continue to offer us visions of extraordinary new breakthroughs with the promise of salvation just as soon as we've harnessed their potential. The new bio-technologies will apparently solve world hunger and pollution and meet all our energy require-ments. And if that doesn't work, the new generation of super-conductors and super-computers are sure to save us. In America and Japan, huge computers are already designing even bigger and yet more powerful computers. When humankind has been relegated to being only the second most intelligent life-form on the planet, will the computers then look after us, managing a world that has become too complicated for lowly mortals to understand?

Sixteen years ago, the Club of Rome's report, *Limits to Growth*, warned against being lulled into a false sense of security by this kind of fix: 'Technological optimism is the most common and most dangerous reaction of our findings ... technology can relieve the symptoms of a problem without affecting the underlying causes. Faith in technology as the ultimate solution to all problems can thus divert our attention from the fundamental problem – the problem of growth in a finite system – and prevent us taking effective action to solve it.'[1] In the meantime, an almost universal faith in science and technology, though still rooted deeply in our culture, has begun to wear a little thin. The Green Movement remains intensely suspicious of the consequences of that faith in science, pointing consistently to other 'miracle' technologies, like nuclear power, which have invariably arrived brimming with fervent promises of a better world, but have often ended up by making things still more dangerous.

Some forms of denial are more to do with political ideology than personal paralysis. Stung by the Greens' claims to being more radical than themselves, Marxists have launched something of an ideological counter-offensive, branding the Greens as an expression of a classically naïve and selfish middle-class perspective. By ignoring the analytical framework of Marxism, Greens are accused of failing to understand the structure and nature of the industrialism they claim to be tackling, of 'biologizing history' and of being 'politically ambiguous'. According to David Pepper, in his book *The Roots of Modern Environmentalism*, Greens see 'present environmental dilemmas in terms of fixed and unchanging natural limits upon human action. This determinist stance leads to fatalism and a pessimism about man's ability to create harmony with nature through enlightened social reform. This is politically reactionary.' The whole approach of the Green Movement is thus 'deeply conservative'. It 'advocates measures which strengthen social "order" and "stability" and negates the importance of class struggle and the need for revolution.'[2]

Greens are often baffled by the durability of this particular denial mechanism. To them, it's just so much angry sputtering from worn-out ideologues who have long since lost touch with the real world. The quotes in the paragraph above exemplify the kind of sterile jargon that makes much of the language of socialism so utterly antipathetic to many Greens, who understandably continue to stress the similarities between capitalist and socialist countries, as they are united by the 'super-ideology' of industrialism. Rudolf Bahro, once an East

German communist but now a leading green theoretician, claims: 'The Greens are to Marx and Marxism what Einstein was to Newton and Newtonian physics – in short, a qualitative transformation of a worthwhile system whose time, however, is up.'[3]

Repressing the knowledge of painful facts or events, such as the death of a loved one, is a familiar method of coping with everyday life. Accordingly, the Green Movement often seems cast in the role of Cassandra, the tragic daughter of the Trojan King Priam, who was blessed by the gods with the gift of prophecy but doomed never to be believed. Greens should not delude themselves into thinking that simply because their message is true, urgent and desperately important, anyone is automatically going to listen to or act upon it. Modern history is full of horrific examples of evidence that the opposite is true.

Between 1942 and 1945, for example, the world at large was silent in the face of the steady trickle of news from Nazi-occupied Poland that the entire Jewish population of Europe was being systematically murdered in pursuit of an unprecedented policy of genocide. The Allies, including Britain, ignored the most desperate Jewish pleas for help and refused to take action to try to stop or slow down the slaughter. In the late 1970s, despite clear signals that new, barely imaginable atrocities were being perpetrated by the Khmer Rouge, the world was equally deaf to the Cambodian genocide, reacting with food aid and worldwide compassion for the survivors only *after* the killings had been halted by the Vietnamese invasion.

It is important to be clear about the nature of the problems which face us. We are not threatened by a demonic, all-powerful totalitarian régime determined to murder us all. Nor are we victims of a ruthless and sophisticated process of deception, as the Jews were. We are not powerless. Above all, we *do* have many escape routes, if only we choose to make use of them. If the dangers facing the planet are recognized and taken seriously enough, early enough, we will have *relatively* little to worry about. The resources that could be directed to our problems by individuals and governments around the world are massive.

However, even if the psychological denial and avoidance mechanisms can be overcome, other problems await us. The loss of any widely shared social or collective hope means that people have to come to terms with their knowledge of the dangers we face more or less on their own. Decisions about what sort of changes have to be made are often taken in a psychological and philosophical vacuum. Even the most mundane level of green activity requires a tentative turning of a corner, the taking of a first step towards deeper green awareness and activity. And each step after that imposes an additional personal challenge, as the barriers to effective and constructive action become ever higher.

The many organizations involved in the Green Movement are playing a vitally important role in this respect, by giving people a focus and by arming them with new ideas. They can also provide people with intellectual and emotional tools, and in this respect the use of language is desperately important. Language shapes our imaginations and gives us the insights we need to make our way through alien territory. The very process of naming the things which frighten us is an important weapon in any attempt to confront our fears or realistically articulate our hopes.

One of the great achievements of the peace movement has been to raise the *implicit* logic of the nuclear weapons business to an *explicit* level, revealing to millions of people a reality which had been hidden. No pro-nuclear politician has ever referred to their nuclear missiles as 'weapons of mass destruction designed to murder a million men, women and children in an instant'. 'Independent deterrent' sounds much more acceptable. The methods of making sure these weapons of mass destruction reach their innocent civilian targets are referred to as 'delivery systems', a friendly sounding phrase summoning up images of mechanized milkmen on their rounds.

Equally, the uncompromising language of green politics gives us some of the same tools to help us draw back from and look critically at the old loyalties to ideologies, beliefs and assumptions which have got us into our present mess.

The more people who use that language, the greater its penetration into everyday social discourse. Hence the frustration of many Greens that there are so few 'opinion-shapers' who are prepared to take this on. In her interview with us, Anita Roddick bitterly regretted the dearth of suitable role models, especially for young people, as does Tim O'Riordan:

> The people who really influence public media, the media and senior scientists, the distinguished men and women of letters, simply don't peddle the green message. Nor do you get it from the Church, nor from leading politicians, nor from the other

professions. It is not really recognized as a legitimate part of the establishment in any shape or form.

One of the few exceptions in this respect is Prince Charles, who has managed to espouse quite radical green ideas without creating a storm of political controversy. The media, of course, simply do not know what to make of this, and the gutter press has revelled in taking the royal mickey by portraying him as a bit 'dotty'. And it's not just the media. In October 1986, Lord Northfield (head of the House Building Consortium) claimed that Prince Charles must have been 'hijacked by the Loony Green Brigade' – why else would he be taking the house-building industry to task for wanting to destroy yet more greenfield sites rather than building houses in the Inner City?

Both the bafflement and the gratuitous insults of such people provide complete confirmation (if any were needed) that in Prince Charles the Green Movement has a unique and invaluable supporter. Although circumscribed by the unwritten laws of the British Constitution as to what he can and cannot say, the breadth of Prince Charles's green concerns over the last few years is impressive: as we saw in Chapter 8, his concern about healthy food and alternative medicine has had a big impact on the medical profession: his decision to convert his Gloucestershire farm to organic farming may have helped a few more waverers to take the organic plunge; and his opening speech to the North Sea Summit in November 1987 was tantamount to sticking poor old Nicholas Ridley in the stocks and pelting him with nuggets of green wisdom:

> Some argue that we do not have enough proof of danger to justify stricter controls on dumping or to warrant the extra expenditure involved. They say that we must wait for science to provide the proof. If science has taught us anything, however, it is that the environment is full of uncertainty. It makes no sense to test it to destruction. While we wait for the doctors's diagnosis, the patient may easily die.

Nor is this beneficial influence limited to mere exhortation. His support for practical projects, particularly in the inner cities, and his advocacy of enlightened self-reliance, have spurred many people into action who might otherwise have remained as bystanders. This is doubly important in that another of the Green Movement's problems derives from the difficulty it has in pointing to successful long-term projects that demonstrate the viability of their alternative ideas. As

Paul Ekins says: 'I don't believe the Greens will succeed in persuading people that their alternative makes any sense until there is something there of sufficient scale, operating successfully, so that people can actually see that it makes sense.'

To be able to do this, he feels, will allow Greens to point to some tangible *benefits*, rather than to have to go on all the time about the *costs* of our current way of life:

> Our big political problem has always been that people are basically interested in benefits. They are not interested in costs. If they happen to become aware of any costs, they simply call on the people who give them the benefits to sort them out! The only way they will shift their political allegiance is if other people can be seen to be giving them bigger benefits. And if we can't learn how to do that, then the green economy is a no-hoper.

Establishing some good practice and creating viable alternatives that make a real difference to people in their everyday lives will also help in two specific ways. First, it will help to guard against the danger of green ideas solidifying into a rigid set of rules, dogmas and prejudices. It is a danger inherent in all political movements – even a self-styled radical 'anti-ideology' like that of the Greens – that it doesn't take long before dogmatism sets in. In any programme of ideas which has as its end-goal nothing less than a fundamental restructuring of human society, disagreements and the emergence of contradictory positions is inevitable. The 'realos' versus the 'fundis' in West Germany, the Deep Ecologists versus the Social Ecologists in the USA, or the light Greens versus the dark Greens in the UK, are all examples of disagreements that can and should lead to constructive convergence rather than negative divergence. Greens must guard against these disagreements becoming sterile or violent internal feuds of the kind that have plagued the political Left for most of the last eighty years.

Second, it will help to discourage those who have decided simply to sit back and wait for those long overdue, much hoped-for changes in our culture, values and assumptions, often referred to as 'the paradigm shift'. There is a whiff of waiting for Godot about the way this phrase has been tripping off green theorists' tongues in the last few years. It is also reminiscent of so much self-deluding talk on the Left about 'when the revolution comes' or 'raising the class-consciousness of the masses'. Throughout this book, we have tried to trace the many ways in which people are choosing to live greener lives. Activities as diverse as going to a homeopathic doctor, becoming a vegetarian or, if you are an industrialist, looking for products to manufacture which do not damage the environment, may all (for all we know) be symptoms of the paradigm beginning to shift. But very few of the millions of people now doing these things are doing them for that reason.

Let us take a seemingly trivial example: a person decides to switch from using ordinary washing-up liquid to a biodegradable alternative. It may hardly seem a world-shaking decision. Yet at the very least, such a move implies distrust of the chemical industries who make the old washing-up liquid. And to feel strongly enough about so apparently banal a product that you are prepared to pay something over the odds for an ecologically benign equivalent suggests a very deep antipathy indeed to modern patterns of consumption and technology. In its modest way, it is a radical and even subversive act.

In most cases, industry, business, politics and even religion are *responding* to this greening, not leading it. The process of change is coming from the bottom up. Individual consumers see a TV film or hear of a speech by Prince Charles about the destruction of the ozone layer and stop buying CFC-based aerosols. A few months later, executives at Boots and Tesco's refuse to sell CFC-based aerosols, and McDonald's promise to phase out their CFC-blown burger-box containers. For reasons of health and (occasionally) conscience, individuals decide to change their diet; when market research picks up signals that this marks the beginning of a trend, the food and advertising industries duly respond with 'natural' products and images. Time and again, this sort of pressure from individuals is responsible for forcing and prompting change.

And herein lies one of the great hopes of the Green Movement. If it is true, as argued by Jeremy Seabrook and others, that social hope has been transformed or 'privatized' into varying patterns of individualism, then is it not with the individual that the healing process must start? Rather than banging endlessly on about social transformation and political revolution in that strangely depersonalized way favoured by the far Left, might it not be more sensible to aim first to convert crude earth-bashing self-interest into a form of environmentally friendly, enlightened self-interest?

The fact is that many of the things favoured by Greens cannot be brought in by government at all. They require a

261

kind of green cultural revolution – the rebuilding of communities around economic institutions that are most compatible with the environment. What is needed is a slow process of education and grass-roots organizing through which people can learn that they have much to gain by a life that is not geared to 'more, bigger, faster'. The Greens must work out and communicate a set of proposals that give people a sense that their lives here and now could be enriched by doing things differently.

Not everyone would agree with such an optimistic forecast. Not even every fully paid-up Green, as witnessed here by Tim O'Riordan:

People are continually thinking about the well-being of life in terms of material goods – mortgages, houses, job security, all of these things remain top of the agenda for most people. The environment is always seen as something that can be dealt with as an afterthought. If you actually strip away a lot of the rhetoric and the various polls, you will find that the majority of British people don't want to change *anything*. They don't have to. They even see the Green Movement as a threat to their standard of living or, at least, to their aspirations to a *higher* standard of living. The green message of a more frugal existence and a more constructive use of resources simply has not come across at all.

On the basis of the research done for this book, we would quite strongly dissent from that view, whilst acknowledging the difficulty of quantifying the extent to which green ideas really *have* 'come across'. And we would agree that a certain amount of caution is needed. For one thing, the widely held assumption that the next generation will necessarily do a better job than this one is not actually justified by the available evidence. McCann-Ericksen's extensive Youth Study, carried out in 1987, showed that teenagers today tend to be *less* concerned about the environment than those in previous years, but far more concerned about their own individual prospects of success:

The 'New Wave' young want personal success, and in this they are in marked contrast to their predecessors ten years back, who wanted happiness and fulfilment. By success they mean getting a good job, getting a foot on the ladder, making it on your own terms. The image of the upwardly mobile self-made young adult has caught on: over a third would like a job in the City and a quarter in marketing, higher than any choice of professional or public service option.

A survey question enquired about the main three constituents of happiness. Health came first (as it did in 1977), then a happy family life – largely because young women rated family life highly. Money came third overall, but second for young men. Nowhere else in Europe was money put so high on the list of essentials – friendship or love always came higher elsewhere. In the UK 10 per cent of New Wave males even picked money first above health. Other questions confirm how strongly the young in Britain are attracted to consumption and feel constrained or limited over shortage of cash, as if wholeness as a person was unachievable without funds.

And beyond that, there is the crucial question of just how *deeply* green ideas are penetrating when pitched at this level. As we saw in Chapters 3 and 6, Greens have recently found many businessmen and politicians to be increasingly sympathetic to environmentalism. If one probes a little deeper, and suggests that our problems require solutions more radical than a spot of superficial environmentalism, mental portcullises start rattling into place. There is still a considerable, and very understandable, reluctance to start questioning the most basic assumptions on which our society and economy rests.

Yet sooner or later the realization will dawn on more and more people that solving the planet's problems is going to require breathtakingly radical action and international co-operation on a scale not seen since the Second World War. The 'sooner or later' time scale relates directly to the brinkmanship theory of ecology: that the only way to persuade world governments and policy-makers to take effective action is to hold them over the brink of disaster and let them stare into the abyss in order to shock them into pulling back in time – i.e. only when a major catastrophe looms will the necessary international co-operation, awareness and solidarity be forthcoming. There is some hope in such a strategy, but it entails high risks as the timing required is extremely delicate! By the time we get to the brink, the momentum and systemic inertia which took us there may well be too strong to reverse.

Writing about East–West rivalries and the Cold War, E. P. Thompson has explored the psychological and political dynamics which make it so difficult for nation states to co-operate:

Every nation needs the idea of an Other (or others) to bind itself together, and to that degree the Other is a projection of its own need. And nations need the Other most of all when their own identity is blurred or insecure or when the rulers fear internal disaffection. Of course, if the Other presents itself as an actual enemy, then internal bonding against it becomes stronger and the problems of the rulers are solved. The question, then, is: must the Other perforce be the enemy? Is humankind doomed because the very same social mechanics which bond them together in nations require an enemy to bond against?[4]

But what if 'the Other' is not another nation, but the threat of ecological devastation on an unprecedented scale? Might not our targeting of that as the enemy pull us back from the brink before it's too late? In Chapter 10, Norman Myers argued that the more serious the international threat confronting national economies, the greater the opportunity for the kind of international solidarity which is essential for solving our problems. Fay Weldon puts it like this: 'The threat we face is rather like an invasion from Mars. If the Martians invaded, everyone in the world would be obliged to get together to fight the common enemy. We have to oblige people to work together.'

Nuclear weapons provide the classic case of international brinkmanship. Throughout the 1980s, Europe has lived in a permanent state of fear that a nuclear war was not only thinkable but imminent. The rapid build-up of nuclear arms on the continent, and the intensity of Cold War enmity and rhetoric fuelled those fears. In the wake of Mikhail Gorbachev, the 1987 INF Treaty and a significant lessening of the intensity of tension between the superpowers, those fears have receded somewhat. The nuclear nightmare is, of course, far from being over. Even if the superpowers are able to agree further, really significant cuts in their stockpiles, the nuclear genie is out and about all over the world. Countries like India, Israel and South Africa already possess the Bomb. Soon Iran, Iraq, Brazil and Argentina also will. A world in which each regional conflict could 'go nuclear' is now a real possibility and a thoroughly terrifying prospect.

Nevertheless, the enormous and rapid shift in superpower attitudes that led to the INF treaty does hold out real hope, and it is important here to emphasize the role of the Peace Movement. Seldom has the language of street protest become that of superpower rhetoric so quickly. Much of what the anti-nuclear campaigners were saying in giant demonstrations throughout Europe in the early 1980s about the insane futility and unwinnability of nuclear war, the need for dialogue, and the fragility of the planet, was being repeated at the top tables by 1987. In his book *Perestroika*, Gorbachev speaks like a true Green: 'There is a need for new political thinking ... We are all passengers aboard one ship, the Earth, and we must not allow it to be wrecked. There will be no second Noah's Ark.'[8]

It is as well not to be too dewy-eyed about Gorbachev. He represents a huge improvement on his predecessors, but his motives and his plans for the Soviet economy could hardly be described as green. His desire to improve the wretched state of the Soviet economy is his underlying motivation. He has clearly concluded that if the Soviet Union continues to spend its resources on vastly expensive and utterly useless nuclear weapons, it will permanently erode its capacity ever to improve the quality of life for its people.

As yet, Gorbachev's calculations clearly relate only to arms expenditure. But it would be possible to take the nuclear arms race as just one example of what the Greens call 'inappropriate investment', a description which could equally well be applied to old-style, unsustainable industrial development. If that analogy was accepted in the West as well as the East, the ecological costs of *every* financial and political decision might eventually be perceived to be acute enough to provide the motivation and momentum for radical change. There is now some genuine prospect of this.

Though it may not always be thought through in precisely these terms, this sort of analysis may explain why there is infinitely less gloom and doom in the Green Movement today than there was in the early 1970s even though, scientifically speaking, we have plenty more to be gloomy about. In the 1970s, the evidence of impending apocalypse was confined to fairly speculative computer models of the type used by the Club of Rome. In the late 1980s, not only do we know much more about the problems which confront us, but the hard scientific back-up for the Green Movement's apocalyptic warnings is now much more robust than ever before. The gap between scientists and environmental activists is narrowing by the day as we discover more and more about the dangers of acid rain, low-level radiation, the greenhouse effect and the destruction of the rainforests. This, ultimately, is what gives us such a firm basis for argument and action.

It is in this context that the enormous importance of the Gaia hypothesis can be appreciated. Though at one level it provides absolutely no vindication of the attempts of green organizations to protect the planet (in that life on Earth will almost certainly survive our most concerted assaults, be they biological, chemical or nuclear), at another it provides the most powerful links in the chain showing people exactly why their each and every action has an impact on all other living creatures: 'There is no one who can take our place. Each of us weaves a strand in the web of creation. There is no one who can weave that strand for us. What we have to contribute is both unique and irreplaceable. What we withhold from life is lost to life. The entire world depends upon our individual choices.'[9]

This is what allows the Greens to work for the future not only in terms of environmentally friendly, enlightened self-interest, but through a new and inspirational vision of collective solidarity and *social hope*. Individual well-being and salvation provide no automatic answer to the exhaustion of life-support systems. In the long run, therefore, only the Greens will be able to temper individualism with the kind of social and ecological conscience that arises out of the knowledge of the interconnectedness of all people and all living creatures. Equally, as we saw in Chapter 11, the compelling power of the Gaia idea opens up the possibility of a new synthesis between the scientific, the political and the spiritual. John Boorman believes it is only at this level that there is any genuine hope for humankind:

> You can legislate, pass laws, have international commissions and campaign to improve things, but one cannot help feeling that all these will only be marginal improvements which are going to be outweighed and overwhelmed by the perpetration of new tragedies and travesties. The root of the solution has to be so radical that it can scarcely be spoken of. We all have to be prepared to change the way we live and function and relate to the planet. In short, we need a transformation of the human spirit. If the human heart can be changed, then everything can be achieved.

This kind of 'co-evolutionary solidarity' cannot come too soon for those parts of the global environment currently under greatest threat, let alone for the millions of people that are dependent on them. But Boorman's visionary approach contrasts starkly with the pessimism of people like David Puttnam, who can't help but conclude from their knowledge of the world that it's all down to the rather baser aspects of human nature:

The problem is not technology, but human beings. I just don't believe we are capable of the self-discipline required to survive. We can do it in short cycles, but the negative cycles are stronger. People's inherent destructiveness is so extraordinarily powerful. People will climb on to the green bandwagon through self-interest, but self-interest will also have them jumping off again. Every time I brush hard against human beings, I see their instinctive self-interest. It's in the genes. I don't have a sense that we are learning how to improve ourselves. But while there's life there's hope. Perhaps if we can win an extra 100 years, we might see a turnaround in human nature. Ironically, though, I believe in God and I don't believe God is going to let the whole thing go without a struggle.

Need it really take so long? Doesn't the problem lie not so much 'in the genes' as in the prevailing culture? The gap between the daily *practice* of humankind and the ultimate *potentiality* of humankind is of such dimensions as to provoke fear in some but hope in others. William James wrote:

> I have no doubt whatever that most people live, whether physically, intellectually or morally, in a very restricted circle of their potential being. They make use of a very small portion of their possible consciousness, much like a man who, out of his whole bodily organism, should get into the habit of using and moving only his little finger. We all have reservoirs of life to draw upon of which we do not dream.[10]

It is fair to say that if the gentle 'Green Revolution' were to stop in its tracks today, the future would indeed look very bleak. Our most pressing and dangerous ecological problems will not go away, and will certainly become much worse if we carry on as we have up until now. Yet things are moving fast. Green ideas have moved decisively from the fringes of society, which they occupied less than ten years ago, into the mainstream. It is actually to our advantage that the values of modern society can change with such prodigious speed. Just consider the bewildering roller-coaster of changing sexual mores over the last twenty years – or the astonishingly swift rise and dominance of Thatcherism. Britain in the late 1980s is a significantly different place than it was in the late 1970s. This volatility is disturbing to many people. But, in a green context, it may also be a cause for optimism.

Despite the many caveats and qualifications which we have felt it right to point out along the way, we can only conclude by stating categorically that green thinking has already had a considerable impact on the way we live, and that the advance of green ideas has been astonishingly rapid. It's often difficult for Greens right in the thick of it to realize just how much is going on all around them, and just how much there is to be genuinely and realistically hopeful about. By its very existence, its diversity and its vitality, the Green Movement has demonstrated the opposite of denial and indifference towards the plight of the planet and its people. It represents an awakening, a refusal to aid and abet humankind in its onward rush towards the abyss. Its influence has only just begun to be felt, but the fact that so much progress has been made in such a short space of time is enough to light a spark of optimism in even the weariest cynic. We have a very long way still to go, but we have at last reached the end of the beginning.

REFERENCES

CHAPTER ONE – The Green Delta
pp. 15–34

1 Tim O'Riordan, *Times Higher Education Supplement*, 26 November 1984
2 All tables from Ken Young, *1987 British Social Attitudes Report* (Gower, 1987)
3 Ibid.
4 University of Surrey Research Paper (1985), quoted ibid.
5 Eric Draper, *New Internationalist*, May 1987
6 Figure from Tim O'Riordan, OECD Discussion Paper, December 1983
7 Ibid.
8 Richard St George, *Resurgence*, November 1987

CHAPTER TWO – The Common Ground *pp. 35–58*

1 World Commission on Environment and Development, *Our Common Future* (Oxford University Press, 1987)
2 John Clark, *For Richer, For Poorer* (Oxfam, 1986)
3 Chris Patten, *Independent*, 20 March 1987
4 Susan Griffin, in Stephanie Leland and Leonie Caldecott (eds), *Reclaim the Earth* (The Women's Press, 1983)
5 Ynestra King, ibid.
6 Ngahuia Te Awekotuku, ibid.
7 Richard North, *Schools of Tomorrow* (Green Books, 1987)

CHAPTER THREE – The Greening of British Politics *pp. 59–85*

1 *Guardian* editorial, 10 August 1986

2 *Daily Mirror*, 17 July 1985
3 Jon Carpenter, *Green Line*, January 1988
4 Friends of the Earth, Critique of Liberal Environment Policy, June 1986
5 Liberal/SDP Merger Document, January 1988
6 Simon Hughes, Address to Young Liberals, January 1988
7 Ibid.
8 Martin Holdgate, quoted in *New Scientist*, 25 April 1985
9 Conservative Party, General Election Manifesto, June 1987
10 Andrew Sullivan, *Greening the Tories* (Centre for Policy Studies, September 1985)

CHAPTER FOUR – Media Matters
pp. 86–108

1 *Financial Times*, 15 July 1987
2 *ECOS*, 8 April 1987
3 *Observer*, 20 September 1987
4 *Campaign*, 28 November 1986

CHAPTER FIVE – Towards a Green Aesthetic *pp. 109–32*

1 *City Limits*, 9 April 1987
2 Daily Express, 13 December 1985
3 Royal Shakespeare Company, programme notes, *Sarcophagus*, Mermaid Theatre, 1987

CHAPTER SIX – We're All Environmentalists Now
pp. 133–53

1 World Commission on

Environment and Development, op. cit.

2 David Puttnam, Speech to CBI Annual Conference, October 1987

3 Steve Robinson (ed.), *Healthier Profits* (Environment Foundation, 1986)

4 Mike Flux, 'The Industrial Tightrope', *Chemistry and Industry*, 6 January 1986

5 Quoted in Steve Robinson, op. cit.

6 John Harvey-Jones, quoted ibid.

7 John Elkington (ed.), *ICI and the Environmental Challenge* (ICI, 1987)

8 John Elkington, *The Green Capitalists* (Gollancz, 1987)

9 *Observer*, 4 April 1987

CHAPTER SEVEN – Green Works *pp. 154–71*

1 Barrie Sherman, *Working at Leisure* (Methuen, 1986)

2 *Guardian*, 24 July 1987

3 Ibid., 20 July 1987

4 *Conservation and Development: the British Approach* (DoE, May 1986)

5 Ibid.

6 Co-operative Development Agency, *National Directory of New Co-ops and Community Businesses (1986)*

7 C. Cornforth and J. Lewis, *Survey of Co-operatives* (ICOM, 1985)

8 James Robertson, *The Sane Alternative* (published privately, 1978)

9 Charles Handy, *The Future of Work* (Basil Blackwell, 1984)

10 James Robertson, *Future Work* (Maurice Temple Smith, 1985)

11 *Guardian*, 21 August 1987

12 Francis Kinsman, *The Telecommuters* (John Wiley, 1987)

13 Charles Handy, op. cit.

14 *The Wealth of Waste*, House of Commons Trade and Industry Committee, October 1984

CHAPTER EIGHT – Life-styles and Profiles *pp. 172–89*

1 PhD on green politics, referring to Enzensberger, quoted by Robyn Eckersley, p. 319

2 *Evening Standard*, 14 April 1987

3 Pietroni, *Holistic Living* (Dent, 1986), p. 171

4 British Medical Association (BMA) Board of Science Working Party on Alternative Therapy, May 1986, pp. 191–2

5 British Holistic Medical Association response to BMA report, 1986, p.63

6 *Observer*, 18 May 1986

7 *Doctor*, 22 May 1987

8 Wharton and Lewith, *British Medical Journal*, 7 June 1986

9 David Taylor Reilly, *British Medical Journal*, 30 July 1985

CHAPTER NINE – Consuming Interests *pp. 190–205*

1 *The Economist*, 12 June 1987

2 Press statement, 11 March 1986

CHAPTER TEN – Greens the World Over *pp. 206–32*

1 Brian Tokar, *The Green Alternative* (R & E Miles, 1987)

2 Mark Satin, *New Options*, June 1987

3 Diana Johnston, *New Internationalist*, May 1987

4 *The Times*, 28 January 1988

5 Sunderlal Bahaguna, *IFDA Dossier 61*, September 1987

6 Lorenzo Cardenal, *Green Line*, February 1987

7 Teddy Goldsmith, *Ecologist*, 1987

8 Bertrand Schneider, *The Barefoot Revolution*, (JT Publications, 1988)

9 Norman Myers, 'Environment and Security', *Environmentalist*, December 1986

Chapter Eleven – Spirits of the Earth pp. 233–53

1 Walter and Dorothy Schwarz, *Breaking Through* (Green Books, 1987)
2 Bishop of Lewes, Speech to International Green Conference, 1985
3 Neil Evernden, *The Natural Alien* (University of Toronto, 1985)
4 Bill Devall and George Sessions, *Deep Ecology* (Gibbs M. Smith, 1984)
5 Bill Devall and George Sessions, *Resurgence*, November 1985
6 Murray Bookchin, 'Deep Ecology vs Social Ecology', Speech to National Gathering of US Greens, Amherst, Massachusetts, 1987
7 Ibid.
8 Fritjof Capra, *Earth Island Journal*, 1987
9 Murray Bookchin, op. cit.
10 Mark Satin, *New Options*, June 1987
11 Gene Sharp, *Ghandi as a Political Strategist* (Porter Sargent, 1979)
12 Wendell Berry, *A Continuous Harmony* (Harvest Books, 1975)
13 *Daily Readings from William Temple* (pamphlet, o/p)
14 Personal statement from Eve Dennis, February 1988
15 Bishop of Durham, 'How Green is Our Future?', Speech at St James's Church, 2 November 1987
16 Sean McDonagh, *To Care for the Earth* (Geoffrey Chapman, 1986)
17 World Wildlife Fund, Harvest Festival Service, 4 October 1987
18 John Vidal, *Guardian*, 19 August 1987
19 George Trevelyan, *Summons to a High Crusade* (Findhorn Press, 1986)
20 David Spangler, *One Earth Magazine*, September 1986
21 John Stewart Collis, *The Vision of Glory* (Penguin, 1975)

Chapter Twelve – Hopes and Fears pp. 254–68

1 Club of Rome, *Limits to Growth* (Pan, 1974), p. 154
2 David Pepper, *Roots of Modern Environmentalism* (Croom Helm, 1984)
3 Rudolf Bahro, quoted in Spretnak and Capra, *Green Politics* (Paladin, 1986), p. 25
4 E. P. Thompson, 'Rituals of Enmity', in E. P. Thompson and Dan Smith (eds), *Prospectus for a Habitable Planet* (Penguin, 1987)
5 Mikhail Gorbachev, *Perestroika* (Collins, 1988), p. 12

BIBLIOGRAPHY

INTRODUCTION

Jonathon Porritt, *Seeing Green*, Basil Blackwell, 1984.
  Though looking a little long in the tooth now, *Seeing Green* does still provide a comprehensive (and, I hope, readable!) account of the *full* extent of green po .ics.
Fritjof Capra, *The Turning Point*, Wildwood House, 1982.
  A quite excellent critique of industrialism, from a fairly philosophical point of view, combined with a very optimistic view of what the future might hold in store for us.
Walter and Dorothy Schwarz, *Breaking Through*, Green Books, 1987.
  A very well-written and accessible account of how green ideas are beginning to make a mark in many different parts of society.
Peter Bunyard and Fern Morgan-Grenville, *The Green Alternative*, Methuen, 1987.
  Another very useful overview of the green scene, particularly as regards nuclear concerns.

CHAPTER ONE The Green Delta *pp 15–34*

Stephen Croall and William Rankin, *Ecology for Beginners*, Writers and Readers, 1981.
  Mostly for beginners, but may be useful for some older hands.
Teddy Goldsmith and Nicholas Hildyard (eds), *Green Britain or Industrial Wasteland?*, Polity Press, 1986.
  A very good presentation of today's environmental issues, giving the full picture of the extent to which this Government has failed in its environmental responsibilities.
Paul Ekins (ed.), *The Living Economy*, Routledge Kegan Paul, 1986.
  Practically the only book on green economics – and a very important contribution to showing people that there *are* alternative economic ideas and examples.

CHAPTER TWO The Common Ground *pp 35–38*

Mike Barker, *Directory for the Environment*, Routledge Kegan Paul, 1986.

The definitive listing of all green organizations (i.e. environment, peace, development, animal rights etc.) with details of their areas of work, membership, etc.

World Wildlife Fund, *Earthrights*, Kogan Page, 1987.
By far the best book on education from a *genuinely* green perspective.

Stephanie Leland and Leonie Caldecott (eds) *Reclaim the Earth*, The Women's Press, 1983.
A varied and fascinating collection of women's voices on feminism and the Green Movement.

Lloyd Timberlake, *Only One Earth*, BBC Publications, 1987.
Produced in conjunction with the BBC TV series of the same name, this still remains one of the best accounts of sustainable development in the Third World.

CHAPTER THREE   The Greening of British Politics *pp 59–85*

Charlene Spretnak and Fritjof Capra, *Green Politics*, Hutchinson, 1984.
An intriguing account of the role and success of the Green Party in Germany, which is still very relevant despite all the developments since the time when it was written.

Green Party, *The Green Party Manifesto*, 1987.
It's important to get the party political bit from the horse's mouth.

Murray Bookchin, *Toward an Ecological Society*, Black Rose Books, 1980.
A robust and entertaining account of green politics from today's best-known exponent of the school of 'social ecology'.

CHAPTER FIVE   Towards a Green Aesthetic *pp 109–32*

Theodore Roszak, *Where the Wasteland Ends*, Faber, 1974.
A fascinating account of how scientific materialism has blighted our artistic and spiritual vision.

Richard Mabey (ed.), *Second Nature*, Jonathan Cape, 1984.
A collection of beautifully written essays on how we relate to nature and our immediate environment.

John Fowles, *The Tree*, Aurum Press, 1979.
A wonderfully rich and evocative essay on trees, their role in our lives, their symbolic and spiritual importance.

CHAPTER SIX We're All Environmentalists Now *pp 133–53*

John Elkington, *The Green Capitalists*, Gollancz, 1987.
An important, bridge-building book. There's no doubt this is the line industry would like us to believe, though scepticism would still seem to be in order!
Fritz Schumacher, *Small is Beautiful*, Abacus, 1974.
A golden oldie, but still one of the best. It's instructive to realise just how much flowed from the ideas in this one little book.
Fred Pearce, *Acid Rain*, Penguin, 1987.
The best book around on Acid Rain.

CHAPTER SEVEN Green Works *pp 154–71*

James Robertson, *Future Work*, Maurice Temple Smith, 1986.
A visionary attempt to break the stranglehold of our hopelessly redundant work ethic.
Charles Handy, *The Future of Work*, Basil Blackwell, 1984.
More academic than Robertson's *Future Work*, but an excellent resumé of current trends.
Mike Cooley, *Architect or Bee?*, Hogarth, 1987.
Mike Cooley raises a cogent and sympathetic voice of dissent amongst all today's technocratic optimists.

CHAPTER EIGHT Life-Styles and Profiles *pp 172–89*

John Seymour and Herbie Girardet, *Blueprint for a Green Planet*, Dorling Kindersley Press, 1987.
A thorough and beautifully presented guide for taking positive action.
Duane Elgin, *Voluntary Simplicity*, William Morrow, 1981.
Explains as well as any book why a green lifestyle is *not* a sacrifice, but actually much better for us (and even more fun!) than living the way we do now.
Patrick Pietroni, *Holistic Living*, Dent, 1986.
This is much more than a book about health: it looks at every aspect of our daily lives in the most practical and inspiring way.

CHAPTER NINE Consuming Interests *pp 190–205*

The Friends of the Earth Handbook, Optima, 1987.
An extremely practical, down-to-earth guide about exactly *how* to be a good environmentalist.

John Button, *Green Pages*, Optima, 1988.
A lively review of all the main areas of green concern today.
John Elkington, *The Green Consumer Guide*, Gollancz, 1988.
As the book's sub-title puts it, 'High street shopping for a better environment: how to buy products that *don't* cost the Earth'.

CHAPTER TEN Greens the World Over *pp 206–32*

World Commission on Environment and Development, *Our Common Future*, Oxford University Press, 1987.
One may not agree with its overall message about economic growth, but this Report is now setting the agenda for discussions about development and aid issues.
Bertrand Schneider, *The Barefoot Revolution*, Intermediate Technology Publications, 1988.
A book of enormous hopefulness, with detailed accounts of grass-roots, sustainable development projects in many different countries.
Sara Parkin, *Political Parties*, Heretic Books, 1988.
A lucid and interesting analysis of *all* the different Green Parties across Europe – and a very mixed bag they are too!

CHAPTER ELEVEN Spirits of the Earth *pp 233–53*

Erich Fromm, *To Have or To Be*, Abacus, 1979.
Still one of the best rebuttals of acquisitive materialism.
Bill Devall and George Sessions, *Deep Ecology*, Gibbs M Smith, 1984.
A good (if somewhat woolly) explanation of what deep ecology is all about.
Sean McDonagh, *To Care for the Earth*, Geoffrey Chapman, 1986.
Written with a specific Christian audience in mind, this attempt to move us towards a new theology is both fascinating and inspirational.
Henrik Skolimowski, *Eco-Philosophy*, Marion Boyars, 1981.
An excellent introduction to a green philosophy.

CHAPTER TWELVE Hopes and Fears *pp 254–68*

Jim Lovelock, *Gaia: A New Look at Life on Earth*, Oxford University Press, 1979.
This book has made a deep impression on many people, and should indeed help to provide a new outlook on life on Earth.

INDEX

277

Powell, Jonathan 122, 124, 125
Prescott, John 156
press, the 94–101
Pritchard, George 152
proportional representation 77, 219, 227
Puttnam, David 92, 114–15, 116, 118–20, 133, 134–5, 266–7

Quick, Diana 110

radio 126–8
Rainbow Covenant 246
Rainbow Warrior incident 26
rainforests *see* deforestation
Ramphal, Sonny 90
Randle, Damien 55
Reagan, President Ronald 13, 121, 226
Rechem company 152
recycling 149, 171, 198–9
Redford, Robert 116
Reggio, Godfrey 116
Research Council for Complementary Medicine 184
Resurgence 99
Ridley, Nicholas 80, 88, 95, 145–6, 259
Rigbey, Liz 127–8
Right Livelihood Foundation 43, 217
Roberts, Allan 69
Robertson, James 155–6, 160, 167–8, 168–9, 170
Robinson, Steve 140
Roddick, Anita and Gordon 190–2, 258
Rodgers, Bill 61
Routledge, Paul 96–7
Rowntree Trust 201
Royal Agricultural Society of England 243
Royal Society of Medicine 188
Royal Society for Nature Conservation 163

Royal Society for the Prevention of Cruelty to Animals (RSPCA) 50
Royal Society for the Protection of Birds (RSPB) 25, 97
Runcie, Archbishop 244
Russia *see also* Chernobyl 131, 222, 265

Saatchi and Saatchi 102
Sachs, Andrew 110
Sadler, Robin 107
Safeways Ltd 195, 196–7
Sahabat Alam (SAM; Malaysia) 223–4
Sainsbury's Ltd 195–6
St George, Richard 32
Sandoz factory disaster 10
Satin, Mark 211, 239–40
Saunders, Ernest 163
Save the Children Fund 38
Sawyer, Tom 66, 67
Scarfe, Gerald 109
Scargill, Arthur 174
Schneider, Bertrand 231
Schonfeld, Victor 51–3
Schroder's Conscience Fund 200
Schultz, Charles 109
Schumacher, Fritz 56, 223–4, 245
Schwarz, Walter and Dorothy 95, 223, 244
science 144–9, 179, 255–7, 265
Scottish National Party (SNP) 78
Scruton, Roger 57
SDP *see* Social Democratic Party
Seabrook, Jeremy 69, 96, 254, 261–2
Searle, Graham 152
Seeger, Peggy 111
Seikatsu Club Consumers' Co-operative 202–3
Sekacz, Ilona 110
Selby, David 55
Sellafield plant 68, 106
SERA 63
Sessions, George 235
Seveso disaster (Italy) 11, 47

285

286

Fontana Paperbacks
Non-fiction

Fontana is a leading paperback publisher of non-fiction.
Below are some recent titles.

Armchair Golf *Ronnie Corbett* £3.50
You Are Here *Kevin Woodcock* £3.50
Squash Balls *Barry Waters* £3.50
Men: An Owner's Manual *Stephanie Brush* £2.50
Impressions of My Life *Mike Yarwood* £2.95
Arlott on Wine *John Arlott* £3.95
Beside Rugby *Bill Beaumont* £3.50
Agoraphobia *Robyn Vines* £3.95
The Serpent and the Rainbow *Wade Davies* £2.95
Alternatives to Drugs *Colin Johnson & Arabella Melville* £4.95
The Learning Organization *Bob Garratt* £3.95
Information and Organizations *Max Boisot* £3.50
Say It One Time For The Broken Hearted *Barney Hoskins* £4.95
March or Die *Tony Geraghty* £3.95
Nice Guys Sleep Alone *Bruce Feirstein* £2.95
Royal Hauntings *Joan Forman* £3.50
Going For It *Victor Kiam* £2.95
Sweets *Shona Crawford Poole* £3.95
Waugh on Wine *Auberon Waugh* £3.95

You can buy Fontana paperbacks at your local bookshop or newsagent.
Or you can order them from Fontana Paperbacks, Cash Sales Department, Box 29, Douglas, Isle of Man. Please send a cheque, postal or money order (not currency) worth the purchase price plus 22p per book for postage (maximum postage required is £3).

NAME (Block letters) _____

ADDRESS _____

_____

_____